EASY &
ELEGANT
beaded
copper
JEWELRY

EASY & ELEGANT
beaded copper JEWELRY

how to create beautiful
fashion accessories
from a few basic steps

Lora S. Irish

FOX CHAPEL
PUBLISHING

© 2011 by Lora S. Irish and Fox Chapel Publishing Company, Inc., East Petersburg, PA.

Easy & Elegant Beaded Copper Jewelry is an original work, first published in 2011 by Fox Chapel Publishing Company, Inc. The patterns contained herein are copyrighted by the author. Readers may make copies of these patterns for personal use. The patterns themselves, however, are not to be duplicated for resale or distribution under any circumstances. Any such copying is a violation of copyright law.

ISBN 978-1-56523-514-4

Publisher's Cataloging-in-Publication Data

Irish, Lora S.
      Easy & elegant beaded copper jewelry : how to create beautiful
   fashion accessories from a few basic steps / Lora S. Irish. -- 1st ed. -
   - East Petersburg, PA : Fox Chapel Publishing, c2011.
         p. ; cm.
      ISBN: 978-1-56523-514-4
      Includes index.

      1. Copper jewelry--Technique. 2. Jewelry making. 3. Wire craft.
   I. Title. II. Title: Beaded copper jewelry.
TT212 .I75 2011
739.27/8--dc22   1104

To learn more about the other great books from Fox Chapel Publishing, or to find a retailer near
you, call toll-free 800-457-9112 or visit us at *www.FoxChapelPublishing.com*.

Note to Authors: We are always looking for talented authors to write new books
in our area of woodworking, design, and related crafts. Please send a brief letter
describing your idea to Acquisition Editor, 1970 Broad Street, East Petersburg, PA 17520.

Printed in China
First printing: April 2011

About the Author and Artist

My earliest memories of home and family are filled with arts and crafts. It seemed there was always something being created in my childhood home. At dinnertime, one of my chores was to clean the dining room table in preparation of setting the table. The table could easily be heaped in piles of cotton print fabrics for Mom's current quilting project, oil paints and canvas, balls of wool yarn for her latest knitting pattern, and even piles of dried flowers, milkweed pods, and pinecones for her flower arrangements.

Growing up, I always knew my avocation would lie in the arts and crafts. Through my years as a craftswoman, I have learned and taught the needle arts, ceramics and porcelain, fine arts painting, limited-edition prints, and even truck lettering and painting. My love of creating finally found my permanent home in woodcarving and woodburning about fifteen years ago.

In 2007, when Mom moved into our home, she wanted to take a class at our local quilt shop. This surprised me as Mom has quilted for more than 20 years. The class focused on a new technique called machine quilt stippling. Most of the students were between their mid-40s to mid-50s and then there was Mom, at age 82, learning the newest techniques for her favorite craft!

Learning the lesson that my mom taught me that day, I began to look around for some new craft or art I had not yet tried. Wire jewelry, with its bright beads, wonderful wire twists and multitude of possibilities, caught my attention. A few dozen beads, a small assortment of tools, and a few pounds of copper wire, and I was hooked.

Dot Cunningham teaching her grandson, Kent S. Irish, a few basics in the art of quilting. Fall 2009.

The results of that lesson are shared here in these pages. As you read through them, please take with you my mother's life lesson—"No matter how old you are you are still young enough to learn something new!"

My goal in preparing this book was for readers to have fun learning all of the possibilities of wire jewelry. I also sought to make the projects as simple as possible while making them interesting to look at, touch, and create. After you have worked with the projects in this book, go to Chapter Ten and learn how to turn your own ideas into beautiful jewelry.

There is an artist in every one of us. Indulge yours.

Thanks Mom for still sharing your life's adventure with me and with my readers.

Lora S. Irish

Contents

**ALL YOU NEED TO KNOW
TO CREATE YOUR OWN**

Easy & Elegant Beaded Copper Jewelry

How to Build a Basic Tool Kit

Page 14

What Materials You'll Need to Get Started

Page 21

The Many Varieties of Beads Available

Page 22

How to Make the 14 Basic Bent-Wire Links

Page 28

**How to Make
Basic Chain Links**
Page 40

How to Connect Links
Page 46

**How to Make
Hook-and-Eye Sets**
Page 52

**How to Use Rattail and
Suede Leather Cords**
Page 60

**What the Complete Set
of Links Looks Like
(and How to Make Them)**
Page 64

**How and When to Add
a Wire-Wrap**
Page 138

**How to Use the Instructions
(and Change Them)**
Page 146

**Tips on Designing Your
Own Jewelry**
Page 154

Step-by-Step Projects
Page 160

Introduction

In 2004, forty-one Middle Paleolithic shell beads were discovered at the Blombos Cave archaeology site in South Africa. At the time of their discovery, the small ornamentations, which date to 75,000 years ago, pushed the time envelope for modern man's earliest known cultural modernity back by nearly 35,000 years. After careful research, the team of scientists determined that shell beads found in Skhul Cave at Mount Carmel in Israel during the 1930s and those found at Oued Djebbana in Algeria during the 1940s may date to more than 100,000 years old.

Each of these three sites are well inland. The Oued Djebbana site, located 120 miles (200km) from the sea, shows that the shells had been moved from their natural environment to the human settlements. Small holes were made in each of these earliest ornaments with either stone or bone awls to string the shells into the first bead necklaces, so our ancestors purposefully altered them.

Whether these shell beads were used for spiritual rituals, personal ornamentation, status symbols, or even trading or gift giving between clans and tribes, may never be known. But their appearance in our distant past marks the period of man's development as he began to create his language, symbolic thinking, religion, and modern cultural interactions.

Jewelry has played an important part in our changing, evolving cultures throughout history and reflects the attitudes, thinking, and events of the era in which it was created. A heavy, bold gold bejeweled ring might show the royal status of a king where a few simple bone beads on a leather string might adorn a peasant girl.

Jewelry has often been exchanged as part of mankind's prenuptial agreements as a bride price paid by the man's family to the woman's family to compensate for her, and therefore her children, leaving the clan. Today's tradition of giving an engagement ring to the bride-to-be by her suitor is a remnant of this distant bride price. Bridal dowry's often included jewelry items, which often were passed from mother to daughter so that the woman came into the marriage with some financial backing. In either situation, the value of the jewelry reflected the value of the union to both families.

The Victorian era of new cultural interactions, the expansion of the sciences, and the explosion of exploration is reflected in its finely detailed, highly intriguing jewelry designs; during the 1960s through 1970s, Op Art- and Abstract Art-Era jewelry is displayed in large single-hoop earrings or the extreme simplicity of the peace emblem.

Today we are hard-wired, networked, and instantly interconnected through electronic circuitry and our jewelry trends show it. Copper, silver, and gold wire have become dominant elements in the necklace, bracelet, and brooch designs, along with intricately coiled or angled bends. Beads that were once the focus points of a necklace have become secondary elements to accent the interlocking metalworkings. Fine delicate chains have been replaced with bold, eclectic twists and turns of bent-wire links.

With a few simple tools, several rolls of copper, silver, or gold wire, and a few bright glass beads you can join today's fine jewelry artisans by creating quality bent-wire jewelry that emphasizes mankind's embrace of the electronic age. As you read through the chapters of this book, you will discover which tools you will need for your new craft, the basics behind the basic wire bends, how to join individual links and bead dangles, and even how to create your own unique jewelry designs.

Modern bent-wire jewelry offers the crafts artisan two very specific features—quick, easy-to-learn techniques and quick-to-complete, unlimited design

possibilities. Because this jewelry style is based on fourteen simple-to-learn-and-execute wire bends, there are very few advanced lessons to learn. Instead of relying on complicated molding, soldering, or sculpturing techniques, bent-wire jewelry depends on how you, the jewelry artist, combine and connect easily reproducible wire links and bead links. Once the basics are explored by working through the step-by-step instructions of the different link styles and by creating practice wire links, you will have mastered the craft and be ready to begin your own jewelry designing. The creation of many of

the projects and designs in this book can be accomplished in one or two short sessions. Most can be done from start to finish during a quiet evening of fun.

As you begin your first project and create those first important practice wire links you will be joining 100,000 years of history and the creative artists that came before us.

Lora S. Irish

Spring 2011

ACKNOWLEDGMENTS

After many years working as a Fox Chapel author writing woodcarving, woodburning, and craft pattern books, I was both surprised and thoroughly delighted when publisher Alan Giagnocavo and editorial director John Kelsey accepted my suggestion for a beaded copper wire jewelry book. Alan has always encouraged me to explore new ideas, new techniques, and new crafts, never limiting the path where each new book takes me. Fox Chapel's willingness to explore new ideas and new arts for book manuscripts has accentuated my growth as a craft artist.

Special thanks are extended to Paul Hambke, Fox's managing editor and developmental editor for this book. I have leaned heavily throughout this last year on his strong shoulders as together we have worked through how to approach the written instructions needed to make each project clear and simple to follow. With his organizational skills, he has taken my multitude of small individual ideas, teachings, and projects and created a logical, easy-to-follow order. Over and over again Paul has offered suggestions and ideas for added text and photos to strengthen an area where he felt you, the reader, would benefit from "just a little more." I believe that I presented Fox Chapel with a good manuscript; Paul made this into a great one.

I also would like to thank the design team at Fox Chapel, especially designers Lindsay Hess and Jason Deller and photographer Scott Kriner, who are responsible for the superb look and wonderful visual layout of the photos and instructions. They worked extremely hard to make sure we could pack every project possible into this one book.

To Sandy Ertz, Gail Larkin, and Roberta VanOrmer, the customer service reps at Fox who man the phone lines, I am so grateful that when I call early in the morning with a new problem to work through I am greeted by a smiling voice. That is a wonderful way to start the working day.

My most lasting gratitude goes to my husband, Michael. Through thirty-three years of marriage and twenty-five years as a working team, he has endured reams of art paper, piles of craft supplies, tons of paint tubes and brushes, and a home that can smell like turpentine or linseed oil, all with a prideful delight in his wife's accomplishments. He has suffered through eating microwave dinners off TV trays because the kitchen table was full of the latest projects and through my creative tantrums when I have too many projects going at the same time.

Michael is the one truly responsible for *Easy & Elegant Beaded Copper Jewelry* going to press. Having taken up bent-wire jewelry as a new hobby just for my own fun and enjoyment, I had a table full of my necklace and bracelet creations. As he looked through my brightly beaded works he simply said, "You are sending those to Paul Hambke in tomorrow's mail!" It was a bold, determined statement that he did not want me to keep my creations all to myself and that I should share the fun and delight I had discovered in jewelry crafting with you. And so, with my husband's insistence, *Easy & Elegant Beaded Copper Jewelry* went from my craft table to yours.

13

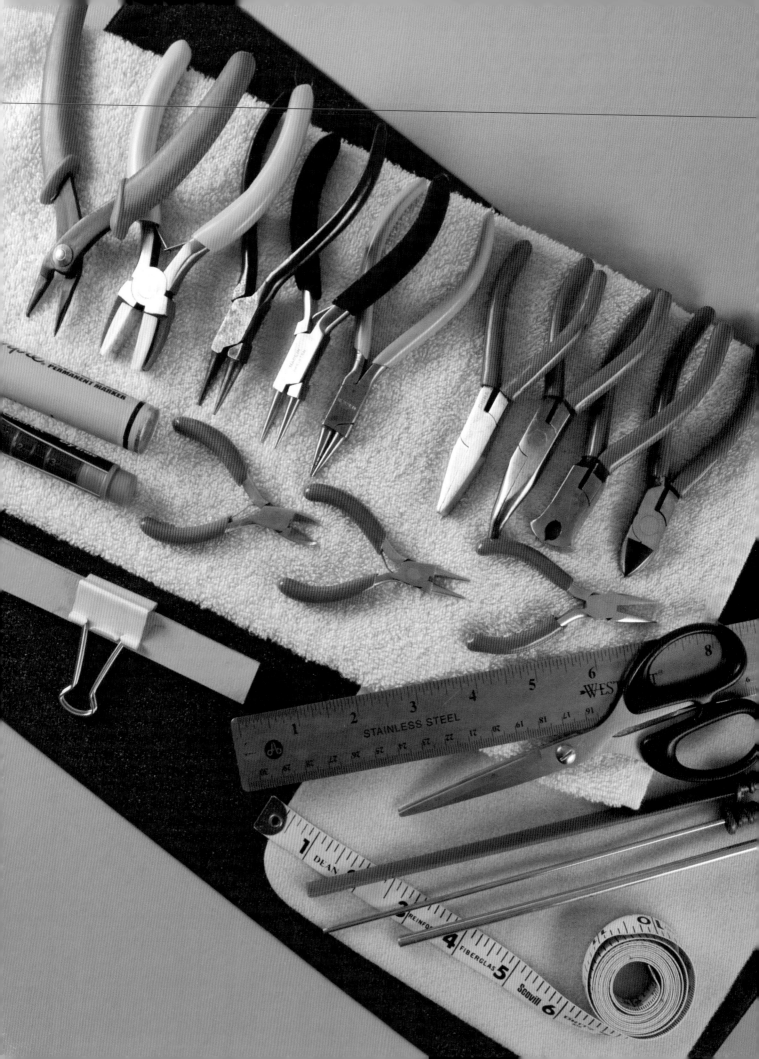

the basic tool kit

A few simple tools and household items compose the jeweler's tool kit. A set of pliers—round-, flat-, and bent-nose—plus a set of wire cutters will quickly get you started. Your kit will need a work surface—use anything from a terry cloth towel to a jewelry pad. Add a steel ruler, measuring tape, scissors, and spring clips, and your tool kit is complete.

Tool sets that include basic pliers, cutters, and even jewelry tweezers for working with smaller diameter beads, are perfect for the new jewelry craftsman. You can also purchase your pliers and cutters individually. Purchasing specific individual higher-quality tools is an excellent option as you advance in your craft.

Flush, end, and side cutters; flat-, round-, and bent-nose pliers; nylon-grip flat pliers; a ruler; a coil maker; and assorted extras compose a jewelry-making tool kit.

Individual Tools

You may already own many of the tools we will be exploring. Flat- and bent-nose pliers and wire cutters are commonly found in household tool kits or in workshops. The large-sized wire cutters and round-nose pliers I use for jewelry projects are from my woodcraft workshop and are 6" (152mm) long from tip to handle. The middle-sized tools—5" (127mm) long—are from my jewelry tool kit and are the tools I use the most for bending links with 18-gauge wire and up. The miniature tools—4" (102mm) long—are also part of my jewelry tool kit. I use the miniature tools when I am working with fine gauge wire in the 26- to 20-gauge range.

Large household tools will get you started and let you create a few practice projects but are not recommended for your jewelry tool kit. The large wire cutters in the photo have been used for everything from mending fence wire and snipping tin to cutting nails. That type of abuse leaves dents and scratches in the cutting edge that transfers to the jewelry wire. The large round-nose pliers still carry a thin layer of epoxy glue from a woodworking project that would quickly mar my copper or silver wire.

Purchase a set of tools that you can dedicate to your new craft and protect from hard daily household use.

Three sizes: Pliers and wire cutters come in three standard sizes. The large tools shown here are common workshop or household tools. Standard jewelry tools come in 4" (102mm) and 5" (127mm) lengths.

WIRE CUTTERS

The profile or cutting edge of a set of wire cutters determines the profile on the point of your working wire. Because of the thickness of the steel, the cutting edge of one side of your wire cutters tapers to make a fine, sharp cut. The backside of the cutters, which are flat, will create a square cut to the wire end where the inside or tapered side of the tool will cut the wire point into a V-shape.

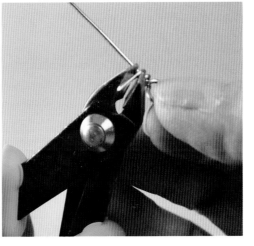

Flush cutters: The inside or face side of this pair of flush cutters shows the V-shape of the tool's profile.

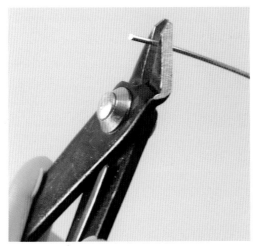

Flattest working edge: The flush cutter has the flattest working edge of the three common wire cutter styles. Use it to pre-cut your working wire from the spool or roll as well as to remove the extra wire from the finished link.

End cutter: The end cutter has a slight curve to the working outside or backside edge that allows you to tuck the tool into very tight areas. This is a favorite tool for working with wrapped loops where there is limited room or space for either the flush cutter or side cutter.

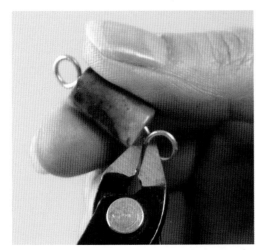

Wire placement: Place the flat side or backside of the cutters into the link to create a flat, square end to your working wire.

Side cutter: The side cutter also has a slight curve to the working side. This cutter has a fine point to the tip that can reach into difficult turns and twists to remove the excess wire from your links.

PLIERS

Use pliers to hold and secure your wire as you work the bends and twists. Which pair of pliers you use depends on the particular bend you are making, as well as how large an area of the link needs to be secured as you add new turns or bends.

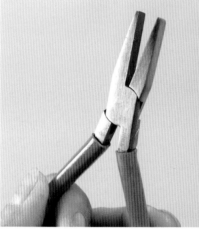

Flat-nose pliers: Flat-nose pliers have a long and wide flat profile. Use them to hold end loops as you add a wire-wrapping, secure large spiral turns, and for making square angles in your links.

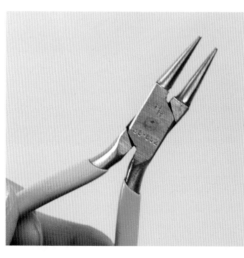

Round-nose pliers: Round-nose pliers have a tapered cone shape to their tips. Use the round profile for rolling perfectly round loops and spirals. One pair of round-nose pliers makes a variety of circle and loop sizes from tight loops made near the point of the pliers, to very large ones made by placing the wire at the base of the sides.

Bent-nose pliers: Bent-nose pliers taper toward the end of the tool, creating a small tip for easy use in tight areas. The bend in the tool's profile makes this a favorite because it places the wire link into a comfortable working position.

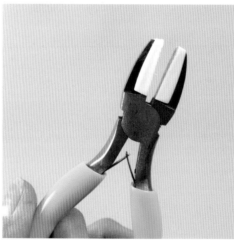

Nylon-grip flat pliers: Nylon-grip flat pliers are flat-nose pliers with a thick nylon pad added to the holding area. Standard pliers can leave small dents and scratches in your links. The nylon pads on this set of pliers eliminate that problem. Their extra-wide profile makes turning large spirals easy and quick.

OTHER WIRE JEWELRY TOOLS

As your interest in jewelry making grows, there is a wide variety of specialty tools that you may wish to add to your kit. Coil makers, wire jigs, measuring tools, and bead tweezers are just a few. For this book, the coil maker is used to create both coil elements—split rings and jump rings.

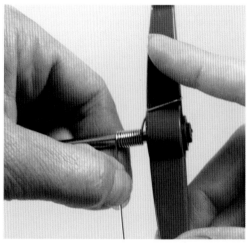

Coil maker: The coil-maker tool comes with a detachable handle and a selection of interchangeable wrapping bars in a variety of diameters. The wire is fed through a hole in the handle, and then placed over the wrapping bar. As you turn the handle in one hand, the wire automatically rolls around the wrapping bar creating a perfectly sized coil of wire.

Party Lights necklace
See page 251 for instructions

Household coil makers: If you start making jewelry without a coil maker, use knitting needles, round pencils, and any other small cylinder-shaped household object as the template for making your coils. There are a series for round objects in the photo (above), but be on the lookout for unusual shapes as well. Coils can be triangular, square, or oval.

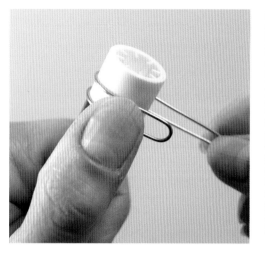

Assorted markers and pens: As you begin working through Chapter 2 on step-by-step creation of bent-wire links, you will quickly learn that the wire is bent around the edge of the bent-nose pliers, around the tips of the round-nose pliers, the coil maker, or other object. For the large open-circle links made throughout this book, I used the base of a large marking pen.

Metal ruler: A steel ruler is handy for both measuring your wire lengths and for sizing beads. My ruler has both Imperial and metric measurements. Use a sewing tape measure to quickly size your projects for necklace, choker, or bracelet lengths.

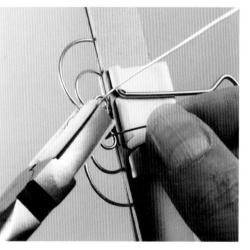

Simple clamp: A simple clamp or 'third hand' can be made with two strips of 1" wide by 4" long (25mm by 102mm) heavy chipboard or cardboard and a spring clamp. When you are working on large open links or wire-wrapping a link, you can secure the link inside of the simple clamp, freeing your hands to complete the bends or wrapping steps. The spring clamp holds the wire while the chipboard protects it from dents.

SCISSORS

I include scissors in my kit but I never use them to cut or snip wire, not even extra fine wire at 26 gauge. Cut your wire with wire cutters and save your scissors for opening bead packages and cutting stain ribbon, and rattail and twine necklace cords.

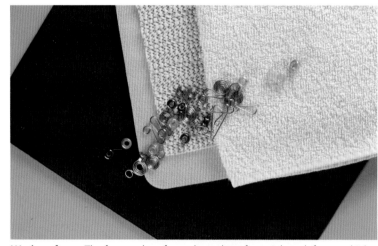

Work surfaces: The four work surfaces shown here from right to left are a thick terry cloth towel, a non-skip rubber pad, a foam core jewelry bead pad, and the foam back of a desk pad. I use the terry cloth towel for when I am working in my lap and the three remaining surfaces for work at the table.

Resealable bags: Assorted sizes of plastic resealable bags are always needed in jewelry making. They are wonderful for storing your loose beads, practice links, and usable lengths of scrap wire.

WORKING SURFACE

Whether you have a dedicated area in your craft room for jewelry making or whether you are working in your lap as you watch the evening television programs, you will want some type of working surface that catches the small wire clipped ends and keeps the beads from rolling.

A terry cloth towel or foam pad will capture the small wire clippings from your work, as well as secure the beads from rolling off the table or work surface. Flexible surfaces, such as a terry cloth towel, make clean up easy because the normal accumulation of small wire clippings can easily be dumped into the trash can at the end of any working session. Stiff or ridged work surfaces such as the office desk pad are great when you want to move a partially completed project into a storage area until you can return to it at a later date.

RESEALABLE PLASTIC BAGS

A jewelry maker never seems to have enough resealable plastic bags. Beads often come either pre-strung on a thread or in a vacuum-sealed bag. After cutting the string or opening the bag, you will need some easy way to store those beads. Resealable kitchen bags are perfect for large storage of coils of wire, assorted shaping tools, and large quantities of beads. Most craft stores offer smaller sized resealable bags for small amounts of beads, loose extra links, and reusable scrap wire.

Materials—Wire, Beads, and Cord

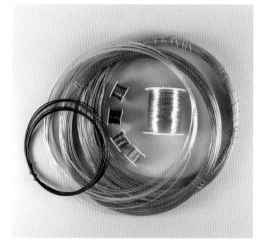

Assorted jewelry wire: Jewelry wire comes in an assortment of metals, gauge sizes, degrees of hardness, and shapes. From left, wires shown in the photo are 16-gauge colored copper wire, 18-gauge sterling silver wire, 18-gauge copper wire, and 20-gauge brass wire. Inside of the ring of wires are four spools of 26-gauge colored craft wire and a spool of 24-gauge copper wire.

METAL WIRES

Jewelry wire comes in a variety of metals or coated metals—gold-filled wire, gold-plated wire, sterling silver, brass, colored copper, copper, and color-coated aluminum are the most common.

Gold and silver wires are usually purchased by the foot, while color-coated copper wire and color-coated aluminum wire are measured by the yard. Brass and copper wire can be purchased by either the yard or by the pound coil. Gold and silver wire are the ultimate jewelry wires that create stunning work with lasting financial value. Colored-coated and copper wires are used for casual jewelry, trendy styles, and for learning our craft.

Throughout this book, we will be using copper wire. For the beginner jewelry crafter, copper has several advantages. It is an inexpensive wire compared to the precious metals and colored craft wires. You can purchase a pound of 18-gauge copper wire (approximately 200 feet) for about the same price you would pay for ten feet of silver wire. This means that you can afford to practice, practice further, and do still more practice as you learn the different bends and twists used in the bent-wire links. Copper has a bright golden orange tone when new but as it ages it develops a deep rich sepia coloring, which enhances your accent beads. Finally, copper is a dead soft wire that bends easily.

WIRE HARDNESS

Precious metal wires, silver and gold, come is three basic degrees of hardness—soft, half-hard, and hard. The copper wire used throughout this book has a soft degree of hardness and manipulates with just your fingers. Using a process called tempering, soft wires need to be hardened after the shaping process. Temper your wire by placing the link under repeated pressure with your nylon grip pliers for about one minute—press, release, press, release—or by gently tapping it with a hammer on a metal block, again for about one minute.

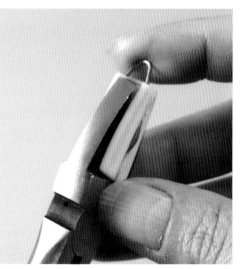

Tempering wires: Soft wires, as copper, need to be tempered after bending to set the link. This is done by repeatedly putting pressure on the link with your nylon grip pliers or by tapping the link on a metal or hard rubber jeweler's pad with a small hammer.

Beads

THE BASIC TOOL KIT

22

Brass, which is also an excellent wire for beginners, tends to be half-hard. You will need more pressure with your hands to complete the bends or may wish to use your bent-nose pliers to pull the wire into position. Brass, like copper, is inexpensive so it can be used for many of your practice projects.

Half-hard wire takes a bit more pressure to bend into shape, but retains that shape once worked. Hard wire may require the use of tools and a fair amount of pressure to create the shape, but retains its final shaping.

WIRE SHAPE

Gold and sterling silver wire comes in four basic shapes—round, half round, square, and twisted. Colored copper wire, copper wire, and brass wire are available in round only. As you grow in this craft and move into the precious metal wires of gold and silver, the added shapes that are available can be used to enhance your link and beadwork.

WIRE GAUGE

Gauge is the measure of a wire's thickness or diameter. The standard sizes for wire jewelry range from 26 gauge to 12 gauge. The higher the gauge number, the finer (or thinner) the wire.

Fine beadwork and the wire-wrapping of bent links is usually done with 26- or 24-gauge wire. Wire gauges 20 through 18 are excellent for small and medium bent-wire links. Make large or thick bent-wire links with 16- and 12-gauge wire.

Assorted glass beads: The variety of beads available can be overwhelming. You can find jewelry beads in precious gemstones, precious metals, pearls, porcelain, resin, acrylics, and glass. You will find rounds, ovals, barrels, and discs. Beads come in fun shapes, such as little frogs holding onto barrel beads, and also in raw nugget shapes.

Material, shape, texture, color, and hole size define beads. Natural materials include semi-precious gemstones, precious metals, bone, shell, and wood. Man-made beads come in acrylic, resin, porcelain, polymer clay, and glass. The color range is infinite from the purest white of mother-of-pearl to bright, dazzling foil glass jewel tones, and even finely decorated multi-colored cloisonné beads.

The best way to explore the variety of beads available to the jewelry maker is by browsing through online bead catalogs

Wire gauges: From top to bottom these pieces were worked in 12-, 16-, 18-, and 20-gauge wire. For comparison, the beads shown in the top necklace and bottom bracelet chain are 6mm sizes. The necklace (top) is *Appalachian Trail* (page 196); the bracelets are *Easy Going* (second from top, page 157), *Day Break* (third from top, page 152), and *Solitude* (bottom, page 158).

Assorted glass beads: For the projects in this book, size, shape, and hole size are more important than the material from which the bead was made, its color, or its texture. The beads in this photo include red turquoise tube beads, red cracked glass, large gold foil glass discs, frosted glass squares, burgundy mother-of-pearl rounds, red crow rollers, and blue, gold, and purple confetti glass rounds.

or through mail order catalogs. Plan to spend some time with those catalogs, as bead browsing can become a full-time hobby itself. A trip to your local bead store can quickly become hours of fun, learning, and excitement.

The beads you choose to use are dependent solely on your preference.

For this book, I have used primarily semi-precious gemstones, hand-blown glass, India glass, foil glass, crow rollers, and lampwork beads to accent the bent-wire links. The necklaces throughout this book may use anywhere from 30 or more small beads for one simple side-loop bead link necklace to three to five specialty lampwork beads for a fancy bent-wire necklace.

For our purposes, the size of the bead, shape of the bead, and size of the bead hole are more important than the material, color, sheen, or texture.

BEAD SIZES

Seed beads are measured by assigned numbers that range from size 15/0, the smallest, to size 1/0, the largest, and are worked with fine thread and needle. Necklace beads are measured by the millimeter. Small necklace bead sizes range from 2mm to 6mm and are worked on 26- through 20-gauge wire. Medium-sized beads are 8mm through 12mm size, which can be worked on wire up to 18-gauge. Large focus beads start around 14mm and go up to 40mm in size or more and may take up to 12-gauge wire.

BEAD HOLE SIZES

As a standard rule, the size of the bead determines the size of the bead hole. Naturally, very small beads only have room for very small holes where large beads may have much larger holes for threading. Size the bead holes to the wire that you will be using for your project. Too large a gauge wire can cause a bead to split or crack with time because of the pressure from forcing the wire through the hole. Large beads need a wire

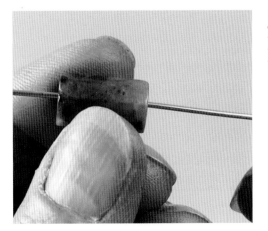

Hole size: The size of the hole through the bead determines the gauge of wire that you can use.

that visually looks strong and supportive. If your wire does not match your bead hole, adjust either by choosing a wire gauge that does fit the bead or by changing to a different bead that fits the wire you want to use.

If you will be using several sizes of beads in one project, you may wish to use two or more gauges of wire in the project. This can be done by being consistent throughout the work. Wire work all the small beads in one gauge and then change to the large gauge wire for all of the large beads.

BEAD SHAPES

Beads comes in a far greater range of shapes than just round. Ovals, flat ovals, discs, squares, rectangles, barrels, and rondelles are a small sampling of possible shapes. Small round, 4mm to 6mm, beads are excellent for adding just a touch of color, while large flattened discs make great focal points. Square and rectangle beads give contrast to sharp-angled bent-wire links. Mix and match your shapes in your projects just as you would mix and match color or size.

24

Small sampling: This is a small sampling of the possibilities that you find in jewelry beads. Everything is available from very fine delicate hand-blown glass rondelles to bold and sassy red agate donuts. A key to the beads in this photo appears on the opposite page.

#	Material	Size	Shape	Wire gauge
1	Foil lampwork glass	35mm	Rounded disc	12 gauge
2	Foil lampwork glass	35mm	Flat disc	12 gauge
3	Marbleized glass	20x15mm	Flat oval	18 gauge
4	Cat's eye glass	10mm	Round	18 gauge
5	Swirled lampwork	18x14mm	Round barrel	16 gauge
6	Hand-blown glass	16x8mm	Rondelle	18 gauge
7	Red agate	50mm	Flat donut	12 gauge
8	Confetti glass	10mm	Round	18 gauge
9	Opaque swirl, ceramic	20x12mm	Rounded rectangle	18 gauge
10	India glass mix	Assorted	Assorted	18 gauge
11	Glass spacers	6x4mm	Spacer	20 gauge
12	Foil lampwork glass	12x6mm	Square	18 gauge
13	Bumpy lampwork glass	15x6mm	Flatten round	16 gauge
14	Ceramic	12x10mm	Twisted rectangle	18 gauge
15	Swirled glass	12mm	Round	16 gauge
16	Porcelain	12x5mm	Tube	20 gauge
17	Acrylic	16mm	Assorted	12 gauge
18	Wood	14mm	Round	12 gauge
19	Antique copper	18x14mm	Flattened barrel	20 gauge
20	Pressed glass	12x10mm	Heart	24 gauge
21	Red agate	Assorted	Nugget	18 gauge
22	Seashell	30mm	Donut	18 gauge
23	Pressed glass	6mm	Cube	24 gauge
24	Laminated acrylic	6mm	Round	18 gauge
25	Cane glass	Assorted	Assorted	12 gauge

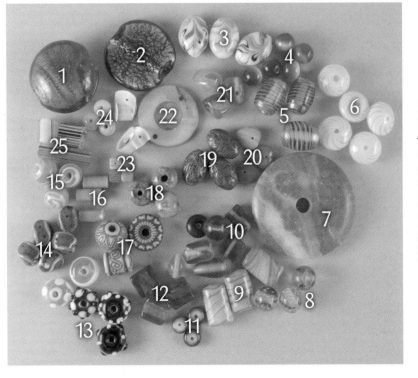

Beads, materials, size, and shape

The above chart displays the number of the bead that corresponds to the photo, the bead's material, size, and shape. The wire size is based on the hole size of the bead. This is an extremely small sampling of the bead sizes and shapes available to today's jewelry maker.

PURCHASING BEADS

Beads are purchased in several ways. Many beads are pre-packaged and sold by a specific number of beads in the pack. Beads can also be bought by the gram weight or they may be sold by strands from 8" to 36" (203mm to 914mm) long. You can obtain packages or strands of one specific bead or choose mixtures that contain an assortment of sizes and shapes. Specialty beads, such as handcrafted lampwork beads, are sold individually.

When purchasing bead strings or packages, be sure to buy more beads than you will need for your project. No bead package is perfect. There can be damaged or irregular beads in any batch. Having a few extra beads on hand means you can make adjustments easily in any project by adding extra links to add length.

Assorted glass beads: Still more beads!

Bead assortments: Assortments are great for the new jewelry maker. They provide a variety of shapes and sizes in a compatible color combination. Mixtures tend to be inexpensive, making them perfect for your practice projects. In this photo you will see six mixtures—from the top left moving clockwise—35mm foil glass discs, assorted-shape cane glass beads, India brown tones glass mix, mixed color iridescent 6mm crow rollers, frosted assorted-shape glass beads, and on the table, 45mm and 50mm large foil glass discs.

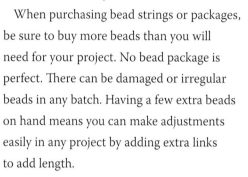

CORD AND TWINE

There are quite a few materials available that can be used as chain, ribbons, and cord to complete your necklaces and bracelets. A few of your options include rattail cord, cotton twine, braided twine, satin and metallic ribbons, and pre-made necklace chains.

You can make your own fine chains by working small links in 24- or 20-gauge wire or you can purchase pre-manufactured chains. Sold by the foot, chain is available in all of the major jewelry metals—gold, silver, brass, copper, and aluminum. Pre-made chain necklaces are also available that include the hook-and-eye or toggle latch where you need only add the decorative links and beads of your choice.

Ribbon makes a fast, fun necklace for your wire link work and is available in a pre-made necklace that includes the hook-and-eye. Twine has recently become popular, especially with fine knit wire projects.

You will see several necklaces throughout this book finished with nylon rattail cord, which is available in several sizes and a variety of colors. It is extremely strong, yet lightweight, and soft to wear. Rattail cord is perfect for projects that use large, heavy focal point beads where a heavy bead needs extra-strong support.

Cord and twine:
A roll of 2mm black rattail cord (back row left), cotton twine (back row right), gold satin ribbon (front row left), pre-made silver chain (front row right), and a pre-made hook-and-eye rattail necklace are among the many alternate materials you can use as you create your jewelry.

Off and running:
A little copper wire, a bowl full of glass beads, and a few simple tools and we are ready to make some fun and exciting bent-wire jewelry.

Using assortments: *Rainbow Road* bracelet was created using a frosted assorted-shape glass bead mixture. This bracelet was worked using 18-gauge copper wire. A 5-turn ribbon link, a double-3-turn spiral link, a two-bead wrapped-straight-loop bead link, a double spiral-heart link and a one-bead straight-wrapped loop bead link were joined using ¼" (6mm)-wide jump rings. A simple hook was added to one side of the bracelet with a large simple side-loop link and jump ring to the second side for the hook eye. Working with 20-gauge wire, three crimped-end one-bead-straight-wrapped loops were interlocked to the wire bend links of the bracelet using frosted glass 8mm to 10mm beads. Three simple side-loop links were created and locked into the wire bend links of the bracelet. A navy blue spacer bead was added to each link.

Rainbow Road bracelet

[See page 251 for instructions.]

14 basic bent-wire links

Any bent-wire link can be broken down into a small set of individual shapes. How the shapes are arranged and placed determines the type of finished link you create. Those basic shapes include simple and wrapped loops, sharp angles, U-shaped bends, full circles, and even spirals. Let us work through how to create each basic shape. Throughout this section of basic wire shapes, I use 18-gauge wire, my nylon-grip flat-nose pliers, round-nose pliers, bent-nose pliers, and flush cutter.

The wire-length measurements given through this section are far longer then you will need when you go to work your links and bead dangles. The extra length will allow plenty of wire as you learn how to make basic bends with consistently smooth curves.

Fourteen simple wire bends are all you need to make bent-wire link jewelry.

SIMPLE SIDE-LOOP

The simple side-loop is often the connecting ring at the beginning and/or end (above left)—and sometimes both (below left)—of a wire or bead link and a primary bend for making quick links for long chains.

1 Start with a flush-cut piece of wire approximately 3" (76mm) long for this practice exercise. Straighten the wire using your nylon-grip flat pliers. Using your round-nose pliers, grip the end of the wire between the two sides of the pliers.

2 Roll the wire around one side of the pliers using the pad of your thumb to press against the pliers.

3 Adjust the wire in the pliers so you can continue rolling the wire around the pliers' profile.

4 The loop is complete when the bent wire touches the original wire starting point at the flush cut.

5 Use your nylon-grip flat pliers to flatten the loop.

SIMPLE STRAIGHT-LOOP

A simple straight-loop (above left) at the beginning and end of a link centers the bead on the working wire (below left) and thus centers the link to the next element.

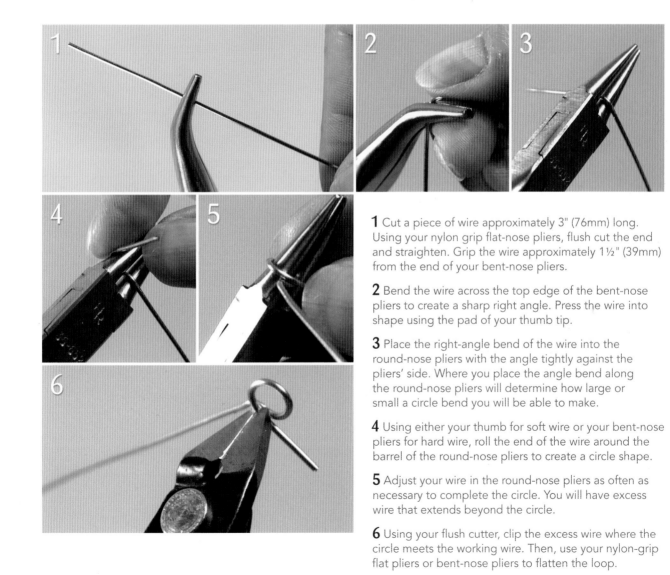

1 Cut a piece of wire approximately 3" (76mm) long. Using your nylon grip flat-nose pliers, flush cut the end and straighten. Grip the wire approximately 1½" (39mm) from the end of your bent-nose pliers.

2 Bend the wire across the top edge of the bent-nose pliers to create a sharp right angle. Press the wire into shape using the pad of your thumb tip.

3 Place the right-angle bend of the wire into the round-nose pliers with the angle tightly against the pliers' side. Where you place the angle bend along the round-nose pliers will determine how large or small a circle bend you will be able to make.

4 Using either your thumb for soft wire or your bent-nose pliers for hard wire, roll the end of the wire around the barrel of the round-nose pliers to create a circle shape.

5 Adjust your wire in the round-nose pliers as often as necessary to complete the circle. You will have excess wire that extends beyond the circle.

6 Using your flush cutter, clip the excess wire where the circle meets the working wire. Then, use your nylon-grip flat pliers or bent-nose pliers to flatten the loop.

WRAPPED SIDE-LOOP

The wrapped side-loop provides strength in the wrap (above left) while keeping the loop to the side of the wire (below left) instead of centered to the long working wire.

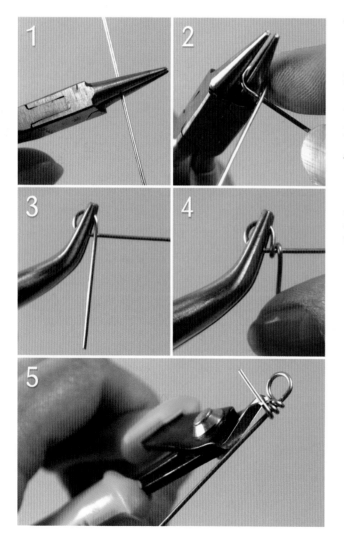

1 Cut a wire 5" (127mm) long; straighten with your nylon-grip pliers. Grip the wire in your round-nose pliers approximately 1½" (39mm) from the end.

2 Create a simple side-loop around the round-nose pliers. Stop the circular bend when the working end of the wire has crossed the gripped wire at a 90° angle.

3 Grip the simple side-loop in your bent-nose pliers.

4 With the pad of your thumb for soft wires or a second pair of pliers for hard wire, roll the end wire around the long wire, completing two to three turns.

5 With your flush cutters, clip the excess wrapping-wire as closely as possible to the wrap. Use your nylon-grip flat pliers or bent-nose pliers to flatten the loop.

WRAPPED STRAIGHT-LOOP

The wrapped straight-loop (above left) locks the beads or link into place (below left) and creates a strong connection.

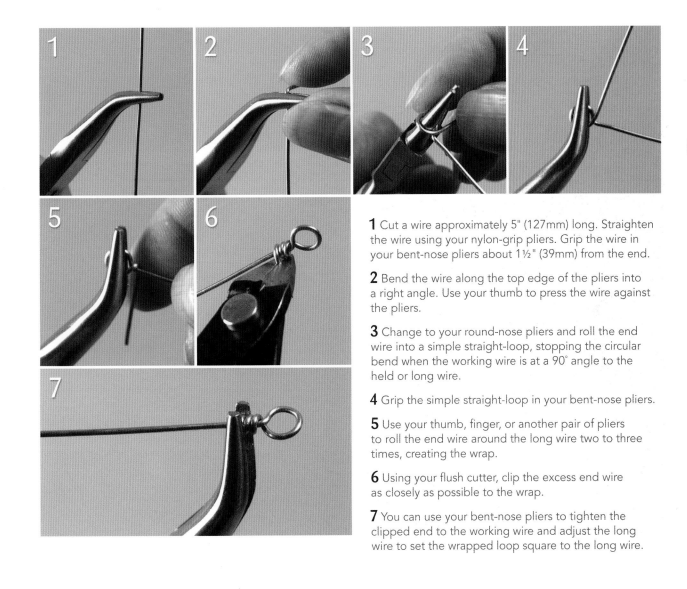

1 Cut a wire approximately 5" (127mm) long. Straighten the wire using your nylon-grip pliers. Grip the wire in your bent-nose pliers about 1½" (39mm) from the end.

2 Bend the wire along the top edge of the pliers into a right angle. Use your thumb to press the wire against the pliers.

3 Change to your round-nose pliers and roll the end wire into a simple straight-loop, stopping the circular bend when the working wire is at a 90° angle to the held or long wire.

4 Grip the simple straight-loop in your bent-nose pliers.

5 Use your thumb, finger, or another pair of pliers to roll the end wire around the long wire two to three times, creating the wrap.

6 Using your flush cutter, clip the excess end wire as closely as possible to the wrap.

7 You can use your bent-nose pliers to tighten the clipped end to the working wire and adjust the long wire to set the wrapped loop square to the long wire.

RIGHT-ANGLE BEND

The right-angle bend (above left) creates a crisp, sharp turn in the wire. That angle is used in straight-loops to center the loops to the wire and in triangle and star elements (below left).

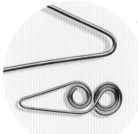

1 Grip the wire with your bent- or straight-nose pliers at the point in the wire where the bend is needed. Use your fingertips to bend the wire across the top edge of your pliers.

2 To set the angle, use the pad of your thumb or your fingertip to press the wire firmly against the pliers' edge.

OPEN U-BEND

An open U-bend (above left) allows you to change the direction of your wire element while leaving room between the two sides of the wire for circles, spirals, and other bends (below left).

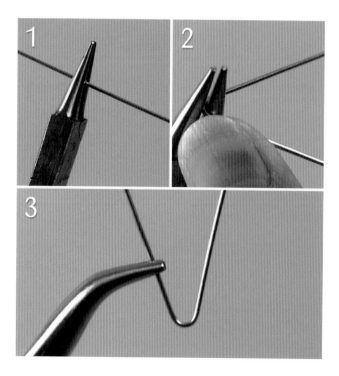

1 Using your round-nose pliers, grip the wire at the midpoint of the wire where you want to work your open U-bend.

2 With the pad of your thumb, roll the wire along the sides of the bent-nose pliers. Turn the wire in the pliers to work the second side of the bend. Bend each side an equal amount along the side of the pliers.

3 As you work, you can adjust the width of the open angle in this basic bend to create tight or wide angles. This is the primary bend in raindrop-shaped elements.

TIGHT U-BEND

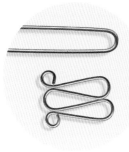

The tight U-bend (above left) creates a hairpin effect in your elements (below left). The bend is worked so that the sides of the wire are curved until the two wire ends are parallel.

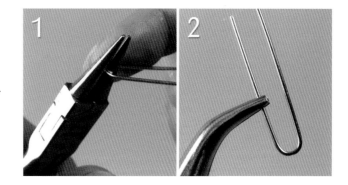

1 Work the tight U-bend exactly as you would an open U-bend. Continue bending each side of the wire until the U-bend has become a half-circle, bringing the two sides of the wire parallel to each other.

2 Multiple tight U-bends in an element create a folded-ribbon effect in your links.

TURN-BACK LOOP

With a turn-back loop you can create a loop on one side of your link (above left) that moves the working wire to the opposite side of the link to continue bending the wire (below left).

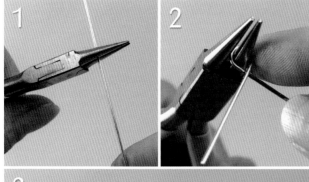

1 Begin this practice loop with a 3" (76mm)-long length of wire. Grip the wire at its center with your round-nose pliers.

2 Bend both sides of the wire into a U-bend using your thumb or fingertip to press the wire against the side of the pliers. Continue rolling the wire until the two working wires cross at a 90° angle.

3 Flatten the turn-back loop using your nylon-grip or bent-nose pliers.

MIDWIRE-CIRCLE

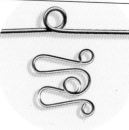

Midwire-circles (above left) add a little dazzle to your link design and create loops for adding beads in the center of the link (below left).

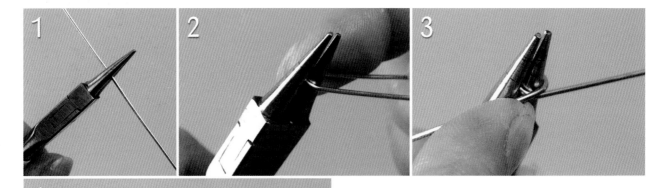

1 Grip the working wire in your round-nose pliers where you want the outside center point of the midwire circle. Where you place your wire in the round-nose pliers will determine the diameter of your midwire circle.

2 Bend both ends of the working wire into tight U-bends.

3 Continue bending the two sides of the wire around the round-nose pliers until you have completed the circle shape. You may need to readjust the position of your wire in the pliers as you work through the final turn.

4 The two wires should cross over with the two sides of the working wire returned to a straight-line position.

MIDWIRE U-BEND CIRCLE

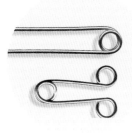

A midwire U-bend circle (above left) brings the two sides of the working wire into parallel while creating a full circle that can be used for adding bead links (below left).

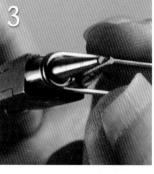

1 At the midpoint in your working wire, grip the wire with your round-nose pliers.

2 Roll the wire into a midwire-circle.

3 Still holding the midwire-circle in your round-nose pliers, continue to bend the two working wires of the link around the pliers' side until they are parallel. You will have created a 1½ turn with the working wires now in the U-bend position.

MIDWIRE LARGE CIRCLE

The large midwire-circle (above left) creates large open spaces in a link that can be wire-wrapped to give a lacy eyelet effect (below left).

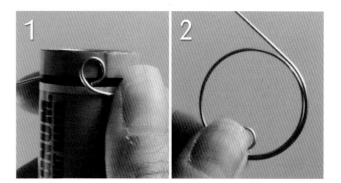

1 For most simple loops and midwire-circles, use your round-nose pliers. For large circles, you can use any form, as in this sample where the circle is being rolled around the base of a marking pen. Hold the working wire against the form where you want the starting point of your circle to be created. Bend the wire around the form, pressing firmly with your fingers to keep the wire tightly shaped.

2 A large midwire-circle may start after a simple side-loop, as shown, or after any hairpin U-bend turn, right-angle bend, or turn-back loop.

SPIRALS

While the large midwire circle adds air space, spirals on any link create dense, tightly packed areas of wire (left).

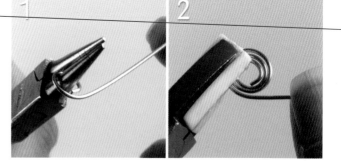

1 A simple side-loop can quickly be pulled into a full spiral. Grip the end of the wire in your round-nose pliers. Begin to roll a simple side-loop. Instead of touching the working wire when you have completed the full turn around the pliers' side, as you would for a simple side-loop, guide the curve of the wire over and past the end point.

2 Transfer the link to your bent-nose pliers and continue rolling the working wire around the outside of the simple loop. You can pull or roll as many turns as you wish to increase the size of the spiral.

38

MIDWIRE-SPIRAL

Spirals (above left) can be worked anywhere in the link to create strong, bold areas of densely packed wire (below left).

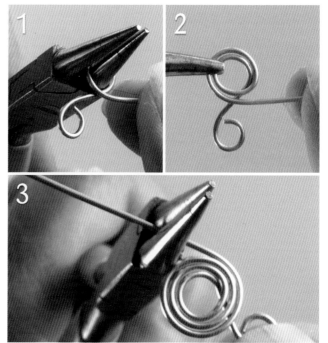

1 A midwire-circle can quickly become a midwire-spiral. Grip the working wire where you want to create your midwire-spiral in your round-nose pliers. Create a midwire-circle.

2 Transfer your midwire-circle to your bent-nose pliers. Gently roll the working wire around the outside of the midwire-circle.

3 You can add multiple turns to any midwire-spiral.

TURN-BACK WIRE SPIRAL

No matter how it's utilized, the double-wire spiral (above left) gives a strong look while adding a little extra interest with its yin-and-yang center (below left).

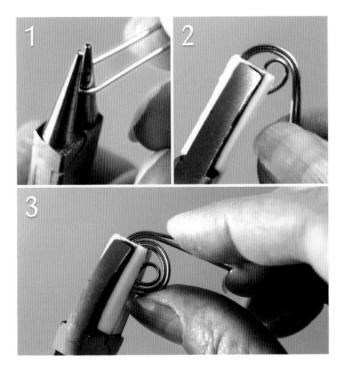

1 Grip your working wire at the midpoint of the wire length in your round-nose pliers. Create a tight U-bend. Holding both wires where they come out of the pliers gently begin bending the U-bend into a spiral.

2 Transfer the U-bend to your nylon-grip pliers and continue gently easing the wire into the spiral shape. Hold both working wires as you work the spiral—treat them as if they were one wire.

3 As you continue bending and adding turns to the spiral shape, adjust the spiral area in your nylon-grip pliers.

Tip 1: Manageable lengths.

Jewelry wire is purchased either by the yard, on pre-packaged spools, or by the pound. Cut your wire into manageable, easy-to-manipulate lengths—between 3" (76mm) long for a small, simple side-loop link and 8" (203mm) or more for a complicated spiral link. The exact amount you will need for each link depends on the bends you incorporate in the link and the gauge of the wire.

basic chain links

You can create every link used in this book by combining the fourteen basic links shown in Chapter Two. This chapter focuses on how to use the bends to create intriguing bent-wire and bent-wire bead links.

Some hints and tricks before you go any further:

1. Cut your wire ends square with the flush cutter before you begin a link.

2. Straighten your working wire with the nylon-grip pliers often.

3. Note your placement of the wire in your round-nose pliers so all of the loops are the same size.

4. As you learn to make a new link, allow a little extra wire for easy bending.

5. Clip the excess wire square with the flush cutters as close to the link as possible.

6. Set the end wire tip by crimping or pressing it into the link with your bent-nose pliers.

7. Flatten your finished link with either your bent-nose pliers or nylon-grip pliers.

8. Practice, practice, practice!

9. Save all of your practice links for fun, link-packed bracelets.

Any of the links shown in this book can be connected and united to make new, long, and interesting chains.

Most Common

The simple side-loop link, simple straight-loop link, wrapped side-loop link, and the wrapped straight-loop link are the most commonly used wire bends for creating chains and bead links in jewelry work.

BASIC CHAIN LINKS

SIMPLE SIDE-LOOP LINK & CHAIN

The simple side-loop is the easiest way to connect or join the links of any chain. The length of space you allow between the two simple side-loops determines how long the link will become and provides space for beads and wire-wrap accents. Links 015 through 020 are all variations on the simple side-loop link and are made in the same manner. (Note: Links are listed on chart beginning on page 66, Chapter 7.)

1 Flush cut a length of wire about 3" (76mm) long, which allows extra wire for easy bending. Grip the end of the wire in between the round-nose pliers' sides. Roll the wire along the outside profile of one side of the pliers. Bring the working wire around to touch the beginning flush-cut end to create a simple side-loop.

2 Reposition the round-nose pliers so the wire lies at the same depth inside the pliers' sides as the first loop. This keeps both loops the same diameter. Slide the wire in the pliers until the first loop touches the side of the wire. This will make a tight or short link with both loops the same size.

3 Roll the working wire around the outside of the round-nose pliers to create a second loop.

4 With your flush cutters, clip the working wire where it crosses the loop wire. Flatten the link using your nylon-grip pliers.

5 Finished, this simple side-loop link has two even loops with little or no space between the loops.

6 Make the second loop farther down the working wire to create a longer link.

7 The simple side-loop link is perfect for quick chains, bead links, and for adding wire-wrap or wire-wrapped bead accents to your projects.

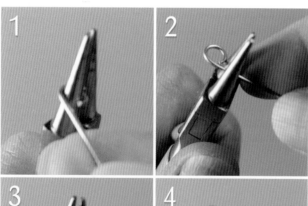

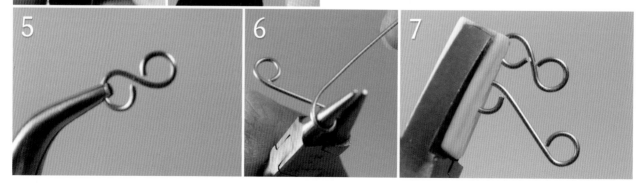

SIMPLE STRAIGHT-LOOP LINK

The simple straight-loop link is another easy way to connect or join the links of a chain. The length of space you allow between the two simple side-loops determines how long the link will become, and provides space for beads and wire-wrap accents. Links 021 through 026 are all variations on the simple straight-loop link and are made in the same manner.

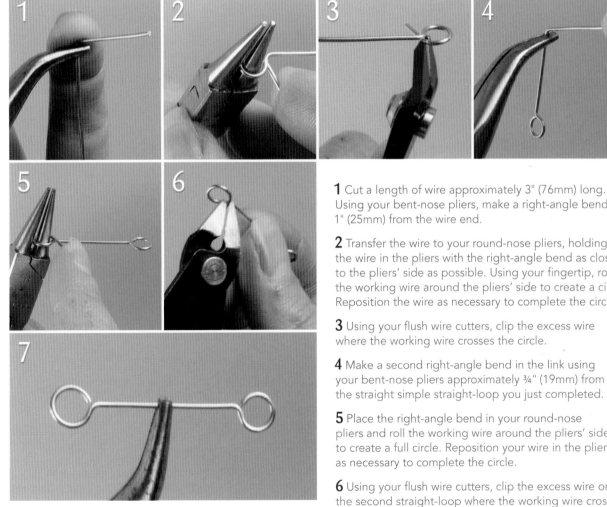

1 Cut a length of wire approximately 3" (76mm) long. Using your bent-nose pliers, make a right-angle bend 1" (25mm) from the wire end.

2 Transfer the wire to your round-nose pliers, holding the wire in the pliers with the right-angle bend as close to the pliers' side as possible. Using your fingertip, roll the working wire around the pliers' side to create a circle. Reposition the wire as necessary to complete the circle.

3 Using your flush wire cutters, clip the excess wire where the working wire crosses the circle.

4 Make a second right-angle bend in the link using your bent-nose pliers approximately ¾" (19mm) from the straight simple straight-loop you just completed.

5 Place the right-angle bend in your round-nose pliers and roll the working wire around the pliers' side to create a full circle. Reposition your wire in the pliers as necessary to complete the circle.

6 Using your flush wire cutters, clip the excess wire on the second straight-loop where the working wire crosses the circle. Use your nylon-grip pliers to flatten the link.

7 The simple straight-loop ends of this link make the link easy to add to any chain. The size of the link can be adjusted from very small links where the second simple straight-loop begins against the first simple straight-loop, or by allowing several inches of wire between the two loops.

WRAPPED SIMPLE SIDE-LOOP LINK

Quick, easy, and very secure, the wrapped simple side-loop link uses the simple side-loop to stagger or offset the links in a chain. Links 027 through 032 are variations of the wrapped simple side-loop.

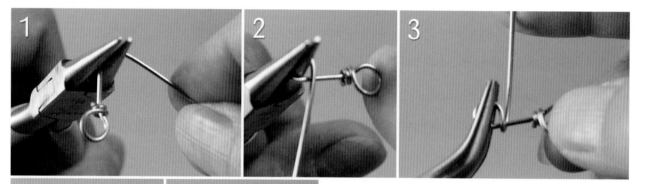

1 Cut a length of wire approximately 3" (76mm) long with your flush cutters.

2 This link has the wrapped simple side-loop worked on both ends. Using your round-nose pliers, roll the working wire into a simple side-loop.

3 Grip the simple side-loop in your bent-nose pliers. Wrap the working wire around the base of the simple side-loop two to three times.

4 Clip the excess wire as close as possible to the wrap. Use your bent-nose pliers to crimp or press the end wire into place.

5 The wrapped simple side-loop link easily adjusts into a link with a long shaft by allowing more wire between the two connecting loops. Often the wrapped simple side-loop link is worked by interlocking one of the loops into the connecting loop of the last link on a chain.

WRAPPED STRAIGHT-LOOP LINK

The wrapped straight-loop both centers the connecting loop to the next link while creating the strongest link because of the wrapping step. Links 033 through 038 are variations of the wrapped straight-loop.

1 With your flush cutters, cut a length of wire approximately 4" (102mm) long. Using your bent-nose pliers, make a right-angle bend approximately 1½" (38mm) from the end.

2 Using your round-nose pliers, create a straight-loop with the bent working wire.

3 Holding the straight-loop in your bent-nose pliers, wrap the working wire around the link wire at the base of the straight-loop two to three times.

4 Use your flush cutters to trim the excess wire from the wrap. Crimp or press the end wire into position with the wrap using your bent-nose pliers.

5 Place the wire into your bent-nose pliers just above the wrap of the first loop. Bend a right angle with the working wire.

6 Using your round-nose pliers, create a simple straight-loop.

7 Holding the straight-loop in your bent-nose pliers, wrap the working end around the link wire at the base of the straight-loop.

8 Clip the excess wire with your flush cutters.

9 Crimp or press the end wire into place with your bent-nose pliers.

10 The size of your wrapped straight-loop link can be changed by changing the number of wraps that you use on each connecting loop and by how much wire you allow between those connecting loops.

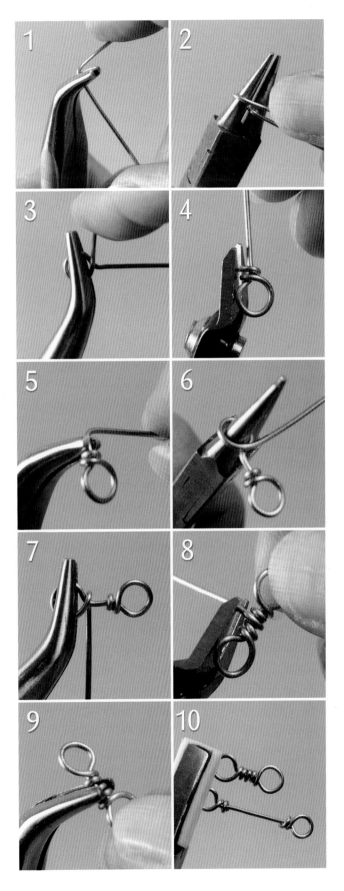

4

connecting the links

There are many ways to connect the links of your jewelry. As the designer, you have a lot of options. Four of the most common ways are jump and split rings, and single and wrapped loops. All four offer versatility and add varying degrees of visual interest to your jewelry. What you use and how you use it are up to you.

Links are connected either through the simple loop or wrapped loop of the link, the use of a jump ring, or the use of a split ring.

Jump Rings

Jump rings are small single circles of wire created with the round-nose pliers or by cutting single rings from a coil. Jump rings have three basic uses in jewelry making—creating chains, connecting links, and adding sparkle to an area of the jewelry. The jump ring is Link 073 in the Complete Links Chart (page 66).

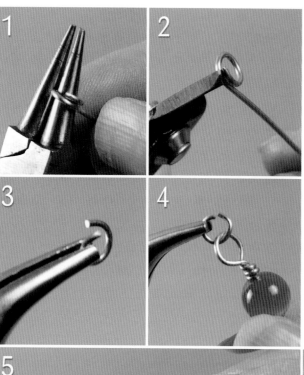

1 Flush cut the working end of your wire to ensure you have a square edge. Working with the round-nose pliers, bend the wire into a full circle. Continue the bend slightly beyond the wire's starting end.

2 Use your flush cutters to clip the working wire at the same point in the circle as the starting end.

3 The completed jump ring is the simplest of links, making a full circle with touching ends.

4 Using your bent-nose pliers, open the ring by pushing one side of the ring away from the second side. Slide the open area over the connecting loop of the last link in your chain or into a U-bend area of a link where you want to place bead dangles.

5 Slide the connecting loop of the next link onto the Link 073, going through the opening. Using your bent-nose pliers, close the opening of the Link 073. Crimp or press the Link 073 to ensure it returns to a flat smooth circle.

6 The simple jump ring creates a strong connection between your bent-wire links.

CREATING MULTIPLE JUMP RINGS

When your project needs only a few jump rings, they are easy to make using your round-nose pliers. For projects that need a large quantity of jump rings, it is quick and easy to first create a coil, and then cut the rings from the coil. This ensures the jump rings for your project are the same size.

The Crystal Fairy bracelet, a 7" (178mm)-long 18-gauge wire bracelet with a lampwork bead, uses three jump rings as one connecting link. The use of multiple Link 073s makes each connection stronger while adding visual interest with the change from the single wire of the hairpin links to the three wires of the Link 073s. Make the extra-large jump rings between the three jump ring links by working the jump ring over the handle of a wooden kitchen spoon. To add just a touch more glitter to the work, I worked a jump ring through the loops of the hairpin links.

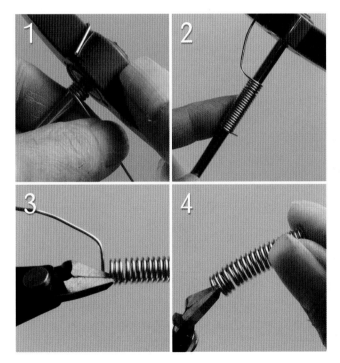

1 Thread an extra-long length of wire through your coil maker. Roll the working wire around the shaft of the coil maker until you have wrapped the entire length of wire.

2 This style of coil maker comes with interchangeable shafts of different sizes and shapes. A knitting needle, wooden pencil, a straight-barreled ink pen, or other similar items also work as coil makers.

3 Flush cut the excess wire at the beginning of the coil. Re-clip the end of your coil wire to ensure the end of the wire is flat and square.

4 Lay the side of your flush cutter against the end of the coil. This frees one full turn of the coil. Cut the first full loop of the coil and continue to cut the Link 073s.

Split Rings

Split rings, Link 074 in the Complete Links Chart (page 66), are very small coils that have two to three full turns to the coil. The coils of the split ring are opened and the loops of the links that are to be connected are threaded through the coil just as you would thread a key on a key ring. Split rings create a stronger connection than jump rings.

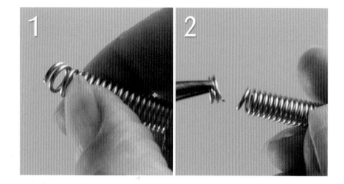

1 Create a coil of wire the width or size of your desired split rings. Flush cut the beginning of the coil wire to square the end of the split ring. Count two full turns in the coil and use your thumbnail to open that coil loop. Use your flush cutters to clip the coil, freeing the split ring.

2 Split rings usually use two to three full turns of the coil but you may create split rings with more than three turns.

Simple Loops

Using a simple loop, whether a side-loop or a straight-loop (links 015 through 026 in the Complete Links Chart on page 66), as the connecting ends of your links makes chain construction quick and easy. If you are working on a new design that you may wish to change by moving or substituting links during the creation process, the simple loop is your choice for link ends.

1 Simple loops, whether worked as side- or straight-loops, make easy connections between links.

2 Open the simple loop using your bent-nose pliers by pulling the loop to one side of the link.

3 Slide the opened loop onto the connecting loop of the last link of the chain.

4 Using your bent-nose pliers, close the simple loop. Crimp or press firmly to reset the loop to square.

5 The simple loop is fast and easy to use.

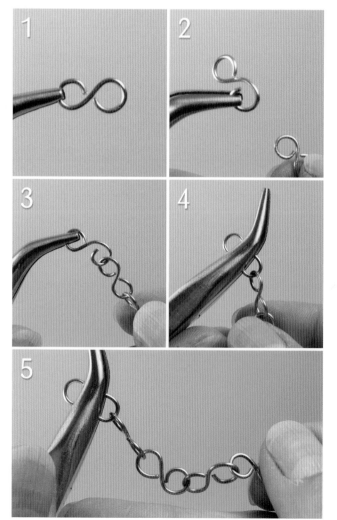

50

Wrapped Loops

Using wrapped looped ends (links 027 through 038 on the Complete Links Chart) as your connecting loops creates the strongest chains. The wrapping process guarantees the links of the chain cannot be pulled apart. Plan your design carefully in advance when using wrapped looped ends as your connection point in a chain because if you need to remove or replace a link, the existing link will need to be cut from the chain, making it unusable.

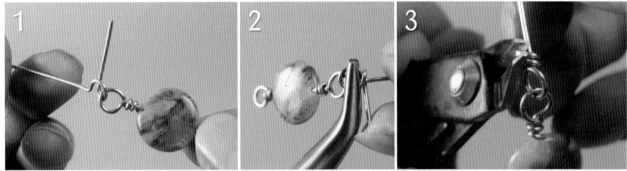

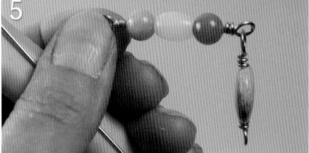

1 Wrapped looped links are worked onto the chain as they are created. Begin work by bending the wire into a right angle, and then pulling your loop around the round-nose pliers. Slide the opening of the loop through the end loop of the last link on the chain.

2 Using your bent-nose pliers, secure the loop by wrapping the working wire end around the base of the loop two or three times.

3 Cut the excess wire from the wrap using your flush cutter.

4 Add any beads or do any bends that you need to create this link.

5 End your link using either a wrapped loop or a simple loop depending on the next link of the design.

5

hook-and-eye sets

Nearly every project you make—from necklaces and bracelets, to anklets—needs some method of latching the two sides of the chain together. The hook and hook eye, links 051 through 062 in the Complete Links Chart (pages 67 to 68), are the standard method, with the hook attached to one end of the chain and the eye to the other.

The eye part of the set can be a simple jump ring, the connecting loop of the last link in the chain, a tight U-bend of a raindrop link, or open center of a spiral link. You can easily use links 015, 033, 046, 073, 074, or other links in the Complete Links Chart (page 66) as basic eyes.

Be creative with the necklace hook. It is seldom seen, yet adding an intriguing bending or a complementary bead to the hook will delight the owner.

Many of the more intricate links shown in this book can easily be turned into hooks and eyes to complete your jewelry designs.

Latch Hooks

As shown, the end of any link can be converted into a hook, making your possibilities endless. As you work your hooks, also consider the size and shape of the curve in the hook. Small curves offer a tight lock into the eye loop but can be harder to use on smaller necklaces, such as dog collars and chokers. Using a larger curve makes latching quick and easy but its size can overpower a fine chain.

For fine wires such as 26- to 20-gauge, keep the total length of the hook small and the curve in the hook bent tight to keep the visual look of the hook in proportion to the visual weight of the chain links.

For large gauge wires such as 18- to 12-gauge, try using large round forms as thick ink pens, wooden spoon handles, or marker pens to create the bent shape. Heavy turned links such as double spirals, 5-turn hairpins, and large beads may need a bold, strong hook to balance the visual weight of the work.

Hook-and-eye sets. *Tornado Alley*, a 7" (178mm) bracelet worked in 16-gauge wire, demonstrates what you can do to create imaginative hook-and-eye sets. The eye area of the bracelet is the open-spiral on the end double-spiral link. The open-spiral has two turns, so the hook can be set in either one, making the length of the bracelet adjustable. The hook was worked onto the end of a spiral three-hairpin-turn link. Instead of working the second or last spiral to the end of the link, I bent the wire to a right angle. After adding a bead, I bent the remaining wire around the handles of a pair of round-nose pliers to make the curve of the hook. Completed, the hook-and-eye for *Tornado Alley* are functional and decorative.

SIMPLE SIDE-LOOP HOOK

The simple side-loop hook (Link 051) is quick and easy to create. Work with the same gauge wire as the main chain links of your project. When connecting this hook to your chain, open the simple side-loop and slide the hook onto the end loop of the last link in your chain.

1 Using your flush cutters, cut a 3" to 4" (76mm to 102mm) length of wire.

2 Using your round-nose pliers, make a simple side-loop on one end of the wire.

3 Using your round-nose pliers, make a U-bend about ¼" to ½" (6mm to 13mm) from the simple side-loop.

4 Using your round-nose pliers, make a shallow open U-bend directly across from the base of the simple side-loop.

5 With your flush cutters, clip the wire about ⅛" (3mm) from the open U-bend.

6 The simple side-loop hook is easy to connect to any necklace or bracelet.

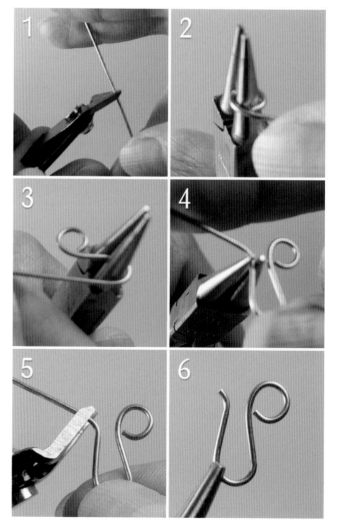

WRAPPED SIDE-LOOP HOOK LINK

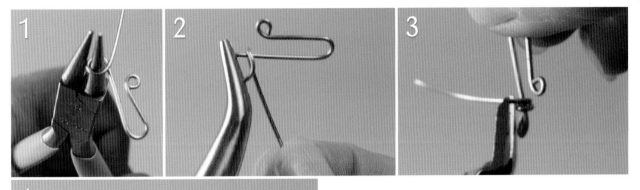

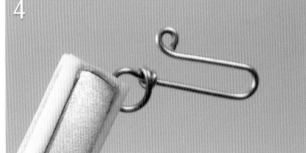

1 Work the hook link as you would a simple side-loop hook. When you have created the second simple side-loop, extend the working wire at a 90° angle to the hook wire.

2 Using your bent-nose pliers, wrap the working wire around the hook wire for two to three turns.

3 Cut the excess wire using your flush cutters.

4 Add the wrapped side-loop hook (Link 055) to your necklace chain using a jump or split ring, by opening a simple loop on the last link of the chain, or by interlocking the wrapped loop end onto the loop of the last chain link.

Tip 2: Cutter position.

The flush-cut wire cutter has a V-shape cut on the inside face of the tool and a flush, flat cut on the back face of the cutter. The flat or flush side of the tool should face the end of the wire at the cut point to create a square angle to the wire end.

WRAPPED STRAIGHT-LOOP HOOK LINK

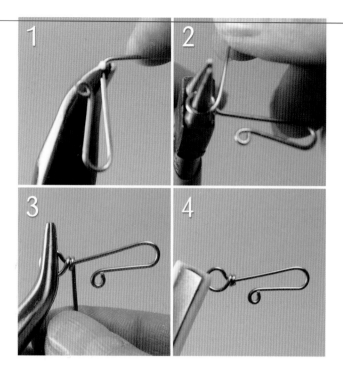

1 Create a small simple side-loop at the end of the working wire. About ¼" to ½" (6mm to 13mm) from that simple loop, create a tight U-bend. Create a right-angle bend ½" (13mm) from the U-bend to begin your wrapped side-loop.

2 Bend the wire around your round-nose pliers to make the loop.

3 Wrap the working wire around the base of the loop two to three turns. Cut the excess wire using your flush cutters.

4 The wrapped straight-loop hook (Link 056) keeps the hook-and-eye set in line with the chain links of your necklace. Like the wrapped side-loop hook, it can be connected to your chain using a jump or split ring, or interlocked into the loop of the last link.

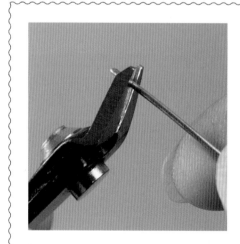

Tip 3: Ensuring square ends.

Ensure you have a square, flat end to the wire, by using your flush cutter. This step is essential when you are using scrap ends of wire left over from previous links.

BENT-SHAFT HOOK

Once you have created the connecting loop of your hook, make a shaft area of straight wire before you turn your hook curve. The right-angle bend of the shaft area offsets the hook so the hook curve locks more deeply into the eye loop. Links 053 and 054 are used to secure beads to the hook link, keeping them from sliding up into the curve area.

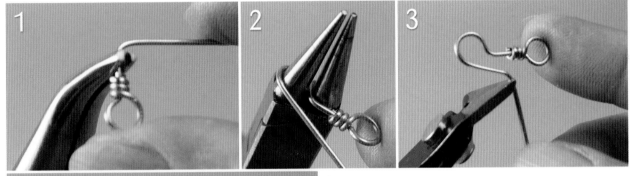

1 After you have created your simple or wrapped loop, grip the working wire with your bent-nose pliers at the top of the loop area. Pull the working wire into a right-angle bend.

2 Grip the working wire above the right-angle bend and pull it into a partial loop.

3 Create an open U-bend at the end of the hook curve, and then cut the wire using your flush cutters.

4 The shaft area of this hook adds a small decorative detail while it off sets the hook from the necklace.

DOUBLE-WIRE HOOK

Folding the wire into a tight U-bend creates a double-wire hook (Link 057). This style of hook is perfect for 26- to 20-gauge wire because it doubles the strength of the hook.

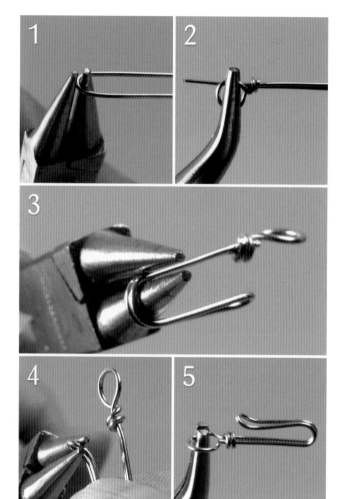

1 Cut your wire extra long, allowing about 2" (51mm) more wire than you would usually use in bending a hook. Grip the wire at the midpoint in the tip of your round-nose pliers. Bend the wire into a full, tight U-bend. Tighten the U-bend by crimping the loop in your flat-nose pliers.

2 Create a wrapped wire-loop on the opposite side of the U-bend. Work the loop by making a right-angle bend in one of the working wires. With the same wire, bend a loop around your round-nose pliers. Hold both working wires in your bent-nose pliers as you work the wrap. Bring the wrap wire over both wires. Clip the excess wire from the wrapping-wire and from the long working wire that extends beyond the wrapped loop.

3 Create the U-bend of the curve of the hook using your round-nose pliers.

4 Using your round-nose pliers, make a small shallow bend at the tip of the hook.

5 Strong and secure, this double-wire hook design is excellent when you need an extra-small hook for your necklace.

ADDING A LITTLE EXTRA

Extra zing. In *Chocolate Sundae* (right), adding beads or using bent-wire links for the hook-and-eye set adds a little extra zing to your work. Also consider adding small chains made of jump rings or simple side-loop links to the loop of the eye link. A chain of about " (51mm) long makes the length of the necklace adjustable, especially when working dog collars and chokers. Small bead links and bead dangles add visual texture and give extra interest to the jewelry when it is worn with a low-back blouse or dress. (See instructions on page 251.)

Chocolate Sundae

EASY & ELEGANT **beaded copper** JEWELRY

BASIC EARRING LOOP

Almost any bent-wire link or bead link can quickly be turned into an earring with the addition of a simple earring loop. Loops can be worked in wire gauges from 26 through 18. You can work the connecting loop of an earring with either a simple side-loop or a wrapped loop.

Earring loops can be worked in a variety of shapes and sizes. Be creative with your loops by experimenting with different shapes for the curve area and different lengths.

1 To create the basic earring wire, links 063 through 072 on the Complete Links Chart (page 66), all variations of the basic earring wire, cut two 4" (102mm) lengths of 20-gauge wire. To ensure the two earring wires will have matching sizes and shape, work them through each of these steps at the same time. Grip the end of the wire in your round-nose pliers and roll the wire into a simple side-loop.

2 Place the working wire against any round shaped form to create the curve of the earring. I used the handle area of my nylon-grip pliers.

3 Holding the earring wire against the form, add a small bend below the curve shape. This gives the earring a shallow turn-back design.

4 Use your flush wire cutters to clip the earrings to length. You can use fine sandpaper or a fine fingernail file to gently sand the end of the earring to make it more comfortable to use.

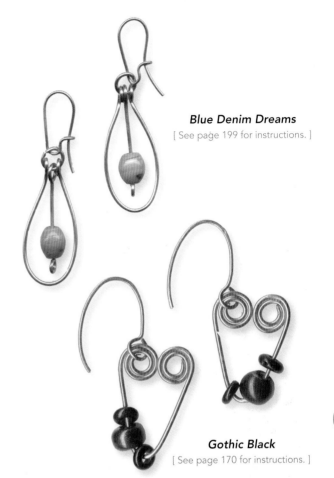

Blue Denim Dreams
[See page 199 for instructions.]

Gothic Black
[See page 170 for instructions.]

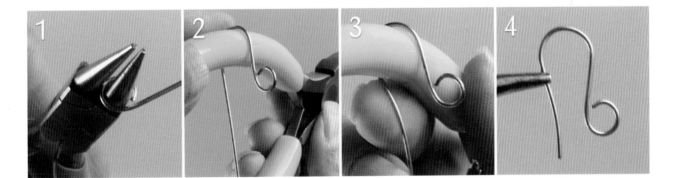

rattail and suede leather cords

A variety of string and cord materials that can replace purchased or hand-bent metal chains are available to the jewelry maker. Ribbons make excellent, soft, and comfortable cording for your finished bent-wire link centerpieces and are available in organza, nylon, velvet, and silk. Suede leather can be purchased in yard-long strips in a range of dyed colors. Also consider trying cotton cording, as well as heavyweight crochet cotton, twine, and knitting cotton. Cotton fabric can be cut into thin strips and sewn into tubes that can become your necklace support.

Nylon cording comes in three basic sizes—bugtail cording is 1mm, mousetail cording comes in 1.5mm, and rattail cording at 2mm. The projects in this book use rattail cording, which can be purchased in 10-, 100- and 200-yard spools.

Adding a cord in place of a chain makes finishing your necklaces quick and easy. There are two primary methods for attaching your cording to your necklace links—coils and wire-wrapping. Through this section, we will look at both methods.

Rattail cord, leather, twine, and even ribbon can be used to create the side chains of your necklace.

COILED RATTAIL CORDING

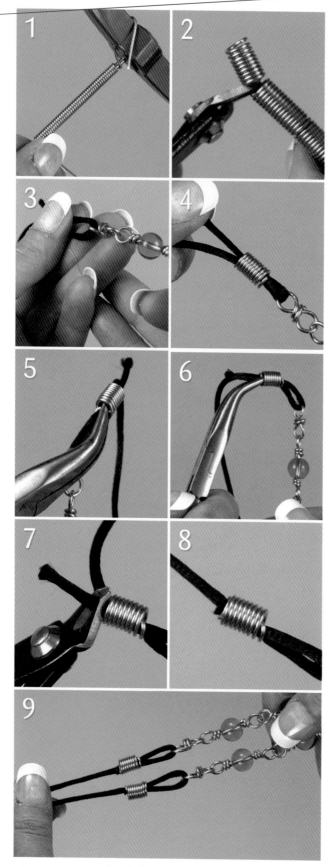

1 Begin this practice session by creating a 3" (76mm)-long tightly packed coil of 20- to 18-gauge wire measuring ³⁄₁₆" (5mm) wide.

2 Remove the coil from your coil maker or form and clip the end loops to start the coil with a clean, square-cut full turn. You will need up to four coils for each necklace—two for securing the necklace links in the center of the project and two for securing the ends at the hook-and-eye point. Cut the coil lengths by measurement or counting the number of coils. For this practice sample, count ten full turns into the coil. Use your flush wire cutters to first slice between the full turns to open an area between the counted coils and the remaining coil length. Cut the counted coil length from the main coil section. You need two ten-count coils for this necklace.

3 Cut two 16" (406mm)-long lengths of rattail cording. Thread one end of one section of the rattail cord through the end-connecting loop of your bent-wire centerpiece. Pull the threaded end of the cord 1½" (38mm) beyond the loop.

4 Slide one ten-count coil length over both ends of the rattail cord. Position the coil so that a 1" (25mm) loop of rattail is below the coil.

5 Hold the coil in position on the two rattail cords and use your bent-nose pliers to grip the first half-turn of the coil. Crimp the half-turn coil wire tightly against both rattail cords.

6 Grip the first half-turn coil on the opposite side of the coil in your bent-nose pliers and crimp the wire tightly against the cording.

7 Use your scissors or flush cutters to clip any excess rattail cord from the short, threaded end of the cording, flush with the coil link's top.

8 A completed crimped coil securely holds the folded cording in position to the last connecting loop of the necklace work. For this project, I used a large coil. You can use tighter, smaller diameter coils that more closely fit the size of your cording. To thread smaller cords, wrap the end of the cording with transparent tape as tightly as possible. This makes a shoestring-type end for your cord and helps with threading the cord through tighter coils.

9 The finished coiled cording secure adds the rattail to the necklace while bringing the sparkle of the wire onto the cord area.

WIRE-WRAPPED CORDING

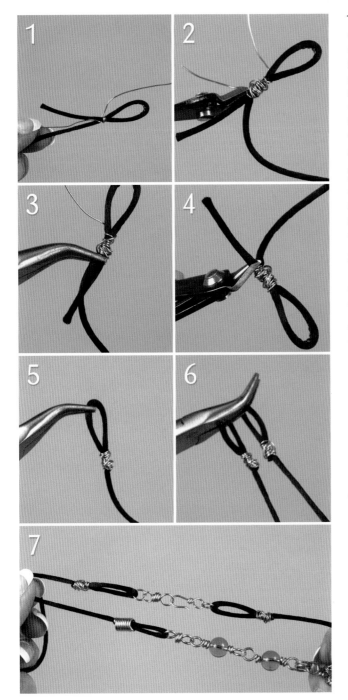

1 To complete this practice necklace, we will use a wire-wrapping to secure the hook-and-eye end of the rattail cord. Begin these steps by measuring the rattail cord from the last connecting loop of the necklace to a length of 11" (279mm). Fold the cord at that 11" (279mm) mark. Cut an 8" (203mm) length of 26-gauge wire. Heavier wires can be used—up to 20-gauge. Grip one end of the wire against the two cords 1" (25mm) from the fold. Wrap the wire into three to four tightly packed coils around both cords.

2 Continue wrapping the wire in either tightly packed coils or, as shown, random loose turns. Wrap at least a ¼" (6mm) wide area of cording. When the wrapping step is complete, clip the excess wire from the end of the wrapping-wire using your flush cutters.

3 Grip the clipped end of the wrapping in your bent-nose pliers and tightly crimp it to the cords. Clip and crimp the excess wire left from the beginning point of the wrap.

4 Use either your scissors or your flush cutters to clip the excess rattail cord from the loop as closely to the wrapping-wire as possible.

5 The completed wire-wrapped cord is strong and secure. As with any wire-wrapping, you can add small bead accents to the wire during the wrapping stage to add bright, small touches of color to the ends of your cords.

6 Repeat these wire-wrapping steps for the remaining hook-and-eye end of your necklace.

7 For this practice necklace, ¼" (6mm)-wide Link 073s were used to connect the wrapped straight-loop hook and the wrapped straight-loop eye to the cord.

Demonstration necklace

For the necklace used for demonstrating coiled rattail cording and wire-wrapped cording, a focal center chain was created using 18-gauge wire and five 8mm olive green cat's eye beads. Five Link 036s using one cat's-eye bead per link were interlocked to create the center chain. Two 033s were created, working one each into the end connecting loops of the chain. The rattail cording was added to the end connecting loops of the 033 links.

63

7

the complete link set

One of the greatest pleasures of creating bent-wire jewelry is creating your own wire bends. Here in Chapter 7, I show you the links I created for the projects in this book, as well as others that were created along the way. When you begin designing your own jewelry—and you will, it's inevitable—indulge the artist inside you by using the links in this chart as a starting point for your own creations. The possibilities of bent-wire links in jewelry design are endless. Explore. Experiment. Enjoy. Those are the secrets to making beautiful jewelry that will be noticed.

The Complete Link Set shows an image of the link, the link number, and a basic description of that link. Each specific link is identified throughout the projects in this book by link number. For example, Link 073 is a jump ring and Link 074 is a split ring. The names of the links may be similar or repeated as they are used only as a general guide to the basic bends used to create those links. To keep it as simple as possible for the reader, we labeled all links, bends, rings, and dangles as links throughout the book and on the complete list.

Many of the links that follow are explained in other portions of the book. Others are slight variations of those explained. I've provided instructions for one link out of each type of link.

Now go for it.

This section will take you through step-by-step instructions to create the links used in this book and to inspire your imagination to create your own unique links.

Link 001	simple side-loop link
Link 002	simple straight side-loop link
Link 003	wrapped side-loop link
Link 004	wrapped straight-loop link
Link 005	right-angle bend link
Link 006	open U-bend link
Link 007	tight U-bend link
Link 008	turn-back loop link
Link 009	midwire-circle link
Link 010	midwire-circle U-bend link
Link 011	midwire large-circle link
Link 012	spiral link
Link 013	midwire-spiral link
Link 014	turn-back wire spiral link
Link 015	simple side-loop link

Link 016	medium simple side-loop link
Link 017	long simple-side-loop link
Link 018	1-bead simple side-loop link
Link 019	2-bead simple side-loop link
Link 020	3-bead simple side-loop link
Link 021	simple straight-loop link
Link 022	medium straight-loop link
Link 023	long simple straight-loop link
Link 024	1-bead simple straight-loop link
Link 025	2-bead simple straight-loop link
Link 026	3-bead simple straight-loop link
Link 027	wrapped side-loop link
Link 028	medium wrapped side-loop link
Link 029	long wrapped side-loop link
Link 030	wrapped side-loop-bead link

Link 031	2-bead wrapped side-loop link		Link 046	wrapped hook eye link
Link 032	3-bead wrapped side-loop link		Link 047	wrapped long loop link
Link 033	wrapped straight-loop link		Link 048	wire-wrapped beaded long loop link
Link 034	medium wrapped straight-loop link		Link 049	horseshoe bead link
Link 035	long wrapped straight-loop link		Link 050	long horseshoe link
Link 036	large bead wrapped straight-loop link		Link 051	simple side-loop hook
Link 037	2-bead wrapped straight-loop link		Link 052	wrapped straight-loop hook
Link 038	3-bead wrapped straight-loop link		Link 053	wrapped straight-loop hook
Link 039	double wire-wrapped straight-loop link		Link 054	basic earring hoop link
Link 040	wire-wrapped simple side-loop link		Link 055	wrapped side-loop hook link
Link 041	3-bead random-wrap straight-loop link		Link 056	wrapped straight-loop hook link
Link 042	small coil link		Link 057	double-wire hook link
Link 043	coil link		Link 058	beaded hook link
Link 044	coil-covered simple straight-loop link		Link 059	wire-wrapped hook link
Link 045	large wrapped straight-loop link		Link 060	2½-turn spiral hook

	Link 061	coiled hook
	Link 062	hook-and-eye set
	Link 063	long-backed simple side-loop earring wire
	Link 064	simple side-loop earring wires
	Link 065	open-curve earring wire
	Link 066	medium-curved earring wire
	Link 067	hairpin earring wire
	Link 068	back-turned simple side-loop earring wire
	Link 069	centered simple side-loop earring wire
	Link 070	right-angle-bend earring wire
	Link 071	deep-set right-angle-bend earring wire
	Link 072	dropped simple straight-loop earring wire
	Link 073	jump ring
	Link 074	split ring
	Link 075	open-eyelet spiral hoop link

	Link 076	medium wire-beaded hoop link
	Link 077	medium wire-beaded hoop link
	Link 078	coil-covered medium hoop link
	Link 079	coil-covered medium bead hoop link
	Link 080	large wire-bead-wrapped hoop
	Link 081	large wire-bead-wrapped hoop link
	Link 082	large open-beaded hoop link
	Link 083	wire-wrapped split ring hoop link
	Link 084	6-turn wire-wrapped spiral link
	Link 085	2-turn spiral link
	Link 086	3-turn spiral link
	Link 087	4-turn spiral link
	Link 088	2-turn 3-turn double-spiral link
	Link 089	double 2-turn spiral link
	Link 090	double 2½-turn-spiral link

	Link 091	double 3½-turn spiral link
	Link 092	wire-wrapped center double-hoop link
	Link 093	double midwire-spiral link
	Link 094	double-spiral bead link
	Link 095	simple parallel spiral link
	Link 096	2-turn parallel spirals link
	Link 097	3-turn parallel spirals link
	Link 098	2-turn parallel spirals link
	Link 099	2½-turn parallel spirals link
	Link 100	3-turn parallel simple side-loop bead link
	Link 101	3-turn parallel spiral bead link
	Link 102	3-turn spiral bead link
	Link 103	parallel simple side-loop bead link
	Link 104	3-turn bent-center spiral bead link
	Link 105	open U-bend simple side-loop link

	Link 106	open U-bend inverted simple side-loop link
	Link 107	simple hairpin link
	Link 108	long simple hairpin link
	Link 109	1½-turn spiral hairpin link
	Link 110	2-turn double-spiral hairpin link
	Link 111	2½-turn double-spiral hairpin link
	Link 112	3-turn double-spiral hairpin link
	Link 113	large U-bend simple hairpin link
	Link 114	beaded simple hairpin link
	Link 115	3-turn double-spiral hairpin link
	Link 116	3-turn spiral wire-wrapped beaded hairpin link
	Link 117	locked double-spiral hairpin link
	Link 118	2½-turn spiral simple side-loop link
	Link 119	3-turn double midwire-spiral hairpin link
	Link 120	3½-turn double midwire-spiral hairpin link

Link 121	midwire-circle simple side-loop hairpin link	
Link 122	1½-turn spiral midwire-circle hairpin link	
Link 123	2½-turn spiral midwire-circle hairpin link	
Link 124	3-turn spiral midwire-circle hairpin link	
Link 125	offset simple side-loop hairpin link	
Link 126	offset 2-turn spiral simple side-loop hairpin link	
Link 127	offset 3½-turn single-spiral simple side-loop hairpin link	
Link 128	offset 2½-turn single-spiral simple side-loop hairpin link	
Link 129	offset 2½-turn single-spiral beaded simple side-loop hairpin	
Link 130	offset 2½-turn double-spiral hairpin link	
Link 131	offset 3½-turn double-spiral hairpin link	
Link 132	offset 4-turn spiral simple side-loop hairpin link	
Link 133	offset 3-turn spiral hairpin link	
Link 134	offset midwire-circle hairpin link	
Link 135	double-hairpin link	

Link 136	3-turn hairpin link	
Link 137	5-turn hairpin link	
Link 138	tapered hairpin link	
Link 139	3-turn open-hairpin link	
Link 140	4-turn stretched hairpin link	
Link 141	hairpin bead link	
Link 142	open 3½-turn spiral hairpin link	
Link 143	open 4-turn spiral hairpin link	
Link 144	open 3-turn spiral 2-turn hairpin link	
Link 145	3½-turn spiral 2-turn hairpin link	
Link 146	2-turn double-spiral hairpin link	
Link 147	3½-turn spiral 3-turn hairpin link	
Link 148	2½-turn spiral 4-turn hairpin link	
Link 149	spiral compressed hairpin link	
Link 150	simple side-loop 2½-turn spiral compressed 5-turn hairpin link	

	Link 151	double-spiral 5-bend hairpin link
	Link 152	turn-back midwire-spiral link
	Link 153	turn-back midwire-spiral high end loops link
	Link 154	wire-wrapped turn-back midwire-spiral link
	Link 155	open-heart link
	Link 156	spiral heart link
	Link 157	heart-shaped spiral bead-dangle link
	Link 158	wire-wrapped heart eyelet link
	Link 159	open-heart wire bead-wrapped link
	Link 160	turn-back loop open-heart link
	Link 161	turn-back loop spiral-end open-heart link
	Link 162	turn-back loop round-sided heart link
	Link 163	turn-back loop straight-sided heart link
	Link 164	turn-back loop compressed open-eyelet heart
	Link 165	open hairpin-bend center open-eyelet link

	Link 166	closed hairpin-bend center open-eyelet link
	Link 167	double-circle, single-circle eyelet link
	Link 168	double-circle eyelet link
	Link 169	wire-beaded eyelet link
	Link 170	wire-wrapped double-circle eyelet link
	Link 171	beaded wire-wrapped hairpin open-eyelet link
	Link 172	beaded wire-wrapped open-circle eyelet link
	Link 173	oval-center double-circle open-eyelet link
	Link 174	oval-center double-circle compressed open-eyelet link
	Link 175	midwire-circle double-hairpin link
	Link 176	3-turn hairpin midwire-circle link
	Link 177	midwire-circle multiple-turn hairpin
	Link 178	midwire-spiral hairpin link
	Link 179	long midwire-circle bead link
	Link 180	2-turn-back loops ladder link

Link 181	4 turn-back loops ladder link		Link 196	2-turn spiral raindrop link
Link 182	6 turn-back loops ladder link		Link 197	3-turn spiral raindrop link
Link 183	7 turn-back loops spiral-end ladder link		Link 198	2½-turn spiral raindrop link
Link 184	5 turn-back loops spiral-end ladder link		Link 199	2½-turn-spiral raindrop link
Link 185	turn-back loop spiral link		Link 200	double 2-turn spiral raindrop link
Link 186	midwire-spiral link		Link 201	2½-turn spiral raindrop link
Link 187	midwire-spiral link		Link 202	double-spiral raindrop link
Link 188	turn-back cross-under loop link		Link 203	wire-wrapped beaded-spiral-center raindrop link
Link 189	spiral turn-back cross-over link		Link 204	wire-wrapped spiral-center raindrop link
Link 190	locked-ends midwire-spiral link		Link 205	2½-turn spiral hairpin raindrop link
Link 191	locked-ends midwire-spiral turn-back link		Link 206	3-turn spiral hairpin raindrop link
Link 192	threaded turn-back loop double-spiral link		Link 207	3-turn spiral long hairpin link
Link 193	turn-back loop spiral hairpin link		Link 208	3½-turn spiral-center 2-hairpin raindrop link
Link 194	midwire-spiral turn-back locked-ends link		Link 209	3½-turn spiral 3-hairpin turn raindrop link
Link 195	simple raindrop link		Link 210	2½-turn spiral 4-hairpin turn compressed raindrop link

	Link 211	2½-turn spiral-center double-raindrop link		Link 226	2-turn spiral raindrop link
	Link 212	2½-turn-spiral double-raindrop hairpin turn link		Link 227	3- and 4-turn spiral raindrop link
	Link 213	double-raindrop bead link		Link 228	large open-eyelet raindrop link
	Link 214	2½-turn spiral turn-back loop raindrop link		Link 229	3-turn spiral-wrapped straight-loop raindrop link
	Link 215	open 3½-turn spiral raindrop link		Link 230	open multi-circle eyelet raindrop link
	Link 216	open 3½-turn spiral hairpin raindrop link		Link 231	3-circle link
	Link 217	open 3½-turn spiral long hairpin raindrop link		Link 232	3-spiral circle link
	Link 218	open 3½-turn spiral 2-turn hairpin raindrop link		Link 233	5-circle link
	Link 219	open 3½-turn spiral 3-turn hairpin raindrop link		Link 234	hairpin spiral raindrop link
	Link 220	open 3½-turn spiral 4-turn hairpin compressed raindrop link		Link 235	1-turn hairpin triangle raindrop link
	Link 221	drop-down simple loop raindrop link		Link 236	1-turn hairpin triangle raindrop link
	Link 222	open 3½-turn drop-down raindrop link		Link 237	1-turn long hairpin triangle raindrop link
	Link 223	4-turn spiral-raindrop link		Link 238	2-turn hairpin triangle raindrop link
	Link 224	3-loop spiral raindrop link		Link 239	rounded triangle link
	Link 225	3-turn spiral raindrop link		Link 240	dual-loop triangle raindrop link

	Link 241	triangle raindrop link		Link 256	5-loop V-link
	Link 242	jump ring spiral triangle raindrop link		Link 257	5-loop crossover link
	Link 243	triangle crossover raindrop link		Link 258	7-loop crossover link
	Link 244	hairpin triangle raindrop link		Link 259	crossover midwire-circle bead connector link
	Link 245	spiral triangle raindrop link		Link 260	midwire-circle 4-turn ladder connector link
	Link 246	spiral crossover triangle raindrop link		Link 261	4-loop crossover-circle link
	Link 247	dueling spirals triangle raindrop link		Link 262	wrapped straight-loop hook
	Link 248	1-bead triangle spiral raindrop link		Link 263	midwire-circle 4-turn ladder connector link
	Link 249	hairpin triangle raindrop spiral link		Link 264	2-loop double-spiral V-link
	Link 250	wrapped-triangle raindrop link		Link 265	crimped-end bead dangles
	Link 251	dual-loop triangle raindrop link		Link 266	simple loop-end bead dangle link
	Link 252	thwarted star-triangle raindrop link		Link 267	coil-end bead dangle link
	Link 253	dual-loop star-raindrop link		Link 268	wrapped straight-loop bead dangle link
	Link 254	spiral-wrapped star-raindrop link		Link 269	2-bead wrapped straight-loop dangle link
	Link 255	midwire-circle bead connector		Link 270	3-bead wrapped straight-loop dangle link

	Link 271	coil-end bead dangle link
	Link 272	wrapped-donut straight-loop-dangle link
	Link 273	wrapped donut loop dangle link
	Link 274	simple-wrapped bead dangle link
	Link 275	long wrapped straight-loop dangle link
	Link 276	2-wire-wrapped-donut link
	Link 277	large end-hoop bead link
	Link 278	wire-wrapped double-circle 3-bead link
	Link 279	wrapped bead-cap dangle link
	Link 280	large-circle bead-cap dangle link
	Link 281	spiral-wrapped bead dangle link
	Link 282	wrapped bead dangle link
	Link 283	wrapped straight-loop bead link
	Link 284	caged wrapped straight-loop bead link
	Link 285	wrapped straight-loop spiral bead link

	Link 286	centered spiral-end bead link
	Link 287	large circle-end center-spiral bead dangle link
	Link 288	coil-end wrapped straight-loop bead link
	Link 289	spiral bead dangle link
	Link 290	double-spiral bead dangle link
	Link 291	double-spiral end bead dangle link
	Link 292	double-center spirals bead link
	Link 293	double-center wrapped-bead link
	Link 294	encircled bead dangle link
	Link 295	looped-circle bead link
	Link 296	wrapped-loop-circle bead link
	Link 297	double-teardrop spiral bead link
	Link 298	wrapped-loop circular-coil link
	Link 299	rolled-wire-end bead dangle link
	Link 300	multiple-wrapped bead dangle link

Link 301	1-bead coil horseshoe loop link
Link 302	3-bead wrapped opposite straight-loop link
Link 303	ball-and-cage bead link
Link 304	open-cage link
Link 305	double-spiral wrapped-bead link
Link 306	S-shaped wrapped-bead link
Link 307	beaded-spiral link
Link 308	simple side-loop spiral bead link
Link 309	simple straight-loop open-spiral bead link
Link 310	simple straight-loop spiral bead link
Link 311	beaded open-spiral dangle link
Link 312	wrapped straight-loop spiral-end bead dangle link
Link 313	3-bead spiral-end dangle link
Link 314	hairpin-spiral wrapped-loop bead link
Link 315	hairpin midwire-spiral bead dangle link

Link 316	inverted raindrop-spiral bead link
Link 317	beaded-spiral turn raindrop link
Link 318	double-raindrop bead link
Link 319	spiral double-raindrop bead link
Link 320	beaded-hairpin raindrop link
Link 321	expanded-hairpin bead link
Link 322	compressed hairpin spiral bead link
Link 323	expanded double-hairpin bead link
Link 324	midwire-spiral symmetry bead link
Link 325	midwire 3-turn spiral symmetry bead link
Link 326	coil-covered hairpin link
Link 327	coil-wrapped simple side-loop link
Link 328	wrapped loop-and-bead dangle link
Link 329	spiral-wrapped loop-and-bead link
Link 330	large spiral-wrapped loop-and-bead link

	Link 331	wrinkle-wrapped bead dangle
	Link 332	coiled-spiral bead link
	Link 333	coiled-hairpin bead link
	Link 334	coiled-spiral hairpin bead link
	Link 335	long wrapped side-loop link
	Link 336	long hairpin bead link
	Link 337	3-bead hairpin link
	Link 338	hairpin bead link

	Link 339	3-bead hairpin link
	Link 340	beaded-wire-wrapped 5-turn hairpin link
	Link 341	3-bead double-triangle hairpin link
	Link 342	midwire-circle wrapped-donut link
	Link 343	spiral-wrapped donut link
	Link 344	3-bead triple-circle jump ring link
	Link 345	3-bead simple side-loop large-circle bead link
	Link 346	beaded double-spiral hairpin link

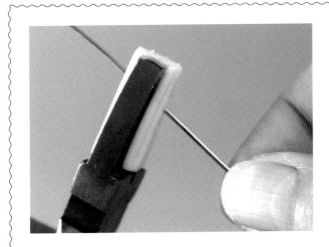

Tip 4: Straighten the wire.

Use nylon-grip flat-nose pliers to straighten the wire before bending. Hold one end of the wire between your fingers and pull the nylon grip pliers from your fingertips toward the end of the length with medium pressure. You can straighten a wire at any time during the bending steps to remove small bends and twists that naturally develop with making your loops and wraps.

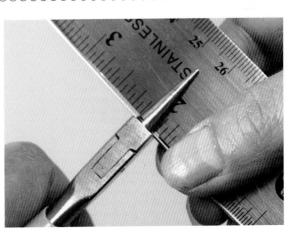

Tip 5: Measure your wire.

A thin, steel ruler can be used to cut your wire into manageable lengths and to find the center point of a wire.

Cornerstone Links

Throughout this section, we will work together to learn and practice a few of many possible bent-wire links used later in the project section of the book. After you have worked a few of the links, you will realize how easy it is to make a simple change, such as replacing a simple side-loop with a wrapped straight-loop or by adding more turns to a spiral.

For this practice section, I used 18-gauge wire, but there is no hard and fast rule. You may use the gauge of wire that you have on hand. When working practice links for a specific project, I would suggest that you use the gauge of wire that you will be using on the finished necklace or bracelet.

Keep all of your practice links. They make wonderful fun bracelets and earrings!

LINK 024: 1-BEAD SIMPLE STRAIGHT-LOOP LINK

Easy bead links can be created using either the simple side-loop or simple straight-loop bend at the beginning and end of the link.

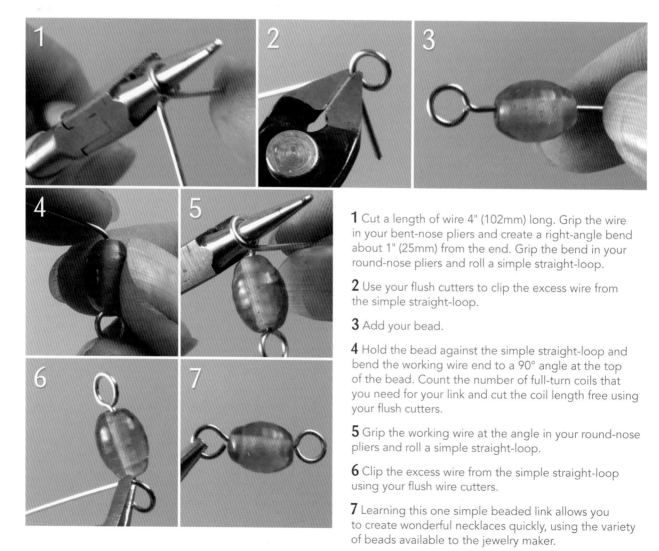

1 Cut a length of wire 4" (102mm) long. Grip the wire in your bent-nose pliers and create a right-angle bend about 1" (25mm) from the end. Grip the bend in your round-nose pliers and roll a simple straight-loop.

2 Use your flush cutters to clip the excess wire from the simple straight-loop.

3 Add your bead.

4 Hold the bead against the simple straight-loop and bend the working wire end to a 90° angle at the top of the bead. Count the number of full-turn coils that you need for your link and cut the coil length free using your flush cutters.

5 Grip the working wire at the angle in your round-nose pliers and roll a simple straight-loop.

6 Clip the excess wire from the simple straight-loop using your flush wire cutters.

7 Learning this one simple beaded link allows you to create wonderful necklaces quickly, using the variety of beads available to the jewelry maker.

LINK 039: DOUBLE WIRE-WRAPPED STRAIGHT-LOOP LINK

Links 027 through 041 follow the same basic steps

Wrapped loops. The wrapped loop link is a basic bending pattern used in many necklaces as a chain link. Because Links 033 and 039 are wrapped on both ends at the base of the connecting loops, there will be an obvious joint line in the center of the link where the two wrapping-wires meet. To avoid this joint line or break in the wrapping-wire of the link you can create a double-wire-wrapped link using one extra-long wrapping-wire from just one connecting loop to coil the expanse of the link.

1 Begin Link 039 by cutting an 8" (203mm)-long length of 18-gauge wire. Using your bent-nose pliers, make a right-angle bend in the wire 1½" (38mm) from one end.

2 Transfer the right-angle bend to your round-nose pliers and roll the wire into a simple straight-loop.

3 Grip the simple straight-loop in your bent-nose pliers and bend the extra wire from the straight-loop to parallel the working wire below the loop.

4 Grip the long working wire of the link in your bent-nose pliers ½" (13mm) from the simple straight-loop and create a right-angle bend.

5 Using your round-nose pliers, roll the wire above the right angle into a simple straight-loop. You will have about 5" (127mm) of excess working wire left after the simple straight-loop.

6 Grip the simple straight-loop in your bent-nose pliers and, working with the long working wire, begin wrapping the working wire around the base of the loop going over both center wires of the link.

7 Continue wrapping the entire double-wire center area of the link using the long working wire.

8 When your long working wire reaches the base of the first simple straight-loop, stop wrapping.

9 Clip the excess wire from the long wrapping-wire with your flush wire cutters. Using your flush wire cutters, clip the excess from the double-center wire that extends beyond the second simple straight-loop.

10 The completed Link 039 has the entire center area of the link wrapped using just one wrapping-wire.

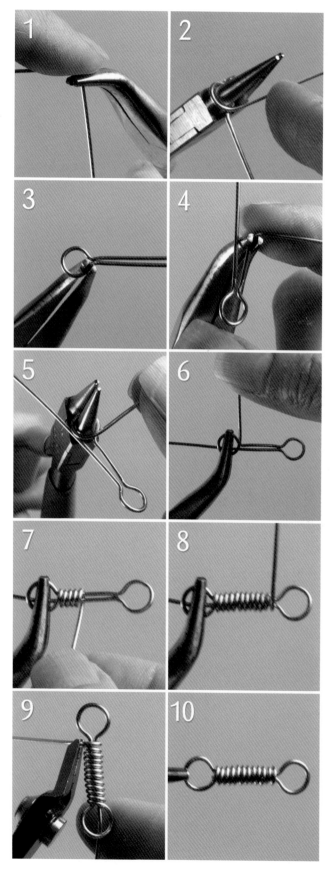

LINK 043:
COIL LINK

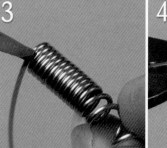

**Links 042 through 043 follow
the same basic steps**

Basic Coils. Coils are used
in jewelry making for jump rings,
split rings, links, and to cover the working wire of
bent links. Here we will look at the steps to creating
a basic coil link.

1 Coils use a large amount of wire. Always cut your
wire length extra long to ensure you have enough to
extend your coil to the size you need for your project.
Save any extra after you have cut your link to use later
as jump rings and split rings. For this practice link, cut
a 24" (610mm) length of 18-gauge wire. Following the
directions on your coil maker, thread the wire onto the
coil maker's handle. Hold the wire over the wrapping
rod and turn the handle to create a long coil length.

2 Wire can be coiled over many forms. If you do not
have a coil maker, try a knitting needle, the barrel of
an ink pen, a round pencil, or any other long cylinder-
shaped item. Here, I'm using a Number 8 knitting needle.

3 Remove the coil from the form. With your flush wire
cutters, clip both ends of the coil to start your coil with
a clean, flat, full turn. Position your flush cutters so that
the end cut is square to the coil.

4 To make cutting sections of coil, jump rings, or split
rings easy, use your flush wire cutters and gently slice
between the coil turns. This does not cut the coil but
does open a space between the turns.

5 With your bent-nose pliers, grip the first full turn
of the coil. Bend this turn to a right angle to the coil.

6 Twist the full turn to center it over the opening of the
coil. Tuck the cut end of the first full-bent turn inside the
opening. This creates a connecting loop at the end of
the coil. Repeat this step for the second end of the coil.

7 The completed Link 043 has both end turns bent
into position as connecting loops.

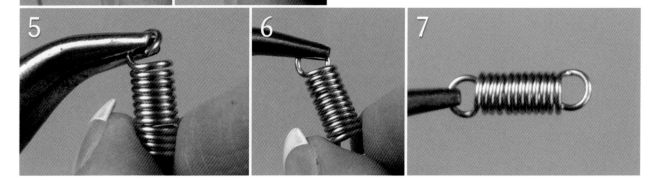

LINK 044: COIL-COVERED SIMPLE STRAIGHT-LOOP LINK

Coil Wrapping. Coils can be created into links of their own, as in Links 042 and 043. They also can be added over the bending wire on another link, just as you would a bead. After adding the coils to the working wire, bend coiled-covered wire into a variety of link designs. Adding coil covering allows you to have coils in one areas of a link and no coils, just the working wire, in other areas.

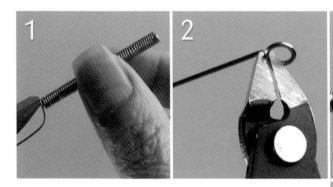

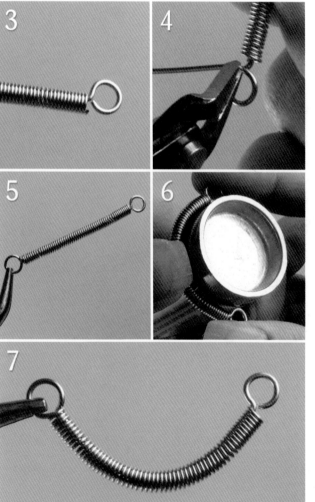

1 Use 20- to 26-gauge wire at least 15" (381mm) long to create a ⅛"-wide-by-1½"-long (3mm by 38mm) coil. Clip the excess wire from both ends of your coil using your flush wire cutters.

2 Cut a 5" (127mm) length of 18-gauge wire. Grip the working wire 1½" (38mm) from the end of the wire and create a simple straight-loop. Clip the excess wire at the base of the simple straight-loop using your flush wire cutters.

3 Slide the ⅛"-wide-by-1½"-long (3mm by 38mm) coil onto the working wire of your simple straight-loop link.

4 With your bent-nose pliers, grip the working wire at the top of the coil covering and create a simple straight-loop. Clip the excess wire from the base of the simple straight-loop using your flush wire cutters.

5 You can add a coil covering to the working wire of most links as a hairpin-turn link or raindrop link during the link-bending process.

6 Once the coil covering has been added, work the link as normal, gripping the coil-covered wire in your pliers to make each new bend.

7 This practice Link 044 has been shaped around the barrel of a large marking pen to create a half-circle bend to the finished link.

LINK 047: WRAPPED LONG LOOP LINK

Links 047 and 048 follow the same basic steps

Loops. Create Link 047 by making two turn-back loops then wrapping the intersection of those loops. This link can easily be created in larger sizes from 1" (25mm) or longer to make quick work of long chains.

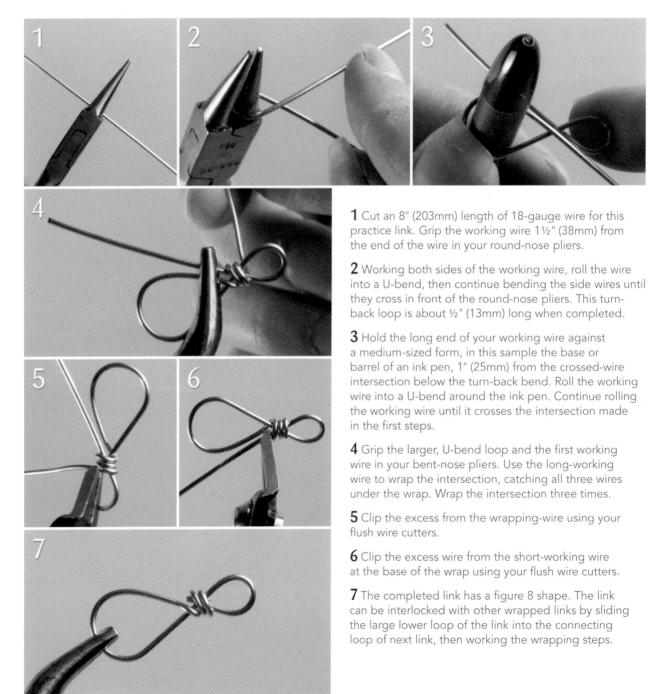

1 Cut an 8" (203mm) length of 18-gauge wire for this practice link. Grip the working wire 1½" (38mm) from the end of the wire in your round-nose pliers.

2 Working both sides of the working wire, roll the wire into a U-bend, then continue bending the side wires until they cross in front of the round-nose pliers. This turn-back loop is about ½" (13mm) long when completed.

3 Hold the long end of your working wire against a medium-sized form, in this sample the base or barrel of an ink pen, 1" (25mm) from the crossed-wire intersection below the turn-back bend. Roll the working wire into a U-bend around the ink pen. Continue rolling the working wire until it crosses the intersection made in the first steps.

4 Grip the larger, U-bend loop and the first working wire in your bent-nose pliers. Use the long-working wire to wrap the intersection, catching all three wires under the wrap. Wrap the intersection three times.

5 Clip the excess from the wrapping-wire using your flush wire cutters.

6 Clip the excess wire from the short-working wire at the base of the wrap using your flush wire cutters.

7 The completed link has a figure 8 shape. The link can be interlocked with other wrapped links by sliding the large lower loop of the link into the connecting loop of next link, then working the wrapping steps.

Ganging Up on Link 047

The long figure-8-shaped 047 link is a favorite of mine, so in working with the different necklace layouts, I have used it multiple times. To make creating this link easy, with consistency in size, use a simple homemade link maker.

1. Chose two different-sized forms for your homemade link form, one small- and one medium-sized. Two sizes of knitting needles—Numbers 2 and 8—work well. A pencil works well as the spacer between the forms. Place the pencil between your two forms, and using transparent tape, secure the three pieces together with the two links forms higher than the center pencil.

2. Hold one end of your wire and wrap the wire in a figure 8 shape around the outside edges of the two knitting needles.

3. Remove the wire-wrapped link from the handmade link form.

4. Using your nylon-grip pliers, flatten the link.

5. Grip the large loop and both working wires of the loop in your bent-nose pliers. Wrap the long working wire around the intersection point between the loops catching all three wires three times.

6. Clip the excess wires. Your handmade link form can be used repeatedly to ensure each link in your chain is the same size. With a little thought and creativity, you can adapt a similar mass production strategy for other links in this book.

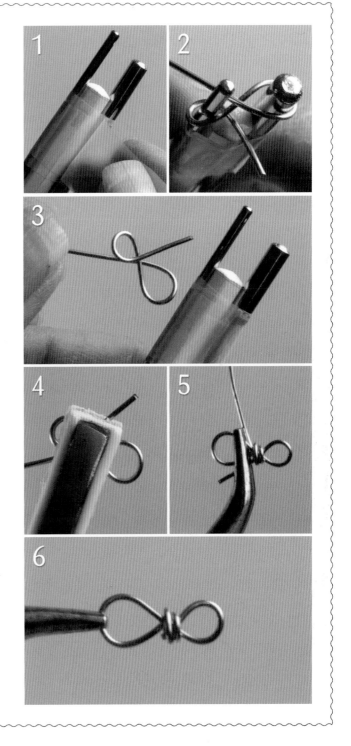

LINKS 075 THROUGH 077: MEDIUM-SIZE HOOP WITH VARIATIONS

Links 075 through 077 follow the same basic steps

Link 075 (left), Link 076 (center), and Link 077 (right). Alter the hoop to add a bead or a beaded wire-wrap, demonstrating that simple changes can make highly individual links.

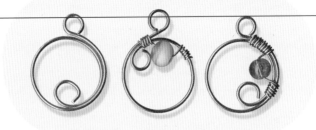

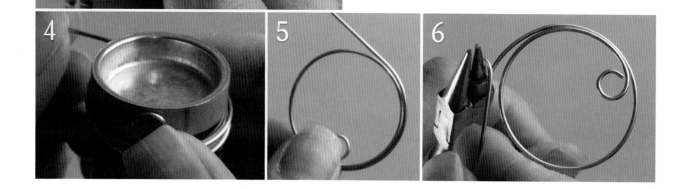

1 Cut an 8" (203mm) length of 18-gauge wire. Grip the end of the wire in your round-nose pliers and roll a simple side-loop.

2 Hold the simple side-loop against the side of a large form. In this sample, I am using a large marking pen. Roll the working wire around the form.

3 Bring the working wire to meet the simple side-loop to complete one full turn.

4 Continue rolling the working wire for one more half-circle. This brings the working wire to the backside of the form, opposite the simple side-loop.

5 Remove the working wire from the form.

6 Grip the working wire at the top of the 1½-turn hoop in your round-nose pliers and create a simple side-loop. Clip the excess wire from the simple side-loop using your flush wire cutters.

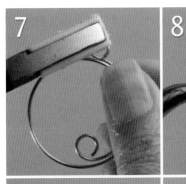

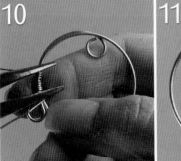

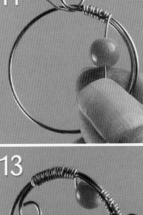

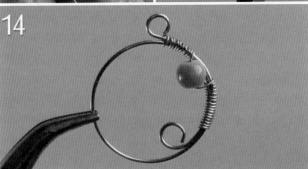

7 Flatten both simple side-loops to match the large 1½-turn circle.

8 The completed 1½-turn hoop link has one connecting loop at the outside top of the link and one near the inside bottom.

9 Adding a wire-wrap to this link strengthens the link and avoids the chance that the circle area can become pulled or stretched. Cut a 16" (406mm) length of 26-gauge wire. Tightly wrap the wrapping-wire into three to four coils, working over both circle wires on the double-wired side of the link. Press or push these tight coils against the base of the simple side-loop.

10 Continue working the wrapping-wire until you have 10 full coil turns. Use your bent-nose pliers to compress the coils.

11 Slide a bead onto the wrapping-wire. This sample bead is a 6mm round glass bead.

12 Slide the bead up the wire to touch the sides of the hoop. Holding the bead in position on the inside of the hoop link, begin coiling the wrapping-wire over the double-wire side of the hoop below the bead. Wrap this area with 18 tightly packed coils. Use your bent-nose pliers to compress the coils.

13 Clip the excess wrapping-wire at both ends and crimp the wire tightly into position using your bent-nose pliers.

14 The completed link is ready to become the center piece of a necklace or part of an earring set.

LINKS 080 AND 081:
BEADED WIRE-WRAPPED LOOPS
Both links follow the same basic steps

Wire-wraps. Large hoop links, such as links 080 (left) and 081 (right), are perfect for adding wire-wraps, with or without beads. This practice link will include a double-hoop link with a beaded wire-wrap and an added bead dangle in the center of the link.

1 Working with 18-gauge wire, cut a length 12" (305mm) long. Grip the end of the working wire in your round-nose pliers and roll a simple side-loop.

2 Place the simple side-loop against a small ½" (13mm)-wide form. For this sample, a small marking pen was used. Roll the working wire around the form to complete one full circle.

3 Using your nylon-grip pliers, flatten the simple side-loop to match the full circle.

4 Place your small full circle against a larger form measuring 2" (51mm) in diameter. I used a medicine bottle cap. Roll the working wire into a full circle around the large form.

5 Using your nylon-grip pliers, flatten the small full circle to match the large full circle.

6 Grip the working wire above the simple side-loop in your round-nose pliers. Roll the wire into a midwire-circle.

7 Clip the excess working wire from the midwire-circle to create a simple side-loop.

8 Your hoop link now has one very small circle created by the simple side-loop, one medium-sized circle worked around the marking pen, and one large circle created with the medicine bottle cap.

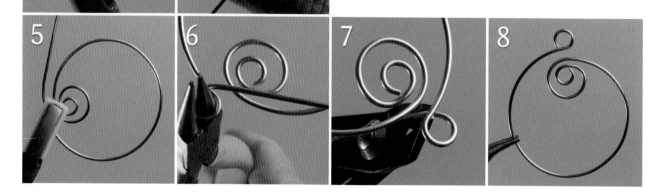

9 To secure the three circles together and to give added strength to the link, cut a short length, 6" (152mm), of 26-gauge wire, to wrap the circle intersection. Thread the wrapping-wire over the outside circle wire next to the upper simple side-loop. Wrap the wrapping-wire over the top wire of the next circle just below the upper simple side-loop. Continue wrapping these two wires together until you have created six tightly packed coils.

10 Cut the excess wrapping-wire.

11 Crimp the ends of the wrapping-wire to secure it to the hoop. Use your bent-nose pliers to compress the coils against the base of the upper simple side-loop.

12 Cut an 18" (457mm) length of 26-gauge wire. Secure this wrapping-wire to the hoop on the simple side-loop wire using six tightly packed coils, ending the wire on the back side of the large hoop. Using your bent-nose pliers push the coils as closely as possible to the first wire-wrapped area.

13 Feed the wrapping-wire through the space between the large and small hoop wires; wrap the wire once around the small hoop. Feed the wrapping-wire back through the space between the hoops, placing the wire to the back side of the large hoop.

14 Roll the wrapping-wire over the top of the large outer hoop wire. Feed it through the space between the large outer hoop and the small hoop. This places the wrapping-wire to the back of the hoop behind the small circle. Feed the wire through the small circle to return the wire to the front of the hoop.

15 Continue feeding the wrapping-wire in this figure 8 pattern until three figure 8s are made, ending with the wrapping-wire at the top of the hoop on the back side of the link. Roll the wrapping-wire over the top of the large circle wire. Add a small bead, a 3mm cube, to the wrapping-wire. Continue working the wrapping-wire in the figure 8 pattern.

16 I worked nine more figure 8 patterns, adding three more individual beads in a random pattern. On my ninth figure 8 wrapping, I added a row of five 3mm cube beads to the wire. At this point, approximately one-third of the circle has been wire-wrapped.

17 With the remaining wrapping-wire, work a series of tightly packed coils around the lower section of the small inside circle wire. When you have used most of your wrapping-wire, clip the excess and secure the end of the wrapping-wire by crimping it into position.

18 This completed Link 081 has the wire-wrapping woven between the two circles with a scattering of beads as accents.

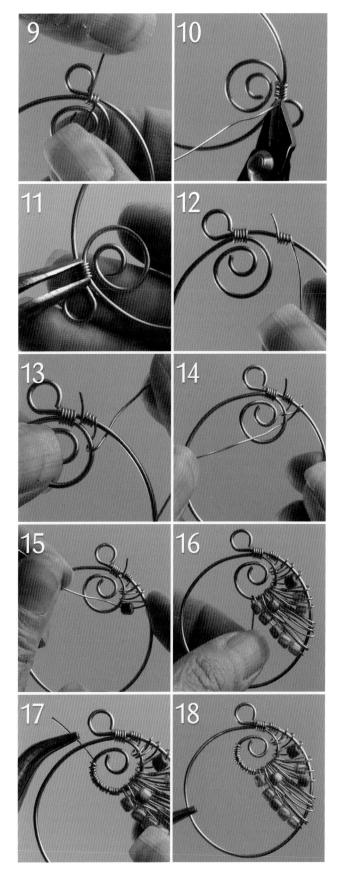

LINK 086:
3-TURN SPIRAL LINK

Links 084 through 104 follow the same basic steps

Making spirals. Link 086 is an adaptation of the simple side-loop link that can become either a chain link or bracelet dangle. Add turns to the simple side-loop or spiral to change the size and density of the link.

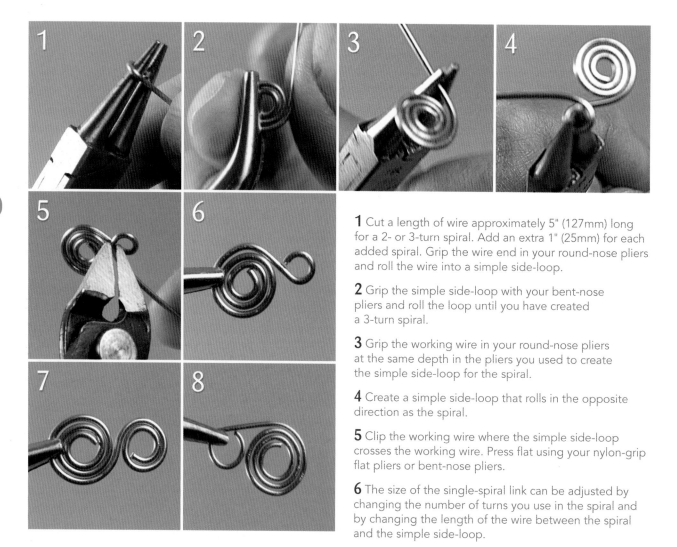

1 Cut a length of wire approximately 5" (127mm) long for a 2- or 3-turn spiral. Add an extra 1" (25mm) for each added spiral. Grip the wire end in your round-nose pliers and roll the wire into a simple side-loop.

2 Grip the simple side-loop with your bent-nose pliers and roll the loop until you have created a 3-turn spiral.

3 Grip the working wire in your round-nose pliers at the same depth in the pliers you used to create the simple side-loop for the spiral.

4 Create a simple side-loop that rolls in the opposite direction as the spiral.

5 Clip the working wire where the simple side-loop crosses the working wire. Press flat using your nylon-grip flat pliers or bent-nose pliers.

6 The size of the single-spiral link can be adjusted by changing the number of turns you use in the spiral and by changing the length of the wire between the spiral and the simple side-loop.

7 The spiral link can easily be changed by varying the number of turns used in the spiral and simple side-loop ends.

8 The placement along the link of the end loops or spirals can also be easily changed.

LINK 093: MIDWIRE-SPIRAL LINK

Links 092 through 095 follow the same basic steps

Double-spirals. Link 093 provides two center-spiral holes to add bead dangles easily in your necklace chain designs.

1 Cut a 15" (381mm) length of 18-gauge wire. Grip the end of the wire in your round-nose pliers and roll the wire into a simple side-loop.

2 Move your round-nose pliers ⅜" (10mm) away from the simple side-loops on the working wire. Grip the wire and roll a midwire-circle.

3 Transfer the midwire-circle to your bent-nose pliers and begin rolling the midwire-circle into a spiral.

4 Give your first spiral three full turns. Bring the working wire to the top of the spiral headed away from the spiral and simple side-loop.

5 Grip the working wire in your round-nose pliers and roll a midwire-circle on the top of the link—opposite side of the link from the first spiral.

6 Transfer the midwire-circle to your bent-nose pliers and roll the circle into a 3-turn spiral.

7 Grip the working wire at the end of the second spiral so that the side of the pliers touches the side of the spiral.

8 Roll a simple side-loop.

9 Clip the excess wire from your simple side-loop using your flush wire cutters.

10 Compress your link so that the two simple side-loops are tucked tightly against the side of their adjacent spirals.

11 The completed loop has a dense heavy feeling while providing extra space—the spiral-center holes—for bead dangles.

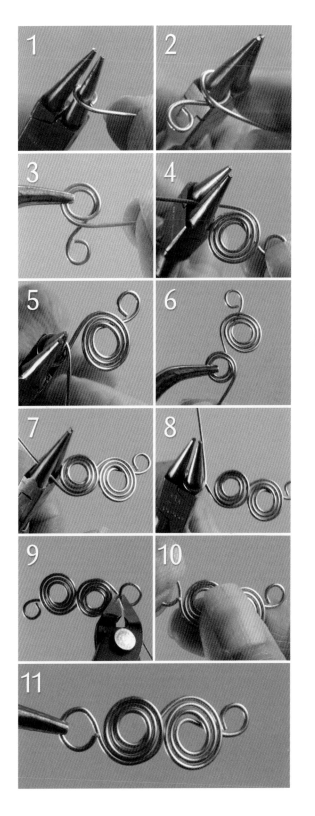

LINK 108 & 110: LONG SIMPLE HAIRPIN LINK

Links 105 through 113 follow the same basic steps

Hairpin links. Use Link 108 to create long chains by joining the simple side-loops of one link to the U-bend of the hairpin in the next link with jump rings or split rings.

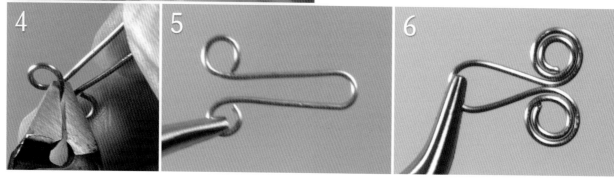

1 Cut a length of wire approximately 4" (102mm) long. Grip the end of the working wire in your round-nose pliers. Create a simple side-loop.

2 Grip the working wire ¾" (19mm) from the simple side-loop in your round-nose pliers. Roll a midwire-circle.

3 Transfer the midwire-circle to your bent-nose pliers and begin rolling the midwire-circle into a spiral. Create another simple side-loop.

4 Using your flush wire cutters, clip the excess wire from the simple side-loop.

5 Here is the completed link. You could accentuate Link 108 with a midwire-circle on the top of the link—on the opposite side of the hairpin (see page 91).

6 Transfer the midwire-circle to your bent-nose pliers and the simple side-loops of this link can easily become spirals by adding extra wire length at the beginning of the link creation.

LINK 114: BEADED SIMPLE HAIRPIN LINK

Hairpins plus beads. Connected to your chain through its simple side-loops, Link 114 drops your beads below the curve of the necklace line.

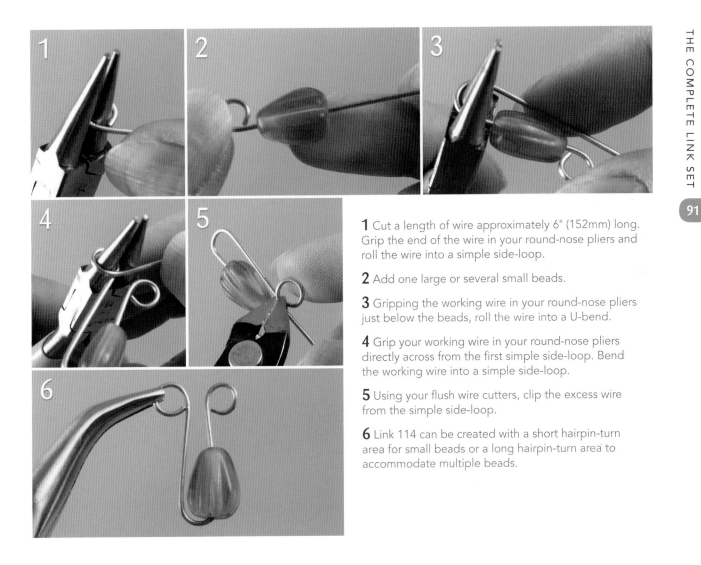

1 Cut a length of wire approximately 6" (152mm) long. Grip the end of the wire in your round-nose pliers and roll the wire into a simple side-loop.

2 Add one large or several small beads.

3 Gripping the working wire in your round-nose pliers just below the beads, roll the wire into a U-bend.

4 Grip your working wire in your round-nose pliers directly across from the first simple side-loop. Bend the working wire into a simple side-loop.

5 Using your flush wire cutters, clip the excess wire from the simple side-loop.

6 Link 114 can be created with a short hairpin-turn area for small beads or a long hairpin-turn area to accommodate multiple beads.

LINK 117:
DOUBLE-SPIRAL
HAIRPINS & CHAINS

Links 115 through 118 follow the same basic steps

Spiral hairpins and chains. Joining Link 117s into a chain creates a fun project. The joining process is done be feeding the U-bend area of one link through the U-bend area of a second link. The U-bend area of the second link—the link with the U-bend on the outside of the joining—is bent to the back of the chain, locking it to the first link.

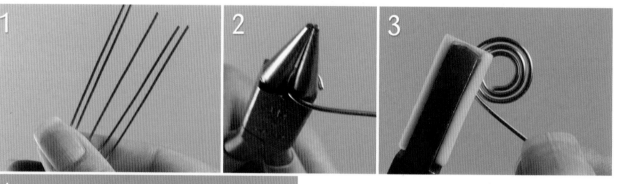

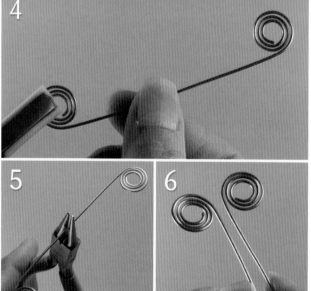

1 Determine how many links you will need to complete your project. It is advisable to plan to make several extra Link 117s beyond what your finished project will need. Cut all of the wires at one time and work each link through each step. Gang working ensures all of the links will be the same size.

2 Cut a 9" (229mm) length of 18-gauge wire. Grip the end of the working wire in your round-nose pliers and roll a simple side-loop.

3 Transfer the loop to your nylon-grip pliers and continue rolling the loop into a 2½-turn spiral.

4 Create a 2½-turn spiral on the second end of the working wire.

5 You should have about 3" (76mm) of straight wire between the two spirals. Measure the wire to find the center point of the straight wire. Grip that point in your round-nose pliers.

6 Create a tight U-bend at the center point.

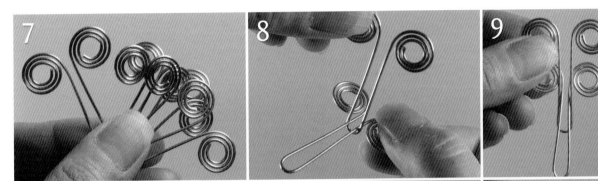

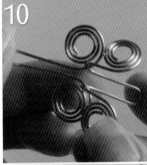

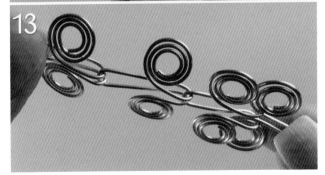

7 Each of your finished Link 117s should measure to the same length with the same number of turns in the spirals.

8 Slide the U-bend area of one link over the U-bend area of another hairpin link. The first link now is inside of the U-bend of the second link. The first link, the link inside of the U-bend of the second link, will become the bottom link of the chain.

9 Slide the inside spiral link toward the bottom of the outside link. The spirals of the outside link should be just above the spirals of the inside link.

10 Turn the two links to the back of the chain. Grip the U-bend area of the outside (top) link and fold that area up toward its spirals. Press the folded area gently to set the link. This folds the hairpin area in half, with one-half of the hairpin on the front and the second half on the back side of the chain.

11 This new fold in the hairpin area of the top link catches the inside edge of the spirals of the link below it.

12 New links are added through the bent hairpin area of the last worked link. Thread the U-bend curve through the U-bend on the last link from the front of the chain—it becomes the inside link. On the backside of the chain, fold the hairpin toward its spiral ends. This photo shows the chain from the backside with the hairpin of the top link ready to be folded up toward its spirals.

13 The hairpins in this photo were created extra long to better demonstrate the folding method of chaining Link 117s.

LINKS 121 THROUGH 124: MIDWIRE-CIRCLE HAIRPIN SPIRAL LINKS

Links 119 through 124 follow the same basic steps

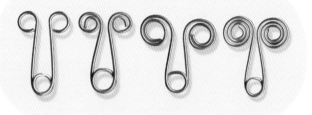

Variations. Links 121 through 124 are variations on the same theme. The midwire-circle in the center of the U-bend of this series of hairpin links creates a strong connecting loop to add the links to a chain or to add a bead dangle to the link. Trim the wire to accommodate the number of spirals you want your link to feature.

1 Cut a 12" (305mm) length of 18-gauge wire. Grip the working wire at the center point of the wire.

2 Roll both sides of the working wire to create a turn-back loop.

3 Continue rolling the wires until you have a midwire-circle with the two ends of the working wire in line with each other.

4 Roll both sides of the working wire into a U-bend so that the two sides are parallel to each other.

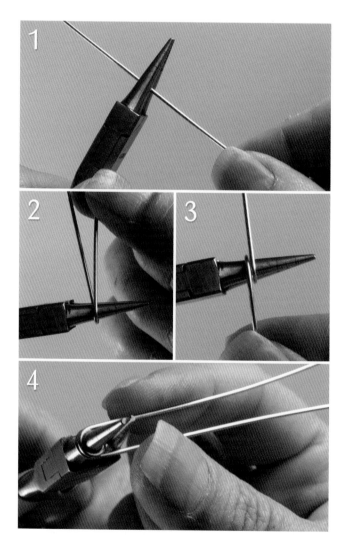

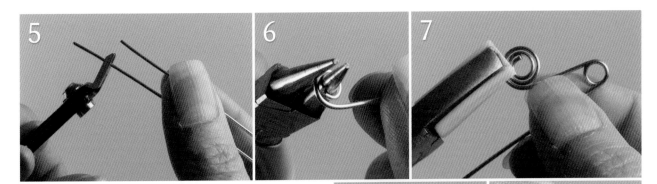

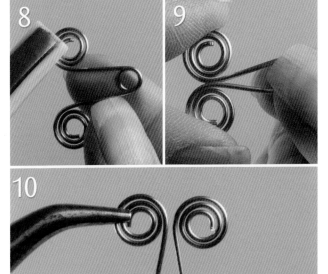

5 Use your flush cutters to clip the ends of the two working wires to make them equal in length. For a 2½-turn spiral end, you want each side to measure about 3" (76mm).

6 Grip the end of one of the working wires in your round-nose pliers and roll the wire into a simple side-loop.

7 Transfer the loop to your nylon-grip pliers and continue rolling the loop into a 2½-turn spiral.

8 Create a 2½-turn spiral on the end of the second working wire.

9 Compress the link to bring the sides of the spirals together.

10 The finished link can be added to your chain through the center holes of the spirals or through one center spiral hole and the midwire-circle in the U-bend.

LINK 128: OFFSET 2½-TURN SINGLE-SPIRAL SIMPLE SIDE-LOOP HAIRPIN LINK

Links 125 to 134 follow the same basic steps

Offset hairpins. The offset hairpin link uses a U-bend turn around the round-nose pliers to join a spiral end and simple side-loop.

1 Cut your wire approximately 5" to 6" (125mm to 150mm) long. Grip the working end in your round-nose pliers and create a simple side-loop. Change to your bent-nose pliers and continue rolling the working wire into a 3-turn spiral.

2 Grip the working wire about 1" (25mm) from the base of the spiral and pull the working wire into a tight U-bend.

3 Grip the working wire in the round-nose pliers about 1" (25mm) from the U-bend, directly across from the base of the spiral turn.

4 Create a simple side-loop that rolls in the direction opposite to the spiral.

5 Clip the working wire where it crosses the simple side-loop.

6 Press the link flat using either your nylon-grip flat or bent-nose pliers.

7 This link can be adjusted by changing the number of turns in your spiral, the depth of the U-bend and by changing the positions of the spiral to the simple side-loop.

8 Changing the number of turns used in the end spirals creates a wide variety of new links.

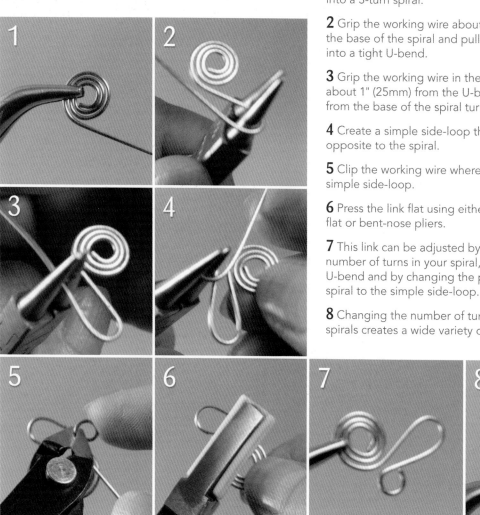

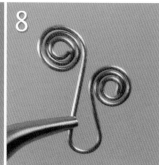

LINK 129: OFFSET 2½-TURN SINGLE-SPIRAL BEADED SIMPLE SIDE-LOOP HAIRPIN

Hairpins with beads. Hairpins, such as Link 129, are perfect for holdings multiple beads. The length of the wire between the spiral and the U-bend easily adjusts to neatly carry any bead size you wish to use in your link.

1 Cut a length of wire about 6" (152mm) long. Grip the end of the working wire in your round-nose pliers and roll the wire into a simple side-loop. Grip the loop in your bent-nose pliers to roll a 3-turn spiral.

2 Straighten your working wire with nylon-grip flat pliers. Slide three small beads onto the working wire. I used 6mm cube beads.

3 Grip the working wire below the beads and roll the wire into a tight U-bend using your round-nose pliers.

4 Grip the working wire directly across from the base of the spiral in your round-nose pliers. Roll a simple side-loop that curves in the opposite direction as your spiral.

5 This spiral-hairpin bead link can be joined to your chain either through the loop in the spiral or with the simple side-loop.

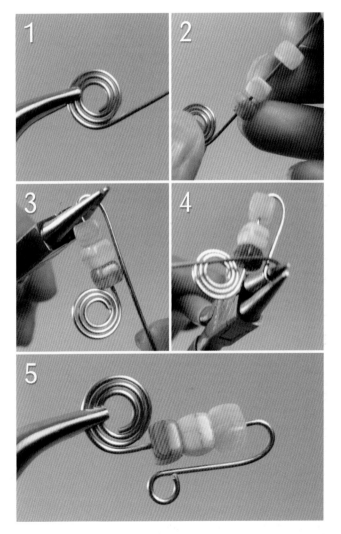

LINK 135:
DOUBLE-HAIRPIN LINK

Links 135 to 137 follow the same basic steps

Two-Turn Hairpin. The Double-Hairpin is a quick and easy link that adds a wide area to your chains when it is connected to those chains through the simple side-loops. Bead dangles can be attached to the hairpin areas.

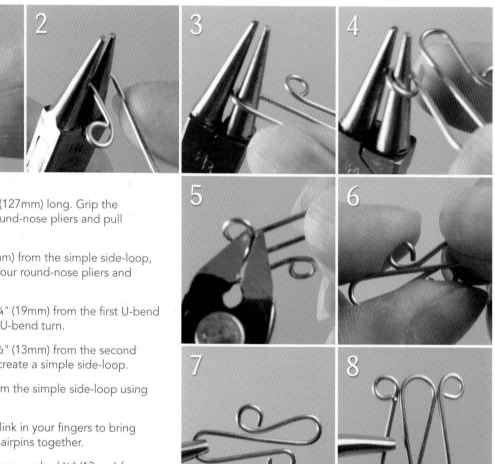

1 Cut a length of wire 5" (127mm) long. Grip the end of the wire in your round-nose pliers and pull a simple side-loop.

2 Approximately ½" (13mm) from the simple side-loop, grip the working wire in your round-nose pliers and create a U-bend.

3 Grip the working wire ¾" (19mm) from the first U-bend hairpin and roll a second U-bend turn.

4 Grip the working wire ½" (13mm) from the second U-bend hairpin turn and create a simple side-loop.

5 Clip the excess wire from the simple side-loop using your flush wire cutters.

6 Compress the finished link in your fingers to bring the sides of the U-bend hairpins together.

7 Because the U-bends were worked ½" (13mm) from the simple side-loops but ¾" (19mm) away from each other, this link has a staggered or offset look. The simple side-loops will connect in line with the chain and the U-bend areas will reach out beyond that chain line, giving added width to the necklace.

8 Hairpin links can have multiple turns and can be worked with parallel end loops or opposing end loops.

LINK 138: TAPERED HAIRPIN LINK

Links 138 through 141 follow the same basic steps

Tapered hairpins. By changing the distance between each U-bend turn, each time making the length a little longer, you can create Link 138 tapered hairpin link. It's a small variation that can make your jewelry more visually exciting.

1 Cut a 9" (229mm) length of 18-gauge wire. Grip the end of the wire in your round-nose pliers and roll the wire into a simple side-loop.

2 Grip the working wire ¼" (6mm) from the simple side-loop and roll the working wire into a U-bend around your round-nose pliers.

3 Move your round-nose pliers ½" (13mm) from the first U-bend and create a second U-bend turn.

4 The third U-bend turn is made ¾" (19mm) from the second using round-nose pliers.

5 The fourth and final U-bend turn comes 1" (25mm) from the last turn. This series of turns, each a little farther from the last, tapers this hairpin link.

6 With your round-nose pliers, grip your working wire ½" (13mm) from the last U-bend turn and create a midwire-circle.

7 Clip the excess wire from your midwire-circle to turn this bend into a simple side-loop.

8 Grip the end loops in your fingers and compress the link to bring the sides of the U-bends together.

9 The finished link can be joined to the chain through the ending simple side-loop.

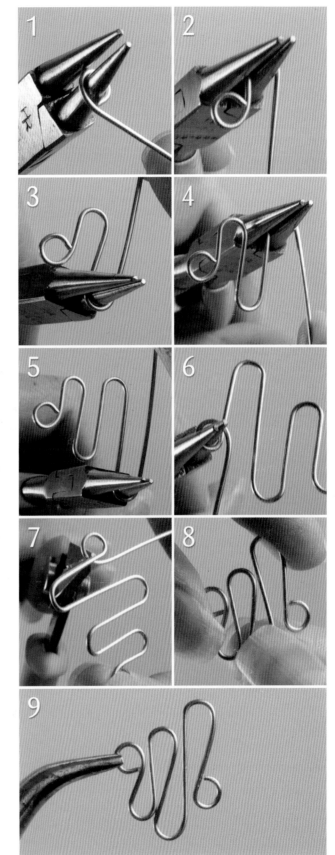

LINK 143:
OPEN 4-TURN SPIRAL HAIRPIN LINK

Links 142 to 144 follow the same basic steps

Air space. Open-spirals give air space to your chain designs. This open-spiral ends with a hairpin turn.

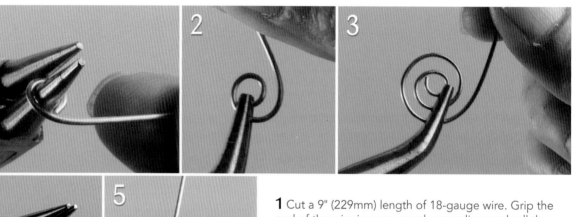

1 Cut a 9" (229mm) length of 18-gauge wire. Grip the end of the wire in your round-nose pliers and roll the end into a simple side-loop.

2 Transfer the simple side-loop to your bent-nose pliers and continue rolling the simple side-loop into a spiral. Do not bring the spiral wire tight enough to touch the simple side-loop. Allow some air space between these two sections of wire.

3 Continue rolling the open-spiral until you have completed 2½ turns.

4 With your round-nose pliers, grip the working wire ½" (13mm) from the spiral end and bend the working wire into a U-bend.

5 Move your round-nose pliers ½" (13mm) from the U-bend turn and roll the working wire into a midwire-circle. Clip the excess wire from the midwire-circle to create a simple side-loop using your flush wire cutters.

6 Hold the spiral and simple side-loop in your fingers and compress the link to bring the sides of the U-bend together.

7 The completed Link 143 can be joined to your chain through the outer ring of the spiral and the simple side-loop.

LINK 145:
3½-TURN SPIRAL
2-TURN HAIRPIN LINK

Links 145 through 148 follow the same basic steps

Spiral hairpin link. Spiral hairpin links add wonderful little areas of dense, compacted wire to your design. The open areas of the hairpin U-bends can be used as the connecting loops or as areas for bead-dangle attachments.

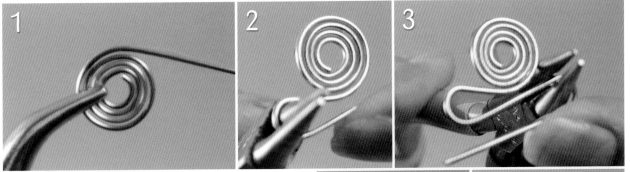

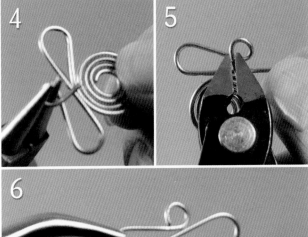

1 Cut a length of wire approximately 6" to 8" (152mm to 203mm) long, depending on how many turns you want in your spiral. Create a 4-turn spiral using your round- and bent-nose pliers.

2 Grip the working wire about 1" (25mm) from the base of the spiral in your round-nose pliers and create a U-bend.

3 Place the sides of the round-nose pliers on the working wire so that the pliers touch the spiral and create a U-bend.

4 Halfway between the two U-bends, create a simple side-loop on the working wire using your round-nose pliers.

5 Clip the excess wire from the simple side-loop using your flush cutters.

6 A spiral hairpin can have any number of turns in the first spiral, multiple U-bends in the hairpin area and end with either a simple side-loop, a wrapped side-loop, or another spiral.

LINK 149:
SPIRAL COMPRESSED HAIRPIN LINK

Links 149 and 150 follow
the same basic steps

Compressed hairpins. Compressing
hairpin turns adds interest to that area of the chain
because of the overlapping U-bends.

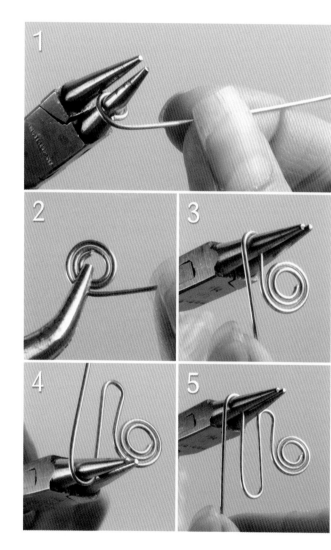

1 Cut a 12" (305mm) length of 18-gauge wire. Grip
the end of the wire in your round-nose pliers and roll
a simple side-loop.

2 Transfer the loop to your bent-nose pliers and continue
rolling the loop into a 2½-turn spiral.

3 Using your round-nose pliers, grip the wire ½" (13mm)
from the 2½-turn spiral and create a U-bend turn.

4 The second U-bend of this hairpin link is made
¾" (19mm) from the first.

5 Create a third hairpin turn ¾" (19mm) from the second
using your round-nose pliers.

6 The last U-bend hairpin is made ¾" (19mm) from
the fourth.

7 Clip the end of the working wire to a 3" (76mm) length
from the last U-bend hairpin turn. Grip the end of your
working wire in your round-nose pliers and roll the wire
into a simple side-loop.

8 Transfer your simple side-loop to your bent-nose pliers
and continue rolling the loop into a 2½-turn spiral.

9 With your nylon-grip pliers, flatten the entire link.

10 Grip the two spirals in your fingers and compress
the link. The spirals should overlap at the adjacent
hairpin turns.

11 This completed link has spiral ends, multiple hairpins,
and lots of visual interest because of the overlapping
U-bend turns.

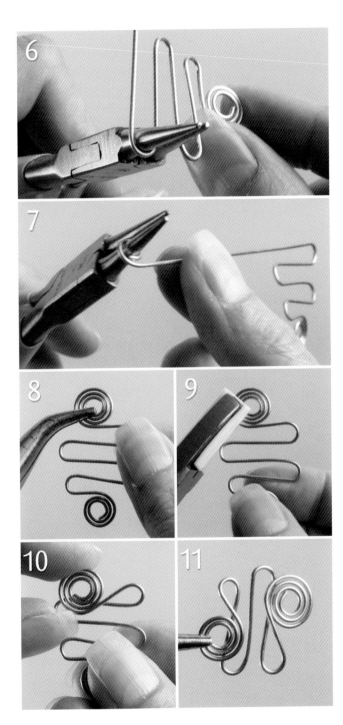

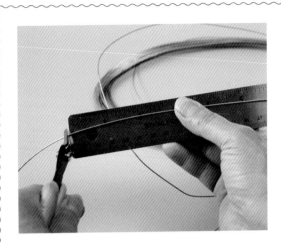

Tip 6: Length and gauge.

There are few exact measurements to offer in making individual links. The length of the wire used depends on gauge, the number of spiral or hairpin turns in the link, and the number and size of the beads used. On average, a simple link with no beads may only need 3" (76mm) of wire while a double-spiral bead link may require 8" (203mm) or more. Cut your wires extra long as you learn to do the bends, about 4" to 5" (102mm to 127mm) for simple links, 6" to 7" (152mm to 178mm) for spirals, hairpins, and two or more beads, and up to 9" (229mm) for multiple-bead spirals or hairpin links. Those few extra inches make bending easier. As you practice, you will learn to accurately estimate how much wire you will need for each link. Use the extra ends of cut wire as jump rings and split rings so they will not go to waste.

LINK 152: TURN-BACK MIDWIRE-SPIRAL LINK

Links 152 to 154 follow the same basic instructions

Midwire-spiral. A turn-back midwire-spiral gives you two central holes in the spiral for your bead dangles. Creating a smooth central turn-back to your spiral does take practice. As you learn to make this link, use a quick even motion when you pull the two wires around the round-nose pliers.

1 Begin with a 12" (305mm) length of 18-gauge wire. Grip the center point of the wire in your round-nose pliers.

2 Bend both sides of the working wire into a U-bend so the two sides are parallel.

3 Grip both wires about 1" (25mm) from the round-nose pliers in your fingers. Keep the round-nose pliers gripped tightly against the U-bend. Pull the two wires into the beginning of a spiral curve.

4 Transfer the curved turn-back loop to your bent-nose pliers or your nylon-grip pliers.

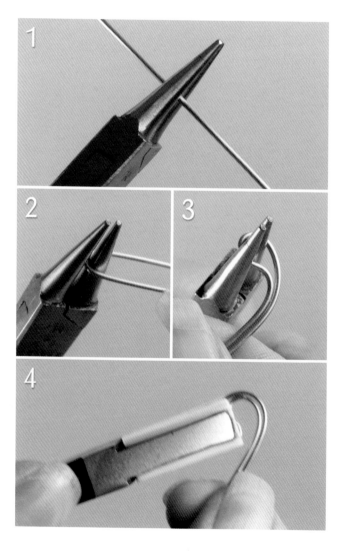

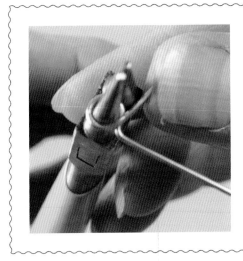

Tip 7: Shaping your bends.

Use the profile ends of your pliers to create the shapes of the bends in a link. Use straight-nosed and bent-nose pliers for sharp right-angle bends. Use round-nose pliers for loops and circles.

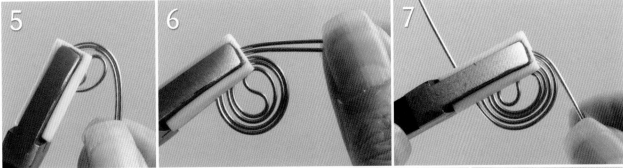

5 Work both wires as one and roll the wires around the outer edge of the turn-back loop.

6 Continue rolling both wires to create a 2-turn spiral.

7 Work the inside wire for one-half spiral turn more. This places one working wire—the outside wire—on one side of the link and the second—the inner wire—on the opposite side of the link.

8 Grip one of the working wires in your round-nose pliers close to the side of your spiral. Roll the wire into a midwire-circle.

9 Create a midwire-circle on the second working wire.

10 Clip the excess on both midwire-circles to create simple side-loop endings for your link.

11 The completed link uses simple side-loops as connecting loops and has a double-hole center.

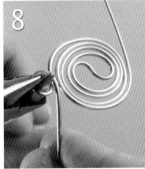

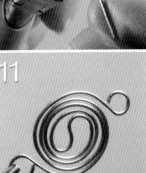

LINK 158:
WIRE-WRAPPED
HEART EYELET LINK

**Links 155 through 164
follow these basic steps**

Easy to make. Heart links are easy to make and a favorite addition to any chain, necklace, or bracelet project.

1 Begin with a 9" (229mm) length of 18-gauge wire. The more wire you allow for the link, the larger the V-space you will create between the two eyelets. Grip the end of your wire in your round-nose pliers and roll the end into a simple side-loop.

2 Place the simple side-loop against a ¾" (19mm) diameter circular form, such as the marking pen (far right, top). above. Roll the working wire around the form, bringing the wire back to the simple side-loop, to create one full-circle turn.

3 Grip the second end of the working wire in your round-nose pliers and roll a simple side-loop.

4 Transfer the simple side-loop to the side of a ¾" (19mm)-diameter form and roll the working wire into one full circle.

5 With your nylon-grip pliers, flatten the simple side-loops into the large open-eyelet circles.

6 Using your round-nose pliers, grip the center point of the wire between your eyelets. Bend the wire to allow the eyelet sides to touch.

7 Continue bending the center wire until the two open-eyelets overlap. (This step completes Link 155.)

8 Place your finger against one side of the V created from the center bend. Hold your finger in place and, using your second hand, gently roll the open-eyelet on that side of the link away from the overlap. This will add a small curve to the V leg. Repeat the step for the second V-leg of your link. (This step completes Link 158.)

9 How many turns you make around your large form changes the shape of the heart eyelet. For Link 159 create a half-turn circle around your large form.

10 Bend the center point of the wire, make the two simple side-loops of Link 159 touch at the top of the link.

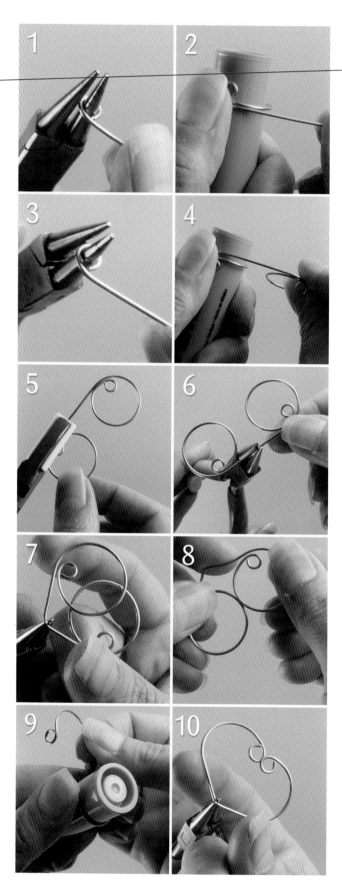

Using a Simple Clamp

1. Many links have open areas that can be strengthened with a wire-wrap. Link 159 is an excellent example because it has a weak point where the two simple side-loops touch.

2. Place the link inside your third hand clamp (page 19). The clamp is two ¾" wide-by-5"-long (19mm by 127mm) strips of heavy cardboard or chipboard held in place by a spring clamp.

3. To secure the link and avoid the chances of it becoming distorted during use, cut a 6" (152mm) length of 26-gauge wire and wire-wrap the simple side-loops together.

4. Thread the 26-gauge wrapping-wire through the simple side-loop of one side-loop on one side of the link, then through the second side-loop on the opposite side. Continue wrapping the center point, working through both simple side-loops for seven to nine tightly packed coils.

5. End the wrap by working both ends of the wrapping-wire to the back of the link. Clip the excess wire from the wrapping using your flush wire cutters. Crimp the ends of the wrapping-wire to secure the wrap to the link.

6. The completed heart makes a wonderful addition to your chain and its open center is perfect for adding bead dangles.

LINK 165:

OPEN-HAIRPIN-BEND CENTER EYELET LINK

Links 165 through 174 follow the same basic steps

Creating air space. Open-eyelet links create large air space areas in your design. The hairpin U-bend in the center is excellent for bead dangles. To keep this link as even as possible, it is worked from the center U and bent outward.

1 Cut approximately 8" (203 mm) of wire. Measure to find the center point of the wire and grip it in your round-nose pliers. Roll the wire into a tight U-bend.

2 Using your round-nose pliers, create a simple side-loop on both ends of the working wires.

3 Place the link over a large, ⅜" to ½" (10mm to 13mm)-diameter, cylinder form. I used a large marking pen. Allow approximately 1" (25mm) of the U-bend end to extend beyond your thumb.

4 Roll both simple loop ends of the link around the cylinder form.

5 Your link, removed from the cylinder, should resemble the photo.

6 Using your fingers and your bent-nose pliers to hold the large open loops, bend the large open circle flat to the tight U-bend of the link.

7 Check that the small simple side-loops are in line with the rest of the link.

8 Compress this link at the sides of the open circles to tighten the center U-bend. This link can have multiple turns changing the simple side-loop into a spiral, multiple turns to the large open circle, or a short or long U-bend center.

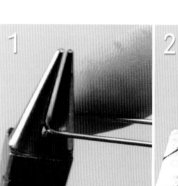

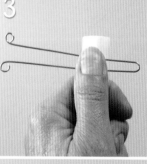

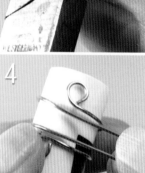

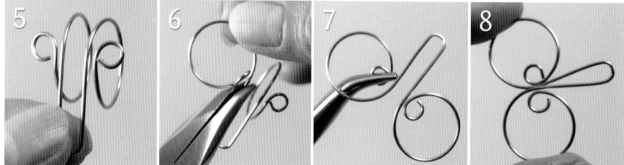

Adding Beads Using Side Wires

You can add a bead to a side wire of a link by wire-wrapping it in place using 26- to 20-gauge wire.

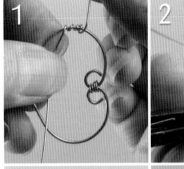

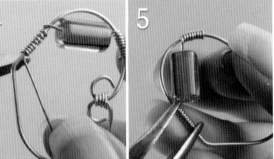

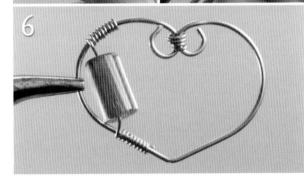

1. Select a link with open air space as any eyelet link, hairpin link, or raindrop link, to add wire-wrapped beads. I'm working this bead wrap on Link 159—an open-eyelet heart. Cut a 12" (305mm) length of 26-gauge wire. Secure the wrapping-wire to one of the side wires of your link by creating two to three tightly packed coils with the wrapping-wire.

2. Clip the excess wrapping-wire at the beginning of the tightly packed coils using your flush wire cutters. Crimp the end of the wire using your bent-nose pliers to secure it in position.

3. Continue wrapping the working end of the wrapping-wire until you have worked ¼" (6mm) of tightly packed coils. Use your bent-nose pliers to compress the coils along the side wire of the link.

4. Slide a bead onto the wrapping-wire. Hold the bead in position with one hand and begin creating tightly packed coils with the wrapping-wire on the side wire of the link below the bead. Work the coils until you have ¼" (6mm) of wrapping.

5. Clip the excess wrapping-wire and crimp the end of the wire tightly into place on the link. Use your bent-nose pliers and compress the second section of tightly packed coils.

6. Adding a wire-wrapped bead to your link allows you to add color and design to your jewelry after the chain or necklace links are completed.

LINK 167: DOUBLE-CIRCLE, SINGLE-CIRCLE EYELET LINK

Multiple circles, different sizes.

Open-eyelet links can have multiple full circles worked around different-sized forms. The link above was first rolled around a small marking pen then around a large sized marker.

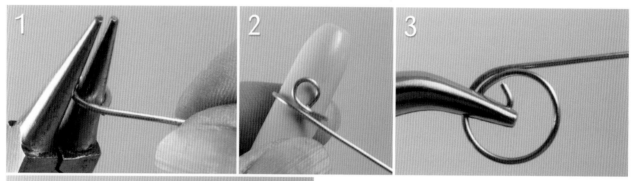

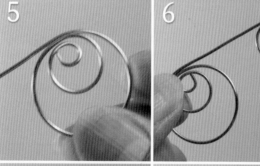

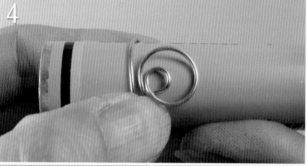

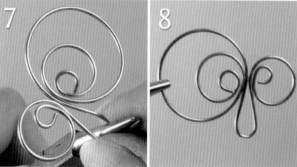

1 Cut a length of wire 10" long. Grip the end of the working wire in your round-nose pliers and roll a simple side-loop.

2 Place the simple side-loop against a medium-sized ½" (13mm)-diameter form. Using your fingers, roll the working wire around the form until you reach the simple side-loop. This makes a one full-turn circle.

3 Use your bent-nose pliers to flatten the two circles—the simple side-loop and the full-turn eyelet. Repeat these steps as you work toward the second side of the wire.

4 Place one eyelet against a large form, ⅝" (16mm) wide. Hold the small eyelet with your fingers and roll the working wire around the form to create a second larger eyelet.

5 Remove the eyelet from the form and flatten the three circles with your bent-nose pliers.

6 Holding the eyelets in your fingers, twist the center wire to bring the two sides of the link into line.

7 Using a ruler, measure the wire between the two eyelet ends to find the center point. Gripping your wire in your round-nose pliers at the center point, bend the wire into a U-bend. Compress the links so the two eyelet sides touch just above the U-bend.

8 You can add multiple rings of eyelets by simply changing the size of the form that you use to roll the eyelet. With each new circle or ring, the form should be slightly larger than the form used in the previous eyelet ring.

LINK 170: WIRE-WRAPPED DOUBLE-CIRCLE EYELET LINK

Adding strength. Adding a small-gauged wire-wrap gives strength to an open link. Wire-wraps can be used on any link to secure two areas of the link, such as two hairpin turns or two large spirals. A wrap can also be worked over one section of wire along one side of an eyelet to add a little extra sparkle to the link.

1 For large open links such as this double-circle eyelet, you may need the assistance of a third hand—a clamp—to hold the link in place while adding the wire-wrap. The clamp is made out of four strips of chipboard and two spring clips. One piece of chipboard is placed on the back of the link and one on the front. The spring clip then is put into position. The clip holds the link wire while the chipboard protects the wire from dents and scratches.

2 Once the clamp is in place, cut a 12" (305mm) length of fine 24- or 26-gauge wire. Thread the end of the wire through one simple side-loop. Leave two inches of wire to hold or secure while you wrap the remaining length.

3 Pull the working wire-wrap across the back of the link and feed the end of the wire-wrap through the second simple side-loop of the link. Use your bent-nose pliers or nylon-grip pliers to pull the wire firmly into place.

4 Continue feeding the working wire through the simple side-loops until you have five to six wraps completed.

5 Feed one end of the working wire through its next simple side-loop so both ends of the wire are on the same side—the back—of the link.

6 Clip the ends of the working wire so that a small length of wire will lap the loops.

7 Use your bent-nose pliers to crimp or firmly press those small laps into the wrap area.

8 The completed wire-wrap secures this open-eyelet link from being pulled apart while adding a little extra sparkle to the link.

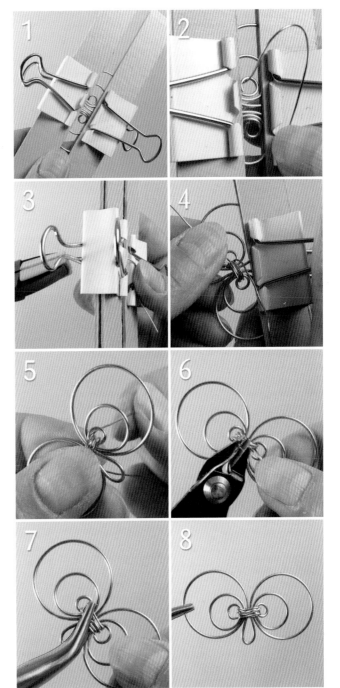

LINK 175:
MIDWIRE-CIRCLE
DOUBLE-HAIRPIN LINK

Adding visual interest.

What would have been a simple
side double hairpin suddenly gains
interest because of the addition of midwire-circles.

112

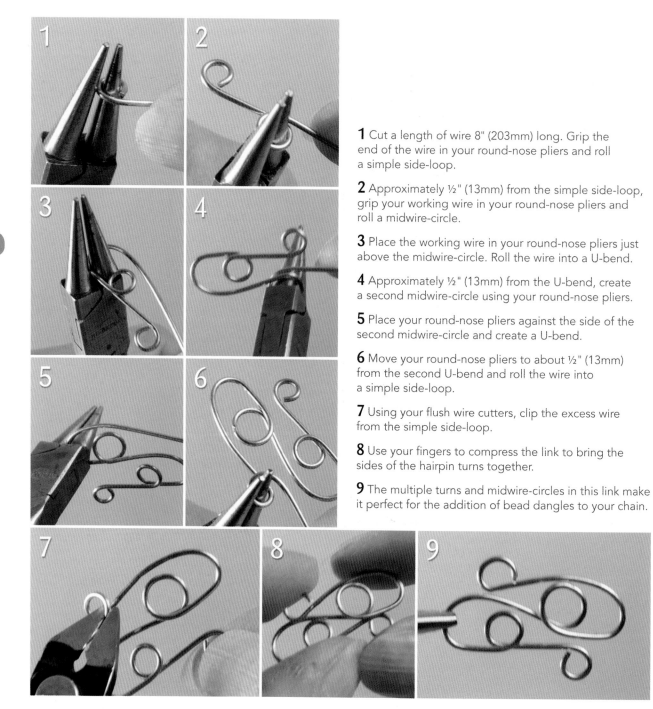

1 Cut a length of wire 8" (203mm) long. Grip the end of the wire in your round-nose pliers and roll a simple side-loop.

2 Approximately ½" (13mm) from the simple side-loop, grip your working wire in your round-nose pliers and roll a midwire-circle.

3 Place the working wire in your round-nose pliers just above the midwire-circle. Roll the wire into a U-bend.

4 Approximately ½" (13mm) from the U-bend, create a second midwire-circle using your round-nose pliers.

5 Place your round-nose pliers against the side of the second midwire-circle and create a U-bend.

6 Move your round-nose pliers to about ½" (13mm) from the second U-bend and roll the wire into a simple side-loop.

7 Using your flush wire cutters, clip the excess wire from the simple side-loop.

8 Use your fingers to compress the link to bring the sides of the hairpin turns together.

9 The multiple turns and midwire-circles in this link make it perfect for the addition of bead dangles to your chain.

LINK 178: MIDWIRE-SPIRAL HAIRPIN LINK

Links 176 through 178 follow the same basic steps

Midwire-spirals. Adding spirals to the center of any link is easy if you use the midwire-circle bend.

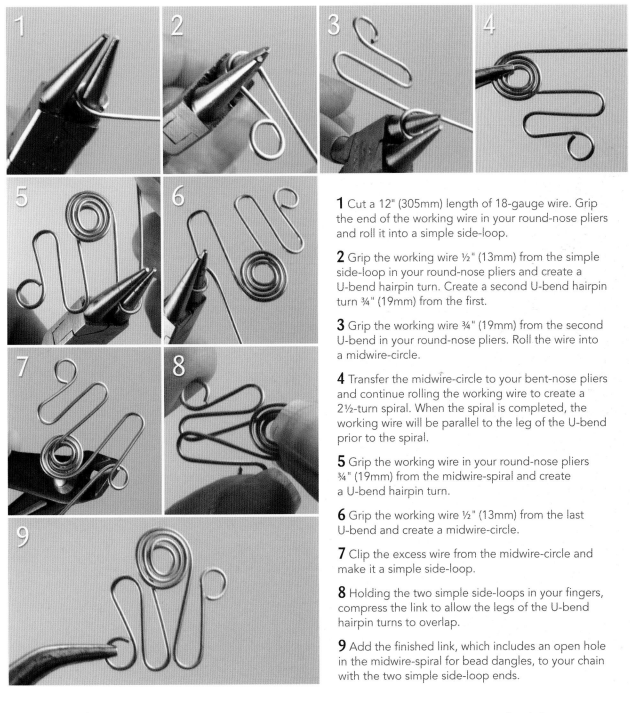

1 Cut a 12" (305mm) length of 18-gauge wire. Grip the end of the working wire in your round-nose pliers and roll it into a simple side-loop.

2 Grip the working wire ½" (13mm) from the simple side-loop in your round-nose pliers and create a U-bend hairpin turn. Create a second U-bend hairpin turn ¾" (19mm) from the first.

3 Grip the working wire ¾" (19mm) from the second U-bend in your round-nose pliers. Roll the wire into a midwire-circle.

4 Transfer the midwire-circle to your bent-nose pliers and continue rolling the working wire to create a 2½-turn spiral. When the spiral is completed, the working wire will be parallel to the leg of the U-bend prior to the spiral.

5 Grip the working wire in your round-nose pliers ¾" (19mm) from the midwire-spiral and create a U-bend hairpin turn.

6 Grip the working wire ½" (13mm) from the last U-bend and create a midwire-circle.

7 Clip the excess wire from the midwire-circle and make it a simple side-loop.

8 Holding the two simple side-loops in your fingers, compress the link to allow the legs of the U-bend hairpin turns to overlap.

9 Add the finished link, which includes an open hole in the midwire-spiral for bead dangles, to your chain with the two simple side-loop ends.

LINK 182:
6 TURN-BACK LOOPS
LADDER LINK

Links 180 through 184 follow the same basic steps

Using a series. Link 182 is created with a series of turn-back loops. Using the same loop in a series can help you create new links with great visual interest, but no investment of time to learn new bent-wire techniques.

THE COMPLETE LINK SET

1 Cut a 9" (229mm) length of 18-gauge wire for this practice link. Grip the end of your working wire in your round-nose pliers and roll the wire into a simple side-loop.

2 Move your round-nose pliers to ½" (13mm) from the simple side-loop and create a turn-back loop. Work the direction of this turn-back loop to bring the working wire to the top of the link.

3 Move your round-nose pliers to ¾" (19mm) from the first turn-back loop. Create a second turn-back loop. Roll the second turn-back loop so that the working wire ends on the top of the link.

4 Move your round-nose pliers to ¾" (19mm) from the second turn-back loop and create a third. Work the third turn-back loop in the direction to bring the working wire to the top of the link.

5 Work your fourth turn-back loop ¾" (19mm) from the third. Work the loop in the direction to bring the working wire to the top of the link.

6 Grip the working wire ⅜" (10mm) from the last turn-back loop. This will place the pliers in the center of the link. Roll the working wire into a midwire-circle.

7 Clip the excess wire from the midwire-circle to create a simple side-loop ending.

8 With your fingers, ease the link apart to evenly space the turn-back loops.

9 Press the link flat using your nylon-grip pliers.

10 The completed link is wonderful for adding bead dangles to both sides of a bracelet or anklet project.

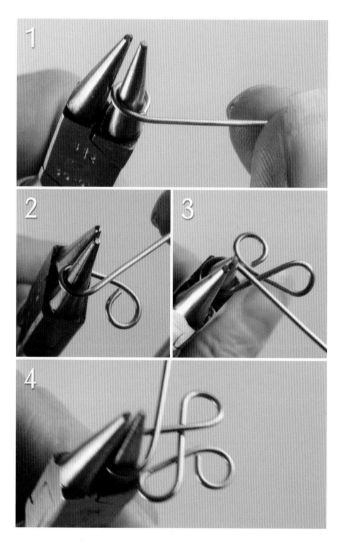

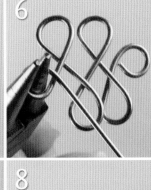

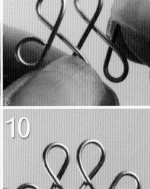

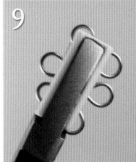

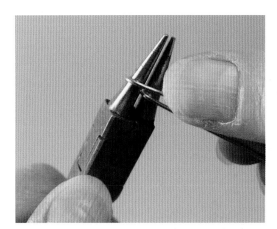

Tip 8: Completing the loop.

Adjust or re-arrange the position of the wire in the tool as needed to complete the bend or loop. Use the tip of your thumb with medium pressure to press the wire against the tool tip.

LINK 186:
MIDWIRE-SPIRAL LINK

Midwire-spiral link. Work
Link 186 with a midwire-spiral that
allows the wires at the beginning
and end of the spiral to become simple
side-loops to connect the link to your chain.

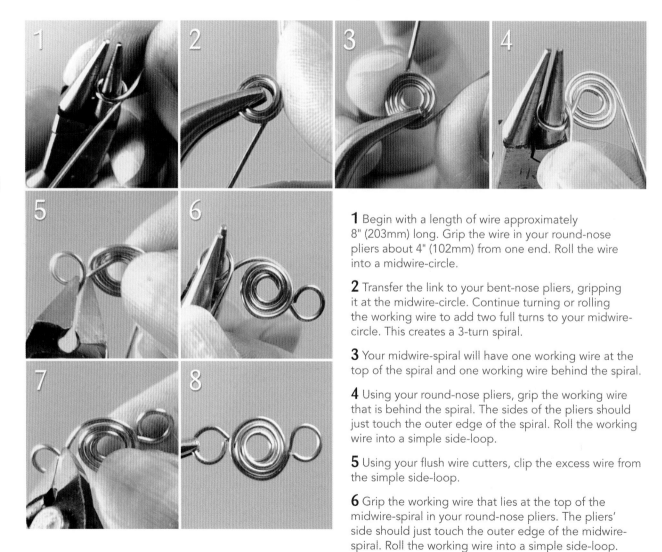

1 Begin with a length of wire approximately
8" (203mm) long. Grip the wire in your round-nose
pliers about 4" (102mm) from one end. Roll the wire
into a midwire-circle.

2 Transfer the link to your bent-nose pliers, gripping
it at the midwire-circle. Continue turning or rolling
the working wire to add two full turns to your midwire-
circle. This creates a 3-turn spiral.

3 Your midwire-spiral will have one working wire at the
top of the spiral and one working wire behind the spiral.

4 Using your round-nose pliers, grip the working wire
that is behind the spiral. The sides of the pliers should
just touch the outer edge of the spiral. Roll the working
wire into a simple side-loop.

5 Using your flush wire cutters, clip the excess wire from
the simple side-loop.

6 Grip the working wire that lies at the top of the
midwire-spiral in your round-nose pliers. The pliers'
side should just touch the outer edge of the midwire-
spiral. Roll the working wire into a simple side-loop.

7 Clip the excess wire from the simple side-loop using
your flush wire cutters.

8 You can bend either of the simple side-loops so they
rest against the spiral sides.

LINK 188:
TURN-BACK LOOP
SPIRAL LINK

Links 185 through 191 follow the same basic steps

Centering a spiral. Placing a spiral on the centerline of your chain is easy when you use a turn-back loop at the end of the spiral. The link is attached to your chain with the turn-back loop and simple side-loop ends and the center hole of the spiral can be used for bead-dangle attachments.

1 Create a 3-turn spiral by rolling a simple side-loop in your round-nose pliers. Grip the loop in your bent-nose pliers and roll the wire for three turns. Straighten your working wire using your nylon-grip flat pliers. Grip the working wire in your round-nose pliers so that the pliers rest against the spiral.

2 Roll the working wire into a turn-back loop with the excess working wire positioned to fall in the center of the original simple side-loop.

3 On the opposite side of the turn-back loop grip the working wire in your round-nose pliers so the pliers lie against the spiral's edge. Roll the wire into a simple side-loop.

4 The turn-back cross-under loop link can be worked so that both the turn-back loop and simple side-loop roll toward one side of the spiral allowing the spiral to hang below the two loops. If you bend the simple side-loop in the opposite direction to the turn-back loop, the spiral area becomes centered to the link.

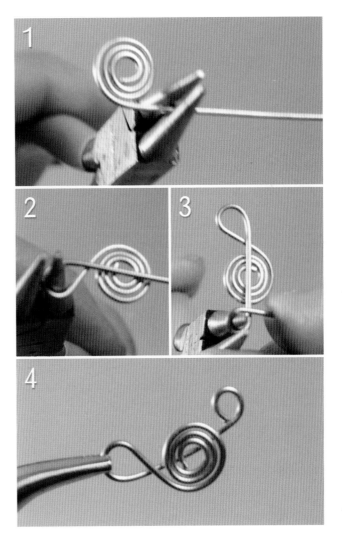

LINK 192: THREADED TURN-BACK LOOP DOUBLE-SPIRAL LINK

Links 192 through 194 follow the same basic steps

Using extra wire. Use the excess wire left from an ending simple side-loop or turn-back loop to create an added spiral for your link.

1 Cut a 12" (305mm) length of 18-gauge wire for this practice link. Grip the end of the working wire in your round-nose pliers and roll the end into a simple side-loop. Transfer the simple side-loop to your bent-nose pliers and continue rolling the loop into a 3-turn spiral.

2 Grip the working wire at the end of your spiral and create a turn-back loop. End the loop with the working wire at the top of the spiral.

3 With your fingers, roll the working wire over the top wire of the spiral, bringing the working wire to the opposite side of the link.

4 Grip the working wire against the side of the spiral and roll the wire into a turn-back loop.

5 Hold the link, especially the spiral, tightly in one hand while you feed the end of the working wire through the center hole of the spiral. You may need to open the second turn-back loop to ease the working wire into position. Once the working wire has cleared the center hole, close the turn-back loop.

6 With your nylon-grip pliers, press the working wire tightly against the back of the spiral.

7 Clip the working wire to a 3" (76mm) length using your flush wire cutters.

8 Grip the end of your working wire in your round-nose pliers and roll the end into a simple side-loop.

9 Transfer the simple side-loop to your bent-nose pliers and continue rolling the loop into a spiral. Roll all of the working wire to place this second spiral over the bottom half of the first spiral. Flatten your link using your nylon-grip pliers.

10 The completed link adds a drop-down spiral that will fall below the centerline of your chain.

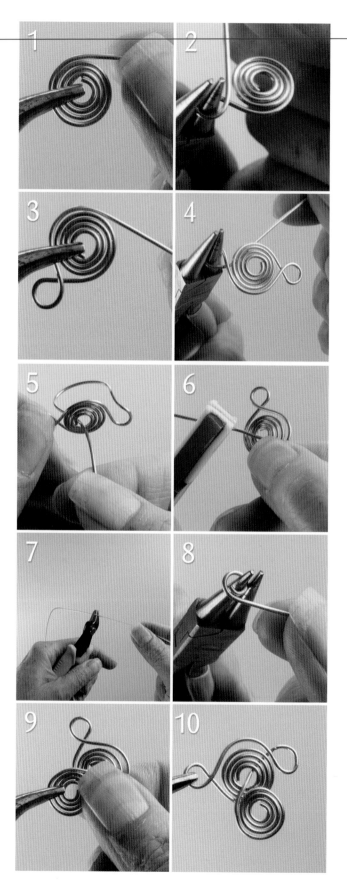

LINK 193:
TURN-BACK SPIRAL-
HAIRPIN LOOP LINK
More uses for extra wire.

An extra-long working wire at the end of a link can be turned into a double-hairpin spiral. The added hairpin turns place extra decorative wire on top of the bends of the link.

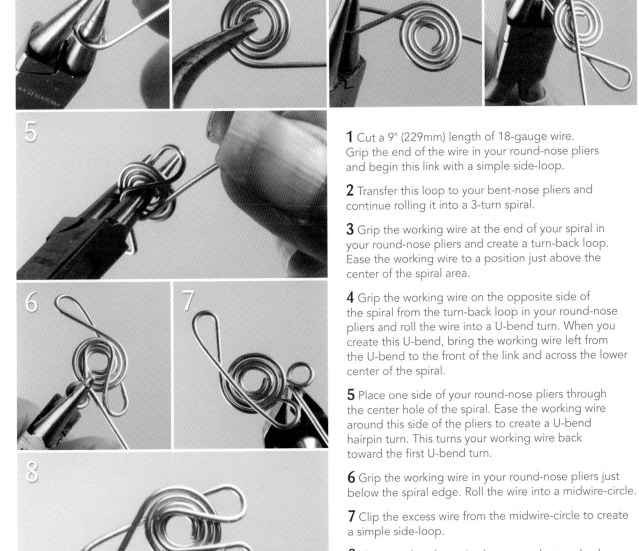

1 Cut a 9" (229mm) length of 18-gauge wire. Grip the end of the wire in your round-nose pliers and begin this link with a simple side-loop.

2 Transfer this loop to your bent-nose pliers and continue rolling it into a 3-turn spiral.

3 Grip the working wire at the end of your spiral in your round-nose pliers and create a turn-back loop. Ease the working wire to a position just above the center of the spiral area.

4 Grip the working wire on the opposite side of the spiral from the turn-back loop in your round-nose pliers and roll the wire into a U-bend turn. When you create this U-bend, bring the working wire left from the U-bend to the front of the link and across the lower center of the spiral.

5 Place one side of your round-nose pliers through the center hole of the spiral. Ease the working wire around this side of the pliers to create a U-bend hairpin turn. This turns your working wire back toward the first U-bend turn.

6 Grip the working wire in your round-nose pliers just below the spiral edge. Roll the wire into a midwire-circle.

7 Clip the excess wire from the midwire-circle to create a simple side-loop.

8 The completed practice loop uses the turn-back loop and the first U-bend loop as its connecting loops. A U-bend circles the center hole of the spiral and ends with a simple side-loop, ready to accept a bead dangle.

LINK 199: 2½-TURN SPIRAL RAINDROP LINK

Links 195 through 204 follow the same basic steps

Center-spiral raindrop. Raindrops use a simple side-loop or a spiral at the center of the link; then, the working wire is bent into a long but tight angle to create an open space below the spiral.

1 Cut a length of wire approximately 8" (302mm) long. Grip the wire in your round-nose pliers and roll a simple side-loop.

2 Continue rolling the side-loop into a 3-turn spiral using your bent-nose pliers or nylon-grip pliers.

3 Grip the working wire about ¾" (19mm) away from the base of the spiral and bend a tight U-bend using your round-nose pliers. Make the bend tight enough that the end of the working wire touches the second side of the spiral.

4 Holding the working wire and spiral in your bent-nose pliers, roll the wire over the top of the spiral so that the working wire extends at a 90° angle from the link.

5 Grip the working wire with your round-nose pliers at the top of the spiral and bend the wire into a simple side-loop. Clip the excess wire using your flush cutters.

6 A spiral raindrop can be linked to the chain through the simple side-loop, the tight U-bend, or through the center hole in the spiral. This particular link is excellent to make long quick links for a chain and can have beads added to the working wire before and after you bend the tight U-bend.

7 Using a longer length of wire that leaves 2 to 3" (51mm to 76mm) of wire after the U-bend turn allows you to replace the simple side-loop end with a multiple-turn spiral end and create Link 202.

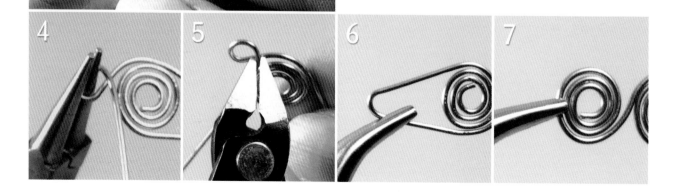

LINK 205: 2½-TURN SPIRAL HAIRPIN RAINDROP LINK

Links 205 through 210 follow the same basic steps

Visual energy. Combining a spiral, a raindrop, and a hairpin creates an interesting flow of visual energy for your jewelry creations. Link 205 can begin and end with a spiral turn.

1 Cut an 8" (302mm) length of 18-gauge wire. Grip the end of the working wire in your round-nose pliers and roll the end into a simple side-loop. Transfer the loop to your bent-nose pliers. Continue rolling the loop to create a 2½-turn spiral.

2 Grip the working wire ¾" (19mm) from the base of the spiral and roll the wire into a tight U-bend turn.

3 Hold the center spiral securely and ease the working wire across the top of the spiral.

4 Grip the working wire in your round-nose pliers ½" (13mm) from the top point of the spiral. Create a U-bend turn that brings the working wire back across the top of the spiral.

5 Clip the working wire to a length of 1½" (39mm) long. Grip the end of the working wire in your round-nose pliers and roll the end into a simple side-loop.

6 Transfer the loop to your bent-nose pliers and continue rolling the loop into a spiral. End the spiral when it is centered over the original central spiral.

7 Grip the upper spiral in your hands and compress the link to tighten the U-bend turn.

8 This completed link can be added to your chain through the ending simple side-loop and the U-bend of the raindrop. A bead dangle can be hung from the U-bend between the raindrop's top edge and the simple side-loop.

9 The number of turns to the center spiral, the size and position of the hairpin turn and the number of turns to the end loop make this a very adaptable link.

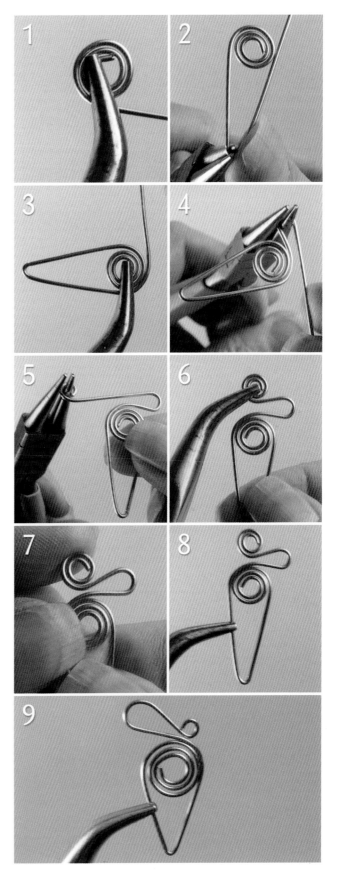

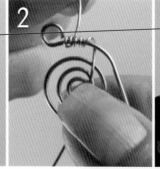

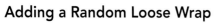

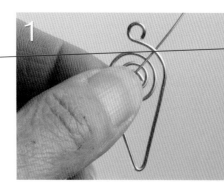

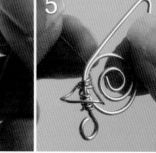

Adding a Random Loose Wrap

Decorative strength. A random loose wire-wrap adds decoration as well as strength to this open 3½-turn spiral raindrop link.

1. Create a spiral hairpin link using an open-spiral center using an 8" (203mm) length of 18-gauge wire. Cut a 12" (305mm) length of 26-gauge wire for wrapping.

2. Secure the end of the wrapping-wire to the outside upper leg of the raindrop link by creating two or three tightly packed coils.

3. Clip the excess wrapping-wire from this end and crimp the end with your bent-nose pliers to secure it.

4. Compact the tight coils using your bent-nose pliers.

5. Begin wrapping the 26-gauge wire around this outside leg of the raindrop using a random pattern with tight and loose wraps.

6. Vary the position of the wraps by working some below the main wrap, then working back to the top of the wrap.

7. End the wrap with three or four tightly packed coils at the bottom of the wrapping area.

8. Clip the excess wire from the end of the wrapping-wire using your flush wire cutters.

9. Compress the tightly packed coils using your bent-nose pliers.

10. This completed link has added sparkle from the wrapping-wire. The wrapping has added strength to the link to avoid the chances of it becoming distorted during use.

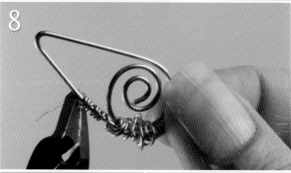

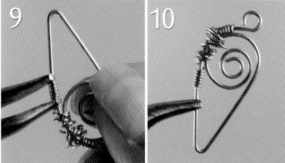

LINK 221:
DROP-DOWN SIMPLE
LOOP RAINDROP LINK

**Links 211 through 227 follow
the same basic steps**

Below the centerline. Bringing the end wire of this raindrop into a downward position allows the raindrop area of the link to land below the centerline of the chain creating more visual interest for your jewelry.

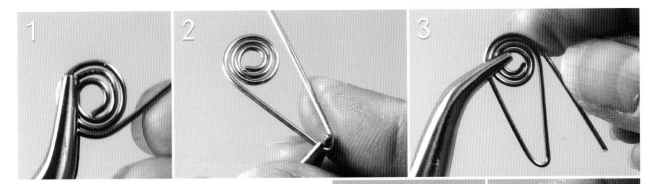

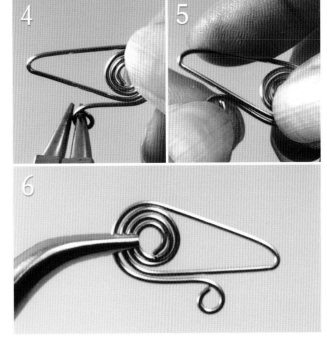

1 Begin with a length of wire approximately 5" to 6" (127mm to 152mm) long. Grip the end of the wire in your round-nose pliers and roll it into a simple side-loop. Grip the simple side-loop in your bent-nose pliers and continue rolling the loop into a 3-turn spiral.

2 About ¾" (19mm) from the base of the spiral, grip the working wire in your round-nose pliers and bend the wire into a tight U-bend so that the working wire touches the second side of the spiral.

3 Hold both the working wire and the spiral in your bent-nose pliers and roll the working wire over the top of the spiral. Continue the roll until the working wire is in a downward position to the link.

4 Grip the end of the working wire in your round-nose pliers and create a simple side-loop. Clip the excess wire with your flush cutters.

5 Use your fingers or nylon-grip pliers to set the simple side-loop into square with the rest of the link.

6 The tight U-bend area of this link creates small downward points in a chain when the link is connected to the chain through the simple side-loop and the center of the spiral.

LINK 228: LARGE OPEN-EYELET RAINDROP LINK

Links 229 through 230 follow the same basic steps

Space for dangles. A large open-eyelet makes the center of this raindrop link. This creates a wide link with lots of space for a cluster of bead dangles.

1 Cut a length of wire approximately 4" to 5" (102 to 127mm) long. Grip the end of the wire in your round-nose pliers and roll a simple side-loop.

2 Place the side-loop against a large round form. In this sample, a marking pen is being used. Secure the side-loop with your thumb and roll the working wire around the form until you return to the side-loop.

3 Continue rolling the working wire until you have created a half-turn that places the working wire on the opposite side of the form.

4 Remove the wire from the form.

5 Use your bent-nose pliers to flatten the simple side-loop into the large open-eyelet. Grip the working wire about ¾" (19mm) from the base of the open-eyelet and create a U-bend. Bring the working wire along the side of the open-eyelet.

6 With your fingers, secure the open-eyelet as you roll the working wire along the top of the link.

7 Grip the working wire in your round-nose pliers at the top of the open-eyelet. Roll the wire into a simple side-loop.

8 The completed link can be connected to your chain through the ending simple side-loop and the U-bend of the raindrop. The open-eyelet area is ready to accept a cluster of bead dangles.

9 Wire-wrap the center open-spiral of this link by working a length of 24- or 26-gauge wire to wire-wrap the center open-spiral of this link by working several tightly packed coils before and after the simple side-loop connection at the top of the link.

10 A few moments of time and a small length of fine wire create this finished wrap, which adds visual interest to the link.

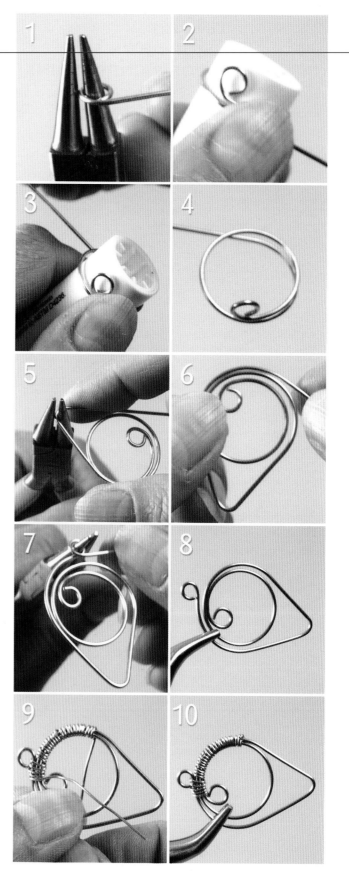

LINK 265: CRIMPED-END BEAD-DANGLE LINK

Links 231 through 278
utilize a combination of
bends already demonstrated

Bead-dangle link. When you want to create a bead dangle without any other bend below the bead, a simple rolled crimped-end will secure it. I have worked this crimped-end bead dangle using a wrapped straight-loop connecting loop, but this link can easily be worked with any simple- or wrapped-loop variation.

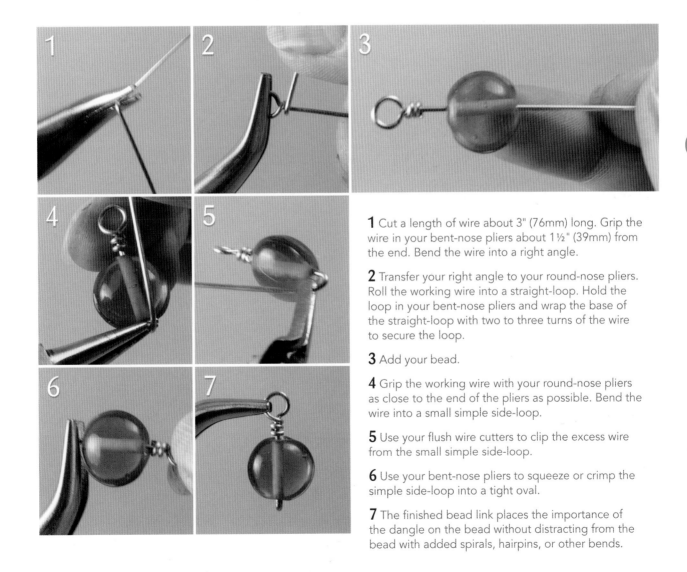

1 Cut a length of wire about 3" (76mm) long. Grip the wire in your bent-nose pliers about 1½" (39mm) from the end. Bend the wire into a right angle.

2 Transfer your right angle to your round-nose pliers. Roll the working wire into a straight-loop. Hold the loop in your bent-nose pliers and wrap the base of the straight-loop with two to three turns of the wire to secure the loop.

3 Add your bead.

4 Grip the working wire with your round-nose pliers as close to the end of the pliers as possible. Bend the wire into a small simple side-loop.

5 Use your flush wire cutters to clip the excess wire from the small simple side-loop.

6 Use your bent-nose pliers to squeeze or crimp the simple side-loop into a tight oval.

7 The finished bead link places the importance of the dangle on the bead without distracting from the bead with added spirals, hairpins, or other bends.

LINK 279:
WIRE-WRAPPED BEAD
CAP DANGLE LINK
Enhancing a solid color.

An otherwise plain solid-colored bead can be enhanced by adding a spiral-wrapped bead cap.

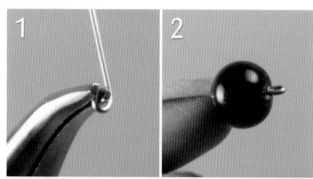

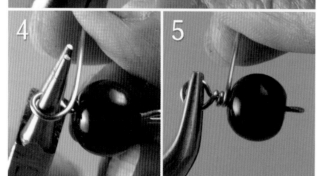

1 Work Link 279 from the bottom of the dangle to the top. Cut a length of wire 7" to 8" (178mm to 203mm) long. The longer you make the working wire the larger your bead-cap area will be. Grip the end of the working wire in your bent-nose pliers as close to the tip of the pliers as possible. Bend a tight U-bend. Move the U-bend inside your bent-nose pliers and crimp the bend firmly.

2 Add your large bead to the wire.

3 With your bent-nose pliers, make a right-angle bend above the bead, allowing room for a loop wrap.

4 With your round-nose pliers, make a simple straight-loop.

5 Wrap the working wire around the base of the simple straight-loop to create a wrapped straight-loop.

6 Continue rolling the working wire around the bead dangle. The spiral wrap will work from the straight-wrapped loop area onto the top of the bead. Continue wrapping the spiral until you have used all of your working wire.

7 Grip the cap in your nylon-grip pliers and firmly set the wire end.

8 This simple black bead catches your attention because of the spiral-wrapped bead cap.

LINK 280: LARGE-BEAD-CIRCLE CAP DANGLE LINK

Links 280 to 285 utilize a combination of bends already demonstrated

Cap and large circle. With a bright bead cap at the top and a large open-circle at the bottom, this dangle will become the center of attention in your necklace or bracelet.

1 Cut a length of wire 12" (305mm) long. The bead dangle is worked from the bottom to the top. Grip the working wire approximately 2½" (64mm) from the end of the wire in your bent-nose pliers. Bend the wire into a right angle.

2 Place the right-angle bend against a medium form, approximately ½" (13mm) in diameter. Holding the right-angle bend with your fingers, roll the working wire around the form to create a full circle.

3 Remove the wire from the form and flatten the circle to the working wire and right-angle bend.

4 To wrap the loop, grip the base of the full large circle in your bent-nose pliers and roll the working wire two to three times around the base of the circle.

5 Using your flush wire cutters, clip the excess wire from the loop wrap.

6 Add a large bead to the working wire.

7 Grip the working wire at the top of the bead in your bent-nose pliers. Bend the wire into a right angle.

8 Transfer the right-angle bend to your round-nose pliers and roll a simple straight-loop.

9 Using your bent-nose pliers, wrap the working wire around the simple straight-loop to create a wrapped straight-loop. Continue wrapping the wire in a spiral turn, letting the wire wrap over the top of the bead. Wrap the spiral until you have used all of your working wire.

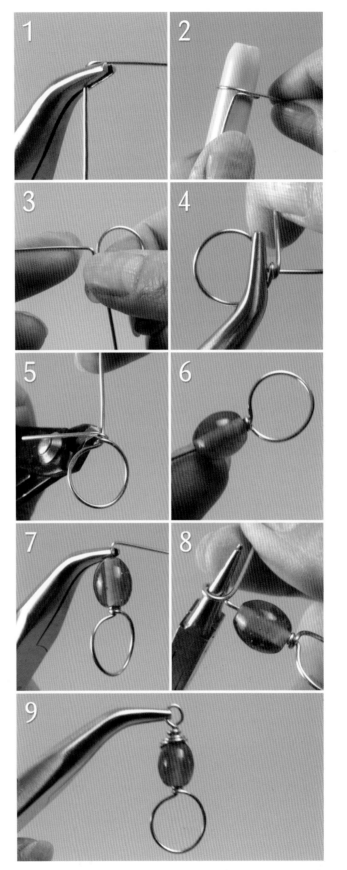

LINK 286: CENTERED SPIRAL-END BEAD LINK

Links 286 through 298 use a combination of previously demonstrated bends

Easy addition. Beginning and ending with a wrapped straight-loop, the centered spiral-end bead link is an easy addition to any chain. The centered spirals on both sides of the bead add a touch of interest to plain or solid-colored beads.

1 Cut a length of wire 10" (254mm) long. Grip the working wire 4½" (114mm) from the end in your bent-nose pliers and bend the wire into a right angle. The extra length of the working wire will be used to create one of the centered bead spirals. Transfer the right angle to your round-nose pliers. Roll the wire into a simple straight-loop. Gripping the simple straight-loop in your bent-nose pliers, wrap the base of the loop two to three times to create a wrapped straight-loop. Do not clip the excess wire.

2 Add a large flat bead—a disc or oval bead works best for this link.

3 Grip the working wire at the top of the bead in your bent-nose pliers and bend to wire into a right angle.

4 Transfer the right angle to your round-nose pliers. Roll a simple straight-loop.

5 Transfer your loop to your bent-nose pliers. Wrap the base of the loop two to three times to create a wrapped straight-loop. Compare the two working wire ends of your link. Use your flush wire cutters to clip the working wires so they are the same length. An even length for each wire will ensure your centered bead spirals will be the same size.

6 Grip one working wire end in your round-nose pliers. Roll a simple side-loop. Transfer the loop to your bent-nose pliers and continue rolling your simple side-loop into a spiral. Roll the spiral until you have used all of your working wire.

7 Set your spiral in the center of one side of your bead.

8 Roll the second wrapped-loop wire into a centered spiral for the opposite side of the bead.

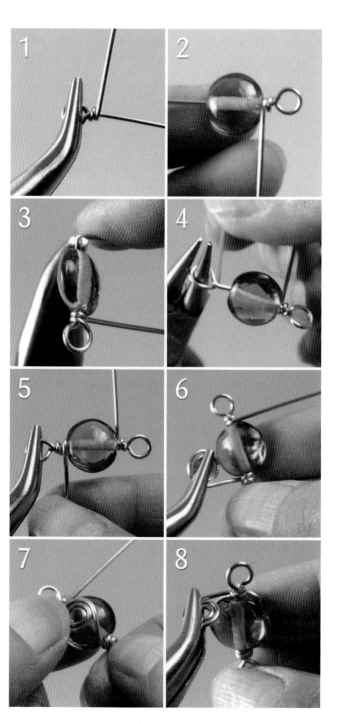

LINK 299: ROLLED-WIRE-END BEAD DANGLE LINK

Links 299 through 306 use a combination of previously demonstrated bends

Running perpendicular. There are times that you want a bead wired vertically—perpendicular to your dangle—instead of the more common horizontal design. Link 299 provides the opportunity for you to create that change in visual energy.

1 Work Link 299 from the center of the wire out to the half-circle bends under the bead. Cut a length of wire 8" (203mm) long. Slide a large bead onto the wire and move it to the center.

2 Holding the bead in position, use your fingers to gently bend the two working wires into right angles. The right angle is created close to the side of the bead.

3 Continue holding the bead in your hand. Gripping one working wire in your fingers several inches from the bead, roll the working wire across the length of the bead.

4 Roll the second working wire along the side of the bead to the opposite side of the bead. The two working wires will cross at the center bottom of the bead.

5 Gently compress the working wires at the bead side until the two wires cross approximately 1" (25mm) above the bead.

6 Using your bent-nose pliers, create an angle in each working wire about ½" (13mm) above the bead that brings the two working wires together in a straight line to the bead link.

7 On one working wire, use your bent-nose pliers to bend a right angle.

8 Grip that working wire in your round-nose pliers and roll a simple straight-loop.

9 Use your bent-nose pliers to grip the link at the simple side-loop base. Catch both working wires in the pliers' grip.

10 Holding both wires with your bent-nose pliers, wrap the simple straight-loop two to three times to create a wrapped straight-loop. Clip the excess wire from the wrapped loop using your flush wire cutters. Clip the remaining working wire at the top of the wrapped loop.

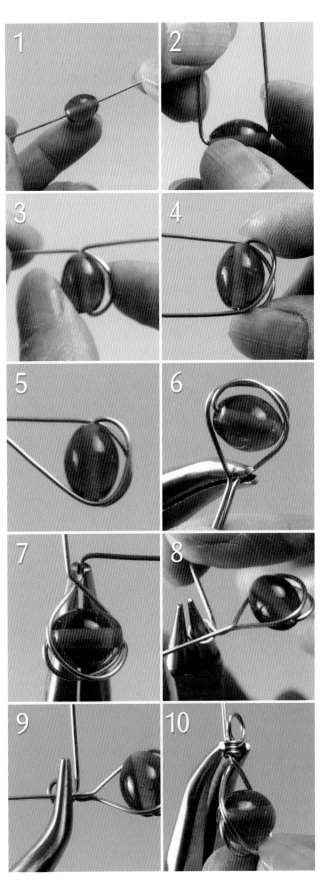

129

Making a Ball-and-Cage Link

LINK 303: BALL-AND-CAGE BEAD LINK

Links 300 through 306 use previously demonstrated bends

The ball-and-cage link captures a bead firmly inside of a spiral wire cage.

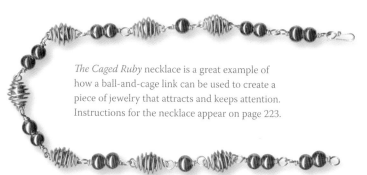

The Caged Ruby necklace is a great example of how a ball-and-cage link can be used to create a piece of jewelry that attracts and keeps attention. Instructions for the necklace appear on page 223.

1. Begin this link with a 12" (305mm)-long section of wire. Grip the end of the wire in your round-nose pliers and roll the wire into a simple side-loop.

2. Transfer the simple side-loop to your bent-nose pliers and continue rolling the loop into a spiral that is one full turn larger than the bead that will be captured inside of the link.

3. Grip the opposite end of the working wire in your round-nose pliers and create a second spiral with the same number of turns as the first. This spiral is worked on the wire on the opposite side as the first.

4. Fold the two spirals along the center connecting wire.

5. Slide the bead between the two folded spirals. With your fingers or your bent-nose pliers, separate the individual turns of the two spirals to cover the bead.

6. Bend the bottom full turn of the spiral into a connecting loop.

7. Bend the bottom full turn of the spiral into a connecting loop. When completed, the bead is firmly set inside the cage with connecting loops on both sides of the link.

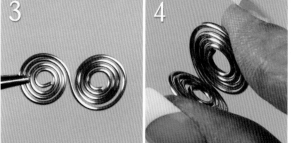

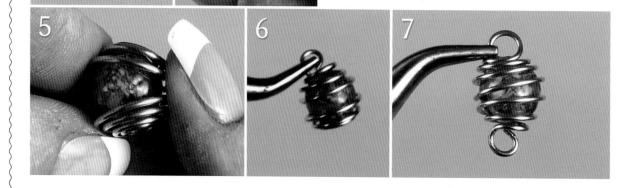

LINK 304:
OPEN-CAGE LINK

A loose fit. To create a loose-fitting bead cage or an empty cage, begin the link by creating two spirals of the same number of turns. You need two more turns in the spiral than the width of the bead to be captured.

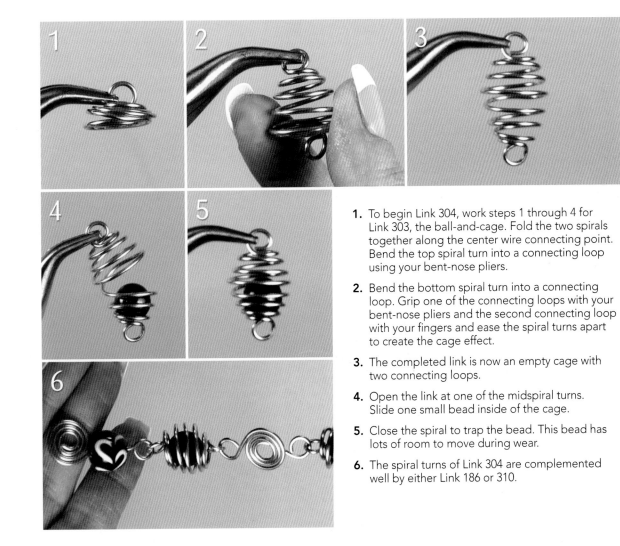

1. To begin Link 304, work steps 1 through 4 for Link 303, the ball-and-cage. Fold the two spirals together along the center wire connecting point. Bend the top spiral turn into a connecting loop using your bent-nose pliers.

2. Bend the bottom spiral turn into a connecting loop. Grip one of the connecting loops with your bent-nose pliers and the second connecting loop with your fingers and ease the spiral turns apart to create the cage effect.

3. The completed link is now an empty cage with two connecting loops.

4. Open the link at one of the midspiral turns. Slide one small bead inside of the cage.

5. Close the spiral to trap the bead. This bead has lots of room to move during wear.

6. The spiral turns of Link 304 are complemented well by either Link 186 or 310.

LINK 307:

BEADED-SPIRAL LINK

Links 307 through 308 use
previously demonstrated bends

Looking light and airy. The beaded-spiral link is a fun bead dangle that adds several beads at once to your necklaces or earrings. The open-spiral keeps the link looking light and airy.

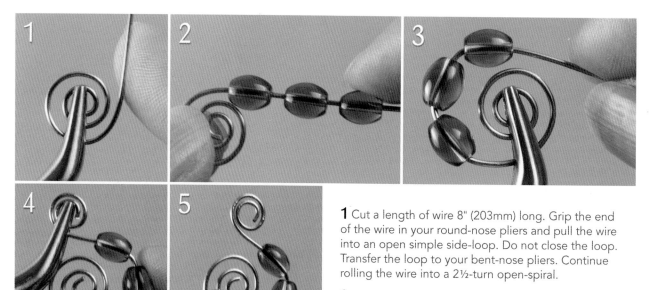

1 Cut a length of wire 8" (203mm) long. Grip the end of the wire in your round-nose pliers and pull the wire into an open simple side-loop. Do not close the loop. Transfer the loop to your bent-nose pliers. Continue rolling the wire into a 2½-turn open-spiral.

2 Add one to three small beads.

3 Continue rolling the wire in the open-spiral shape.

4 Clip the working wire to about 1¼" (32mm) long. Grip the clipped end in your round-nose pliers and roll the working wire into a simple side-loop. Continue rolling the side-loop until your loop sits above the center of your open-spiral.

5 The finished link can be connected to your chain through the spiral arm before the first bead and the simple side-loop.

LINK 309: SIMPLE-STRAIGHT-LOOP OPEN-SPIRAL BEAD LINK

Add a spiral. To enhance the energy of any bead, add a spiral end, using either a tightly packed spiral or an open-spiral, as shown above.

1 Cut a length of wire about 8" (203 mm) long. Using your bent-nose pliers, make a right angle in the working wire 1½" (38mm) from the end. Transfer the right-angle bend to your round-nose pliers and roll the end of the wire into a simple straight-loop. Use your flush wire cutters to remove the excess wire from the loop.

2 Slide a bead onto the wire.

3 Using your fingers or your bent-nose pliers, bend the working wire at the base of the bead into a 90° angle.

4 Cut the working wire to a 5" (127mm) length. Grip the end of the wire in your round-nose pliers. Roll the wire into a simple side-loop, but do not close the loop.

5 Transfer the loop to your bent-nose pliers or your nylon-grip pliers and continue rolling the wire into an open-spiral.

6 The open-spiral ends when it touches the base of the bead. This link adds the interest of the spiral without the heavy feeling of a closed- or tight-spiral.

7 Link 310 is made in the same manner, using a tight-spiral turn instead of an open-spiral turn.

8 In Link 311, the open-spiral end of a bead link can even have smaller bead accents added, just as were worked in Link 307.

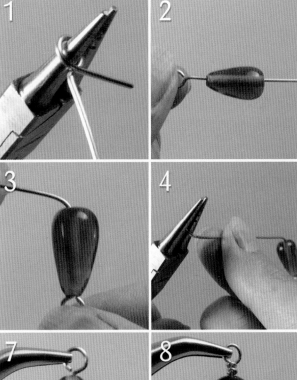

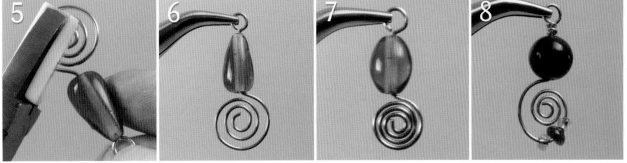

LINK 317: BEADED-SPIRAL RAINDROP LINK

Links 313 through 327 use previously demonstrated bends

Added bead area. The raindrop-spiral bead dangle can be connected to your chain through the simple side-loop, center hole in the spiral, or through the U-bend of the raindrop. It has plenty of open area in the hairpin for added beads.

134

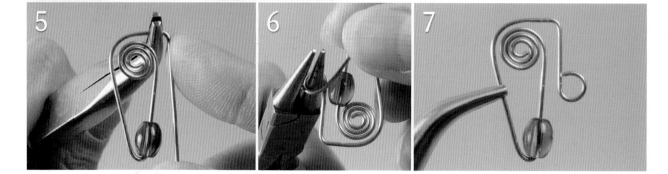

1 Cut a length of wire approximately 8" (203mm) long. Using your round-nose pliers, create a simple side-loop. Change to your bent-nose pliers and pull the simple side-loop into a 3-turn spiral.

2 Add one to three beads to the wire.

3 Using your round-nose pliers, bend the working wire into a U-bend about ¾" (19mm) away from the 3-turn spiral.

4 Hold the spiral area of the link in your bent-nose pliers and roll the working wire across the top of the spiral. End the roll when the working wire is at a right angle to the raindrop.

5 Grip the working wire in your bent-nose pliers so your pliers just touch the side of the spiral. Bend the wire into a tight right angle.

6 About ½" (13mm) from the right-angle bend, roll the working wire into a simple side-loop.

7 Cut the excess wire from the simple side-loop using your flush wire cutters.

LINK 328: WRAPPED LOOP-AND-BEAD DANGLE LINK

Links 328 to 331 follow the same basic steps

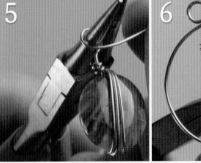

1 To create a center bead dangle for this hoop link, cut a length of 20-gauge wire 12" (305mm) long. Bend the wire into a small, tight U-bend at its midpoint.

2 Slide a 16mm flat disc agate bead onto the wire. Slide the bead into the tight U-bend.

3 While holding the bead in position on the working wire, take the wire at the bottom of the bead and wrap it over the bead three times.

4 Still holding the bead, wrap the working wire used to circle the bead around the wire at the top of the bead. This is the same type of wrapping you would create on any wrapped loop. Clip the excess wire from the wrapping and crimp the wire end into place.

5 With your bent-nose pliers, create a right-angle bend in the wire at the top of the bead. Grip the right angle in your round-nose pliers and roll the working wire into a simple side-loop.

6 Slide the opening in the simple side-loop over the wire to bring it in a straight line to the link. Using the working wire left from the simple side-loop, wrap the base of the simple side-loop two to three times. If you have excess wire, continue wrapping this area to create a thick random wrap.

7 This finished hoop link is ready to become the centerpiece for a long necklace or part of an earring set.

LINK 332:
COILED-SPIRAL BEAD LINK

Delightful dangle. The coiled-spiral bead link can be one part of a necklace chain or a delightful dangle for a sassy bracelet. The coil and spiral combination provide an interesting almost-unending visual line.

1 Begin with approximately 12" (305mm) of wire. Roll your wire around a coil maker or other round shape to create a ten-turn coil that is ¼" (6mm) wide.

2 Clip the short wire end of the coil using your flush wire cutters.

3 Using your bent-nose pliers, lift the side of the first turn of the coil.

4 Bend the first turn into a connecting link using your bent-nose pliers. Tuck the clipped end of that connecting link into the inside area of the coil.

5 Grip the working wire at the opposite side of the coil in the wire at the top of the bead. Grip the right angle with the your bent-nose pliers. Bend the wire into a right angle that places the working wire so it crosses the center hole of the coil.

6 In this sample the simple straight-loop has been interlocked to the small inner circle of a hoop link. The working wire left from the straight-loop was then wrapped in a thick loose random wrap.

7 Add one or more beads.

8 Grip the working wire in your round-nose pliers about ¼" (13mm) from the base of the last bead. Roll the wire around your round-nose pliers to create a midwire-circle. Transfer the circle to your bent-nose pliers and continue rolling the wire into a 3- to 4-turn spiral. Roll the spiral until the last turn of the spiral touches the base of the bead.

9 Wrap the working wire two times around the wire that comes from the bead to secure the spiral. Clip the excess wire from the wrap and crimp.

10 The finished bead link is connected to your chain through the connecting loop of the coil and the open hole in the spiral.

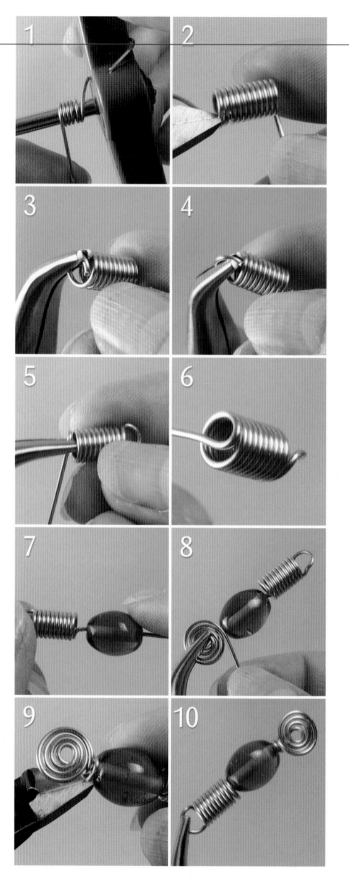

LINK 346:
BEADED DOUBLE-SPIRAL HAIRPIN LINK

Links 333 through 346 use
previously demonstrated bends

More opportunities. Adding beads to
a double-spiral hairpin link drops the beads below the line
of the necklace chain and provides another opportunity to
create attractive pieces of jewelry that draw the eye inward.

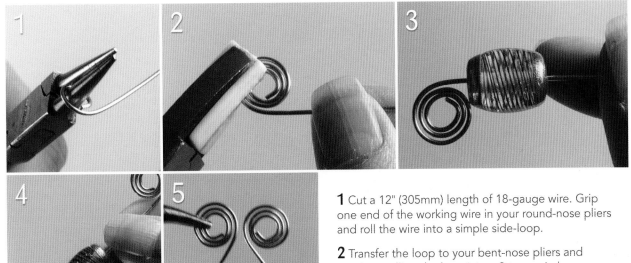

1 Cut a 12" (305mm) length of 18-gauge wire. Grip
one end of the working wire in your round-nose pliers
and roll the wire into a simple side-loop.

2 Transfer the loop to your bent-nose pliers and
continue rolling the loop into a 3-turn spiral.

3 Add your bead to the working wire. Slide it close
to the spiral you just completed.

4 Grip the opposite, unworked end of your working
wire and create a second 3-turn spiral.

5 Bend both sides of the center working wire until
the spiral ends touch. You can use the center hole
of the two spirals as your connecting area to add
the link to your chain.

adding a wire-wrap

Part of the attraction of any piece of jewelry is the beads that are used. The beads add areas of bright color. Another part is the shape and bend of the wire links. The third major part of any jewelry work is the sparkle created by the light that reflects off the wire used to create those bent-wire and bead links.

Enhance the reflected light sparkle of your metal work by adding fine-gauge wire-wrappings to your links. Although a wire-wrap can be added using any gauge wire, 26- and 24-gauge wires are the most common.

There are several methods for adding a wire-wrap. You can carefully roll the wrapping-wire around one leg of your link to create a fine coil, randomly wrap curves and loops over one area of your link to add extra sparkle, or even add small beads to your wire-wrapping to add color accents.

We will look at each method of wrapping through this chapter. Practice your wire-wrapped bead link to determine exactly how long a wrapping-wire you need to complete the link. The more small beads you add to the wrap, the more wrapping-wire you will need. Wrapping over a link that includes large beads will also require more wrapping-wire.

If you run out of wrapping-wire on any link, simply finish the first wrapping-wire according to the instructions. Cut a new length of wrapping-wire, secure it at the base of one of the connecting loops of your link, and continue adding more wraps to your link.

Extra wire can be used to enhance your links, add beads, and create coils around beads.

Simple Wire-Wrap Link

In the photo sequence below, a simple wire-wrap is worked over a 1" (25mm)-long simple straight-loop link worked in 18-gauge wire. The simple straight-loop of the finished link makes this an easy link to add to any chain. The wire-wrapping added to it makes this link wider because of the loose circles created with the wrap and adds fine sparkles because of the number of turns and small loops from the wrapping.

1 Cut a length of 26-gauge wire that is at least 24" (610mm) long.

2 Hold one end of the wrapping-wire and the link that is to be wrapped in your fingers. Using your second hand, roll the wrapping-wire tightly, in closely packed circles, at the base of the simple straight-loop at one end of your link three to four times. Use your flush wire cutters to clip the excess wrapping-wire at the beginning of these closely packed circles.

3 Continue to secure the link and the wrapping-wire in your fingertips. With your second hand, roll the wrapping-wire around the center wire of your link. These wraps are not tightly packed nor evenly spaced— they are wrapped in a random manner. When you reach the opposite side of your link, roll the wrapping-wire several times tightly at the base of the second simple straight-loop.

4 Turn the wrapping-wire and begin adding new wraps over the first layer of wrapping. You are working the wire-wraps back toward the first simple straight-loop of the link.

5 Work the wrapping back and forth across your link until you have used all of your wrapping-wire.

6 To complete the wrap, work two or three tight coils at the base of one of the simple straight-loops. Clip the excess wrapping-wire and crimp the end of the wrapping-wire tightly into place.

7 The completed wrapped link will have a random, chaotic look with some tight circles and some loose, some closely packed and some widely spaced. The more wraps that you were able to add, the more your link will sparkle in the light.

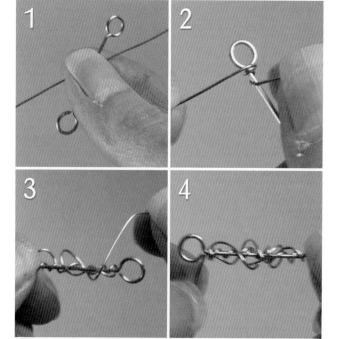

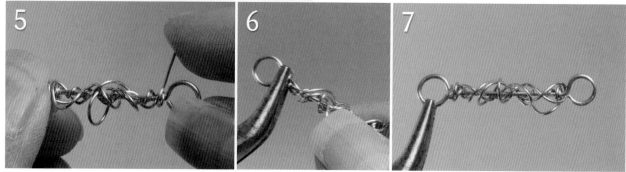

Beaded Wire-Wrap Link

When adding a wire-wrap to a link, string small 2mm and 4mm beads along the wrapping-wire. Wire-wrapped beads stand higher from the link than beads added directly to the link wire, increasing visual depth in this type of finished link. In the following sequence, a sample of wire-wrapping is being worked over a 1" (25mm)-long simple straight-loop link made from 18-gauge wire.

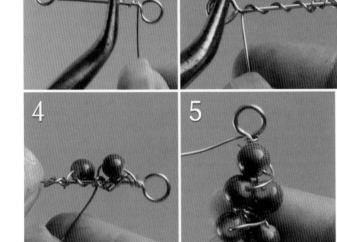

1 Cut a long length, at least 24" (610mm), of 26-gauge wire for the wrapping-wire. Holding your simple straight-loop link in either your fingertips or your bent-nose pliers, wrap the beginning of the wrapping-wire over the link at the base of one of the simple straight-loops. Create three or four tightly packed circles. Cut the excess wire from the beginning of this wrap with your flush wire cutters.

2 Wire-wrap the link using the 26-gauge wire by rolling the wire along the long leg of the link. Roll the wrapping-wire around the base of the second simple straight-loop several times to secure the wrapping-wire. Begin working the wrapping-wire back across the link.

3 When you have reached the center of the link wire, add a small bead to your wrapping-wire. Roll the wrapping-wire around the link, easing the bead into the position you want it to take on your link. Wrap the wrapping-wire one to two times after adding the bead.

4 You can add as many beads to the wrapping-wire as you want but allow one or two non-bead wraps between each.

5 When you have filled your link with wire-wraps and beaded wire-wraps, roll the wrapping-wire into several tight circles at the base of one of the simple straight-loops. Cut the excess wire with your flush wire cutters and crimp the wrapping-wire firmly into place.

6 The completed beaded wire-wrapped link has bead accents that stand away from the center of the link wire, adding color accents beyond the centerline of the link.

Wire-Wrapped Bead Link

Wire-wraps can be added to bead links. This gives the feeling that the beads on the link are caged or enclosed by the wire-wrapping.

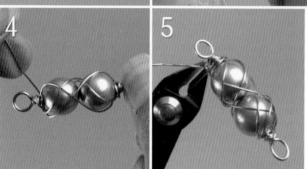

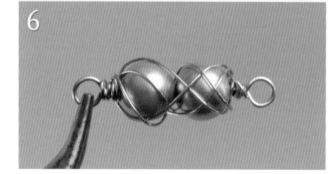

1 This sample is worked over a wrapped straight-loop bead link worked in 18-gauge wire and uses two 10mm frosted glass beads.

2 Cut a length of 26-gauge wrapping-wire at least 24" (610mm) long. Secure the wrapping-wire to the link at the base of one of the connecting loops by tightly wrapping two or three circles. On this wrapped straight-loop link, the wrapping-wire was secured on top of the link wraps that set the connecting loop.

3 Begin wrapping the wire around the link, bringing the wire over the first bead, into the area between the two beads, and then onto the second bead. This brings your wrapping-wire to the second wrapped straight connecting loop of the link. Roll the wrapping-wire over this area for two or three tight circles.

4 Work the wrapping-wire back across the link, again wrapping over the first bead, then rolling the wire into the space between the bead and onto the second bead. When you reach the second connecting loop area of the link, wrap two or three tight circles. As you work back and forth across the link with the wrapping-wire, try to place the wrapping-wire into a new area on the beads.

5 Finish your wrapping at one of the connecting loops by tightly turning the wire in two to three tight circles around the wrapped loop area of the link. Cut the excess wire using your flush wire cutters and crimp the end of the wrapping-wire firmly into place using your bent-nose pliers.

6 The finished link has a netted or caged look with the beads encased inside the wire-wrapping.

Wire-Wrapping to Strengthen a Link

Wire-wrapping can be used to strengthen an open, airy bend such as those found in the open-eyelet links. As you work the wire-wrap, you can add small seed beads and 2mm round beads easily to enhance the link. I worked this example over a Link 166, made with 1⅜" (35mm) of 18-gauge wire. Because the link is worked off a center U-bend, it can easily be pulled apart. A wire-wrapping worked through the small simple side-loops inside of the eyelets will secure this weak area of the link.

1 Once your link has been created, decide where you want to add the wire-wrap. Here, the wire-wrap will be worked between the two simple side-loops in the center of the eyelet-circles. Cut a length of thinner-gauged wire than used for the link. The most common sizes for wrapping are 24- and 26-gauge.

2 Lay the wrapping-wire over the link, secure the end using your thumb, and then feed the working end of the wrapping-wire through one of the simple side-loops. Tightly pull the wrapping-wire across the back of the link to bend it over the wire of the simple side-loop.

3 Feed the working end through the second simple side-loop. Because you are using wire, not flexible string, you may need to adjust the wrapping-wire loop at the back of the link as you pull the wire through to keep it from bending into a tight U-shape.

4 After you have wrapped the wire several times around the center of the link, you can begin adding beads. Feed the wire through to the front of the link, then slide your bead onto the working wire. You can use your thumb to hold the bead in place as you feed the working wire through to the back of the link.

5 Continue adding one bead with each wrap.

6 After all of the beads have been added, continue your wire-wrap for two to three turns. End with the working wire at the back of the link.

7 Clip the working wire so it lies over the back area of the link but does not extend beyond that area. You want just enough wire to crimp into place to secure the wrap but not so much that the end of the wire can be seen from the front of the link.

8 Use your bent-nose pliers to push the end wire deeply into the wire-wrap on the back. Crimp or press the wire end into place using your bent-nose pliers.

9 The completed link has an open, airy feeling because of the large circles in the eyelets. The center divide between the two large eyelets has been secured with the wire-wrap. A few small beads added to the wrap make this link a center focal point link.

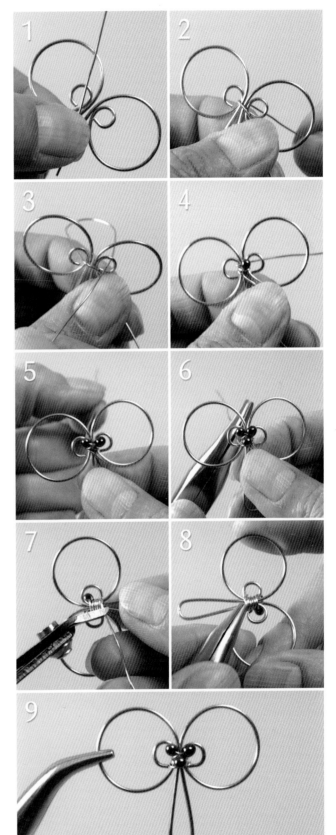

Twisting Coils

Not only can you wrap a link with wire, you can wrap it with coils and long lengths of beads. Let's work through the creation of a wrapped coil and bead link. This sample uses 18-gauge wire for the coil and wrapping-wire, 26-gauge wire for the bead wire strand, and an assortment of 3mm to 6mm glass beads.

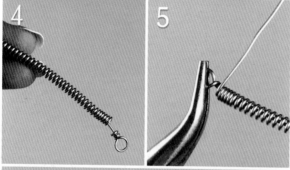

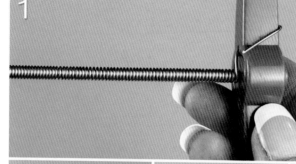

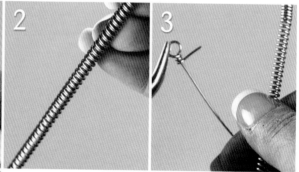

1. Begin the link by creating a long ⅛" (3mm)-wide coil. The sample coil measures 6" (152mm) long.

2. Remove the coil from the wrapping form and gently stretch the coil to allow some space between the individual turns of coil.

3. Cut a length of wire that is 3" (76mm) longer than the stretched coil. Create a wrapped straight-loop in one end of this wire.

4. Slide the coil over the working wire and bring it to touch the wrapped straight-loop.

5. Create a wrapped straight-loop in the opposite end of the working wire at the base of the coil. Clip the excess wire from the wrapped straight-loop.

6. Place the coil-covered wrapped straight-loop link against your coil form. Roll the coil-covered wire around the form to create a loose, open coil.

7. To add a wire-wrap to this link, cut a length of wire 3" (76mm) longer than the original length of the coil. Wrap the end of this wrapping-wire around the base of one wrapped straight-loop for two to three tight turns. Clip the excess wire from the wrapping.

8. Return the link to your coil form and wrap the new working wire around the form, working it between the coil loops.

Finished piece. *Gothic Coils* (see instructions on page 232) makes good use of a 20-gauge wraparound coil to create a double-visual impact. The five large, bold coils are the necklace's focal point, but the center coil, with its added coil wrapping, is the central- focal point.

9. Secure the opposite end of the wrapping wire at the base of the second wrapped straight-loop of the link. Clip the excess wire from the wrapping-wire.

10. To add a bead strand to the coil-covered wrapped link, cut a length of 26-gauge wire 3" (76mm) longer than the original stretched coil length. Thread the wire with an assortment of beads from 3mm to 6mm in size.

11. Secure one end of the 26-gauge wire at the base of one of the wrapped straight-loops with two to three tight wraps. Clip the excess wire from the wrap. Place the link back on the coil form and work the bead strand into a coil wrapping, working the beads between the turns of the coil and the wrapping-wire. Secure the second side of the bead strand wire at the base of the opposite wrapped straight-loop of the link. Clip the excess wire.

12. You can continue to add more coils, more wrapping-wires and more bead strands to your coil-covered wrapped link.

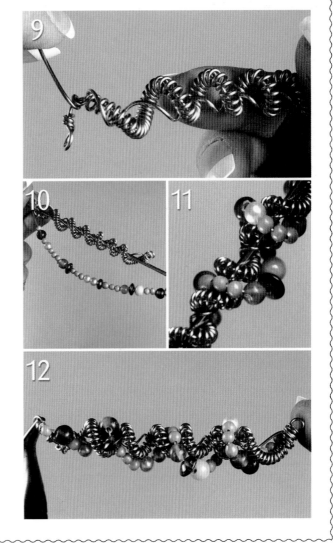

how to use the instructions
(and change them)

We have worked through the 14 basic bends used in bent-wire links (Chapter 2) and we have put those bends to work in the sample link instructions (Chapter 7). If you have already begun making practice links, you have no doubt discovered how easy it is to take the basic bends and create new, unique links of your own.

Many of the links used in the projects in this book are adaptations of the basic link shapes that you have learned to create. When a link used in a project differs from a basic link, instructions will be given on how to adjust your wire bending to create the new variation.

As this chapter details, *Rock Concert* and *Emerald City* are a perfect example of how easy it is to change, adapt, and vary any basic link that you bend to create an entirely different piece of jewelry.

Any project in this book can easily be changed into a new unique design by simply enhancing the links or using different links than shown.

Rock Concert and Emerald City

Rock Concert is a practice bracelet I created while writing this book and it led to the creation of *Emerald City*. That is an important lesson for jewelry makers: one thing will always lead to another, so keep your mind and creative spirit open at all times.

I worked *Rock Concert* in 16-gauge wire using lampwork beads—from 16mm-by-12mm nuggets to 22mm-by-16mm teardrops.

Links used for both projects:

	Link 036	large bead wrapped straight-loop link
	Link 086	3-turn spiral link
	Link 136	3-turn hairpin link
	Link 155	open-heart link
	Link 186	midwire-spiral link

Supplies used for *Emerald City:*

- 18- & 20-gauge wire
- 2 3mm x 6mm spacer beads
- 2 8mm round clear striped glass beads
- 1 6mm cat's eye bead
- 1 14mm lampwork bead
- 1 6mm x 8mm oval frosted bead
- 1 16mm round glass bead

ROCK CONCERT: STEP-BY-STEP

1 Begin by creating a practice *Rock Concert* bracelet using 16-gauge wire and four large glass swirled beads.

2 Read the step-by-step for wrapped loops on page 48 to learn how to interlock wrapped straight-loop links.

3 Create one Link 136 3-turn hairpin link as shown on page 98.

4 Create one Link 073 jump ring as shown on page 48. Join the Link 073 to the Link 136.

5 Create one Link 186 using a 3-turn spiral center as shown on page 116. Join the Link 186 to the chain using the simple side-loop.

6 Create one Link 036 wrapped straight-loop bead link using one 16mm-by-12mm glass nugget bead and interlocking the link to the chain as shown on page 51.

7 Create one Link 036 using one 22mm-by-16mm teardrop glass bead and interlocking it to the chain.

8 Create one Link 086 single-spiral as shown on page 88. Join this link with the simple side-loop.

9 Skip one link and create one Link 155 open-heart link as shown on page 106.

10 Create one Link 036 using one 22mm-by-16mm oval glass bead, interlocking it to the chain with the first wrapped straight-loop and interlocking it to the open-heart link with the second wrapped straight-loop.

11 Create one Link 036 using one 12mm-by-12mm glass nugget, interlocking this link to the open-heart link. The finished bracelet measures 7½" (191mm) long.

Great discoveries. *Rock Concert* is a practice bracelet that led to the creation of *Emerald City*. Often practice work leads to great discoveries and new projects.

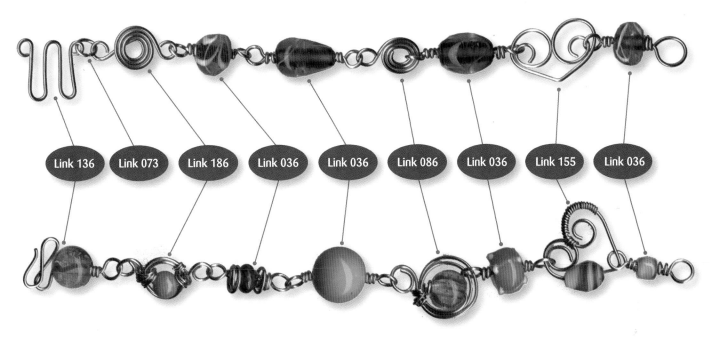

Link 136 · Link 073 · Link 186 · Link 036 · Link 036 · Link 086 · Link 036 · Link 155 · Link 036

For starters. *Emerald City:* an excellent 8" (203mm)-long starter bracelet.

EMERALD CITY: STEP-BY-STEP

Emerald City uses the same links as *Rock Concert.* Before you begin *Emerald City* you may wish to re-read the instructions for those five basic bent-wire links and create several practice links for each. It will be easier for you to learn to make adjustments on a link if you are already comfortable and proficient at making the link. When you're dealing with any set of instructions for a necklace or bracelet, there will be adjustments due to differences in bending styles and the body shape of the person who will be wearing the jewelry, so it's best to learn how to anticipate.

As we work though each link you will learn how easily any link can be altered or embellished to create a new look. This bracelet is worked in 18-gauge wire using a variety of green glass beads.

Variations on a Link—
Rock Concert Becomes Emerald City

LINK 136

Cut a 6" (152mm) length of wire. Begin this Link 136 with the simple side-loop followed by the three hairpin turns. Create a right-angle bend ¼" (6mm) from the last U-bend to center the wire to the link. Add one 8mm clear glass striped bead to the working wire. Create a wrapped straight-loop at the end of the bead. Clip the excess wire from the wrapping. Clip the simple side-loop at the beginning of the link in half to create a small hook bend.

LINK 186

Cut an 8" (203mm) length of wire to create this variation of a beaded Link 186. Slide one 8mm cat's-eye bead onto the working wire. Move the bead 2" (51mm) from one end. Holding the bead in one hand, create your midwire-spiral using the long working wire by bending the wire around the bead for two turns. This will bring your working wire to the opposite side of the beginning 2" (51mm) wire. Cut the working wire to 1" (26mm) from the midwire-spiral on either side and create simple side-loops on both ends. Cut two 12" (305mm) lengths of 26-gauge wire and wire-wrap the midwire-spiral on both sides of the bead, catching the arms of the simple side-loop with about ten tightly packed coils as shown on page 49. Join this link to the chain using one of the simple side-loops.

FIRST LINK 036

Create one variation of Link 036 using a 6" (152mm) length of wire and one 3mm-by-6mm spacer bead. Slide the bead to the center of the working wire. Create a wrapped straight-loop at the ends of the bead, interlocking one loop into Link 186. Grip the excess wire from the wrapping in your bent-nose pliers and continue wrapping this wire around the loop areas of both loops in large random loops until you have used all of the working wire.

SECOND LINK 036

Create one Link 036 with no variation changes using one 16mm round glass bead, interlocking this link to the chain.

LINK 086

Begin this Link 086 with 10" (254mm) length of wire and using one 8mm round bead. Create a small simple side-loop in the end of the wire. Bend the loop to a right-angle. Slide the bead onto the wire. The simple side-loop holds the bead in place. Holding the bead, bend the wire at the base of the bead into a right-angle. Wrap the working wire around the bead into a 2-turn spiral. Clip the working wire to 1½" (38mm) at the end of the spiral and create a simple side-loop. Cut a 12" (305mm) length of 26-gauge wire and wire-wrap the spiral on this link catching the simple side-loop arm for six to ten random loose coils. Join this link to the chain through the simple side-loop.

THIRD LINK 036

Create one Link 036 using one 14mm lampwork bead interlocking this link to the chain through both spiral arms of Link 086. Stop this link after you have created the simple straight-loop step for the second loop—do not finish the wrapping steps for this link.

LINK 155

Create one Link 155 using one 6mm by 8mm oval glass bead. Start with a 7" (178mm) length of wire. Add the bead to the center of the wire. Create the heart's open-eyelets as shown in the step-by-step instructions for this link. Bend the center of the wire with your bent-nose pliers, placing the bead onto one side of the bend. Cut a 12" (305mm) length of 26-gauge wire. Wire-wrap through the inner loops of both open-eyelets for four tightly packed coils. Continue wire-wrapping along the top portion of one open-eyelet for twenty tightly packed coils. Clip and crimp the wrapping-wire into place. Link 155 is added to the chain by sliding the unwrapped open-eyelet into the unfinished second wrapped straight-loop of Link 036 above. Finish wrapping the straight-loop of Link 036.

FOURTH LINK 036

Create one Link 036 using one 3mm by 6mm spacer bead, interlocking this link to the wrapped open-eyelet of Link 155.

Emerald City is now complete. What was a simple link bracelet, *Rock Concert*, has become a heavily embellished wire-wrapped bracelet because of a few simple variations on each link.

Those variations included changing simple side-loops into wrapped straight-loops, adding beads to the inner arms of the links, adding wire-wrappings, and using extra wire in the wrapped loop stages of the work.

Tip 9: Making matching links.

To keep the beginning and ending loop the same size, place your working wire for the second loop at the same depth along the pliers' side as you worked the first. You can mark your round-nose pliers with a permanent fine marker to denote where you want to place the working wire if you are creating a group of matching links.

Simple Changes for Your Links

There are quite a few simple changes you can make to any link or bead dangle that will dramatically change the look and feeling to your jewelry.

1. Jewelry wire comes in many widths, called gauges. Changing the gauge of your wire is a quick and easy adjustment that you can make to any project. Fine wire gauges such as 26 through 20 create delicate chains and links. Thick wire, gauges 16 through 12, gives a heavy, strong look to your chains.

   When you change wire gauge, adjust either the length of your individual links or the number of links that you use in your project. Going to a finer gauge of wire may mean you will need to add extra links to make your project the correct finished length. Projects using larger-gauge wire may need a smaller number of links to fulfill the needed finished measurement of the work.

Copper Coils bracelet used Link 043 worked in 20-gauge wire with 6mm crow roller beads worked into Link 038s. The small-sized wire and small 6mm beads give a lightweight feeling to the finished work. (See instructions for *Copper Coils* on page 250.)

Day Break also uses Links 043 and 038 worked in 16-gauge wire. This bracelet has a stronger, more imposing feeling because of the change in wire gauge. (See instructions for *Day Break* on page 250.)

2. You can easily change the number of spiral turns or U-bends that you use in one link. Any simple side-loop can quickly become a spiral by continuing to add spiral turns.

All That Jazz includes two Link 198s that use a 2-turn spiral as the center element and end with a simple side-loop. *Day Break* (above), also uses a raindrop link but that link uses four turns to the center spiral and its ending simple loop became a 2½-turn spiral. (See instructions for *All That Jazz* on page 250.)

Deep Sea Adventure uses a basic Link 036 and a five Link 136s throughout the chain. This is a simple layout with the beads worked in one style of link and the wire bending in the hairpin links. (Instructions for *Deep Sea Adventure* are on page 184.)

3. Any wire link can have beads added to the working wire and become bead links.

4. Many link styles can be expanded or compressed after the link is completed. Link 043 coils can be pulled apart to expand the air space between the coil turns. Hairpins can be compressed to cause the U-bend to overlap.

Ribbon Rock bracelet also uses Link 136 but places the beads on the hairpin links. By adding the beads directly to the hairpins, this bracelet has more hairpin turns and more beads than *Deep Sea Adventure* (above). (Instructions for *Ribbon Rock* are on page 251.)

Golden Moments uses four Link 043s to create the main section of the necklace. I create the coils by working the wire tightly around a ¼" (6mm)-wide form. When the coil was completed, I gently pulled it to expand the coils and open the space between the turns. Compare these open, expanded coil links to the tightly packed coil links used in *Day Break* bracelet (left center page). (Instructions for *Golden Moments* necklace are on page 251.)

10

designing your own jewelry

You will be surprised at how quickly you will be ready to create your own designs and layouts for your bent-wire jewelry. Any necklace, bracelet, or earring design in this book can easily be adjusted to include different bent-wire links or to accept a different style of bead. Creating jewelry is all about you selecting bends and beads you like and putting them together in the things you wear. Through this section, we will look at a few design ideas that may guide you in creating your own unique work.

With any creative or artistic effort, the key is to experiment and practice. That is truly the only way to discover what you like, what you don't like, and all of the ways in which you can express yourself. Let your mind go; let your feelings flow. Don't allow yourself to be held back. Experiment and enjoy.

The sky is the limit when you are working with bent-wire links and creating new designs unique to you.

Create a Practice Piece

Practice makes perfect...new bracelets. *Blueberry Pie* (below), a practice bracelet, was created from practice links and beads left over from several other projects. The links vary in their wire gauge because they were made at different times. By joining individual links you have already made and adding leftover beads, you can do a sample layout in advance of working your final project. Practice pieces allow you to make adjustments in which links you want to use, where each link will be used, and where you want bead accents.

Practice guides final version. *Blueberry Muffin* (right) is the finished project made from the practice work of *Blueberry Pie*. The practice layout guided the link sizes, link placement, and the bead accents.

156

Blueberry Muffin
[Final version]

ONE STYLE/VARIETY OF BEADS

Repeating elements. Unite a variety of link shapes by repeating one element or part of the design several times. In *All That Jazz* (below), the links included raindrops, hairpins, and coils. Five identical amethyst tube beads were worked into the links. By using the same bead throughout the design, you unite the changing links into one work.

Blueberry Pie
[Practice piece]

All That Jazz
[One style/variety of beads]

Instructions for *Blueberry Pie*, *Blueberry Muffin*, and *All That Jazz* bracelets appear on page 250.

REPEATING BEAD COLOR

Creating visual tension. *Emerald City* (below top) uses a variety of bent-wire links and several bead styles and sizes. When designing your own jewelry, uniformity is not always necessary, and sometimes, the visual tension resulting from multiple styles and sizes can bring a lot of life to a jewelry piece. What unites this design is the repeated use of color—every bead is some shade of bright green. The bright green color flows from start to finish through this project.

REPEATING BEAD STYLE

Repeating styles. Baby blue, passion pink, sun yellow, and lime green beads are used in the bracelet *Rainbow Road* (below middle). Each link uses its own color of bead. Yet, all of the beads are frosted, striped beads that came from one bead mixture. You can repeat the style of a bead—all foil-lined beads, all faceted-cone beads, all lampwork beads— as a way to give a chain made of varying bent-wire links a uniting element.

REPEATING A VISUAL ELEMENT

Repeating lines. *Easy Going* (below bottom) repeats the use of color, with green beads throughout, but more importantly, it repeats the use of vertical lines within the bent-wire links. The coil links of this bracelet look like a row of vertical lines. That vertical line feeling shows up in the wire-wraps, in the spiral dangles, and in the use of the split rings in the connecting loops of the spiral hairpin. Even the hairpin link shows vertical lines in the sides of the U-bends.

Instructions for *Emerald City* appear on page 149. Instructions for *Rainbow Road* and *Easy Going* are on page 251.

Emerald City
[Repeating bead color]

Rainbow Road
[Repeating bead style]

Easy Going
[Repeating a visual element]

REPEATING A BENT-WIRE LINK

Solitude (below top) was made to showcase several different styles of bead dangles with each dangle slightly different from all of the others. What holds this bracelet together as a strong design is the repeated wrapped straight-loop bead link that makes up the two chains of the bracelet. This simple repeat link helps your eye move across the changing dangles easily.

REPEATING A BASIC BEND

This bent-wire bracelet (below middle) uses a hairpin link that ends with a spiral turn, a single spiral-wrapped-loop link, and a double-spiral link. No matter where your eye looks, this bracelet project has a spiral. By repeating the basic bend and using it in each of the links, this bracelet becomes a bold, strong design.

USING STRONG FOCAL ELEMENTS

Crystal Fairy (below bottom) uses a hairpin link and jump rings to quickly create a simple chain. The chain leads to a center ring where one large lampwork bead becomes the focal point of the bracelet. Showcasing one element, such as this lampwork bead, creates a stunning design.

Solitude
[Repeating a bent-wire link]

Bent-Wire Bracelet
[Repeating a basic bend]

Crystal Fairy
[Using strong focal elements]

Instructions for *Solitude* bracelet appear on page 251.

Instructions for Bent-Wire bracelet appear on page 250.

Complete step-by-step instructions for *Crystal Fairy* bracelet appear on page 183.

High Tide
[Mirrored design]

Hot Summer Night
[Just have fun]

Charm Bracelet
[Fully packed]

Instructions for *High Tide*, and *Hot Summer Night* appear on page 251, and instructions for *Charm Bracelet* appear on page 250.

MIRRORED DESIGN

High Tide (above) uses one large foiled glass bead as its center point. One hairpin link and one spiral link rest on both sides of the bead. By mirroring the links as they work away from the center of the bracelet, you strengthen the importance of your focal element.

FULLY PACKED

This *Charm Bracelet* (above right) is packed full of beads of different sizes and colors worked on a jump ring chain. The focus is neither the links nor how each bead dangle was created. The emphasis is on the number of bead dangles used. Charm bracelets are designed to be fully packed and even overloaded with dangles. To avoid overloading the bracelet, the beads were first sorted by size with the smallest beads at the end of the chain and working toward the center where the largest beads fall. Controlling the placement of the beads by size gives this bracelet some feeling it was planned instead of random creation.

JUST HAVE FUN!

Hot Summer Night (above center) uses spirals throughout the bracelet. Four spiral links are included in the bracelet chain, two bead links have been wrapped with a spiral around the bead, and even the bead dangles have a colored spiral stripe. All of the beads used in this design, even though they are different styles of beads, are some shade of blue. The bracelet has a strong central focus with the three blue-striped bead dangles. But what makes this pattern a strong bracelet is that it simply was fun to create.

11

projects

You now know everything you need to know to create beautiful bent-wire and beaded jewelry. Try some of the examples I provide, and practice your links many times before committing to a specific project. After practicing, and then practicing more, you will be ready to create your own beautiful pieces. Let your inner artist flow to the surface and create the perfect piece of jewelry for every outfit and event.

The projects in this section are simply a starting point for you to use your own creativity in jewelry making.

Classic Scroll

Adding a coil to the working wire gives these double-hairpin link earrings lots of bright sparkle. A small adventurite bead gives just a little touch of color. This link is worked with two large U-bends that create an S-shaped link.

PROJECTS

162

earrings

Links used in this project:

	Link 043	coil link
	Link 052	wrapped straight-loop hook
	Link 073	jump ring
	Link 135	double-hairpin link
	Link 265	crimped-end bead dangles

Supplies needed for this project:
- 18- & 26-gauge wire
- 2 8mm adventurite beads (same color)

1 For each earring, create one Link 043 using a 20" (508mm) length of 26-gauge wire.

2 Create two coil-covered Link 135s using steps 2 through 4 of Link 135 (page 98). Cut a 9" (229mm) length of 18-gauge wire for the earring link. Grip the end of the wire in your round-nose pliers and roll the wire into a small simple side-loop. Use a medium-sized form, such as the barrel of an ink pen, to create a U-bend ½" (13mm) from the simple side-loop.

3 Slide the 26-gauge coil over the 18-gauge wire and move it into the last one-third of the U-bend turn. Place the coil-covered working wire against your medium-sized form 1¼" (32mm) from the first bend and roll the wire into a second U-bend.

4 Using your round-nose pliers, roll a simple side-loop in the working wire 1" (25mm) from the second U-bend turn. Clip the excess wire from the side-loop.

5 Create three ¼" (6mm)-wide Link 073s. Open one Link 073 and thread this ring through one of the simple side-loops and over the center wire of the S-shape. Repeat for the second Link 073. Close the rings.

6 Create two Link 051s or 052s. Open the last Link 073 and thread it through the loop in the earring wire and the top U-bend of the S-shaped link.

7 Using 8mm adventurite beads, create two Link 265s by cutting a 5" (127mm) length of 20-gauge wire. Using your bent-nose pliers, create a simple side-loop 1½" (38mm) from the end. Grip the right-angle bend in your round-nose pliers and roll the wire into a simple side-loop. Open the loop and thread it over the lower U-bend of the S-shaped link. Wrap the base of the simple side-loop three times using the excess working wire from the simple loop. Clip the excess wire. Add one 8mm adventurite bead to the working wire below the wrapped loop. Grip the working wire at the base of the bead and bend it into a tight loop. Clip the excess wire from this tight loop.

Wire length estimates

It can be difficult to give exact measurements of wire length needed to turn each and every link used in making wire-wrapped jewelry. Once you have learned how to make each of the basic bends and sampled a few of the instructions on how to make each link, you will quickly be adapting those links to fit your designs.

Adding a bead, including an extra turn to a spiral, and even placing a midwire circle in a link can mean that you need several extra inches of wire.

Below is a chart that shows the estimated wire length needed to work on one part or basic bend to any link. These estimates were worked using 18-gauge wire.

Large-gauge wire, such as gauges 16 through 12, will require greater lengths. Small-gauge wires—20 gauge and down—will use less.

As an example, if I were creating a link that has a simple straight-loop beginning, then flows into a ½" (13mm)-long coil, I would need at least 1" (25mm) for the loop and 12" (305mm) for the coil. If I want to add a bead, I need to allow another 1" (25mm) of wire. If the link ends with a 4-turn spiral, I add 5" (127mm) more—a total of at least 19" (483mm) of wire to complete that link. I would also add at least 3" (76mm) extra to allow enough wire to comfortably work the bends. So I would start this link using at least 22" (559mm) of wire.

Some guidelines for working in 18-gauge wire:

5" (127mm) of wire equals a 4-turn spiral

12" (305mm) of wire equals a ½" (13mm) coil

9" (229mm) of wire equals a 2-turn turn-back spiral

2" of wire equals a ½" (13mm) straight-looped link

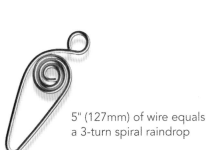

5" (127mm) of wire equals a 3-turn spiral raindrop

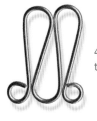

4" (102mm) of wire equals three hairpin turns

3½" (89mm) of wire equals a one full-turn ⅝" (16mm) circle

½" (13mm) of wire is needed for a small bead (6 to 8mm) and up to 1½" (38mm) for a large bead (20mm)

Coils

Four different sets of earrings from same links:

	Link 023	long simple straight-loop link
	Link 043	coil link
	Link 047	wrapped long loop link
	Link 051	simple side-loop hook
	Link 053	wrapped straight-loop hook
	Link 073	jump ring
	Link 265	crimped-end bead dangles
	Link 266	simple loop-end bead dangle link

Supplies needed for this project:

- 16-, 18- & 20-gauge wire
- 2 14mm oval glass beads
- 2 16 x 12mm fire agate flat rectangles
- 6 8mm round silver foil beads
- 18 spacer beads
- 4 spacer beads

BRANDYWINE

Big bold coils are used to hold a fire agate rectangle for the *Brandywine* earrings.

1 For each earring, cut a 12" (305mm) length of 16-gauge wire. Create one ½" (13mm)-wide-by-six-full-turns Link 043. Create the link by rolling the wire around the outside of a ½" (13mm)-wide form. Clip the excess wire from both ends of the coil using your flush wire cutters. Lift the first loop on both ends of the coil and bend that turn into a connecting loop using your bent-nose pliers.

2 Cut a 6" (152mm) length of 16-gauge wire to create a Link 265 using one 16mm by 12mm fire agate flat rectangle bead. Create a Link 004 wrapped straight-loop 1½" (38mm) from the end of the wire. Add the bead to the working wire. Grip the working wire at the base of the bead and roll the wire into a tight coil. Clip the excess coil wire.

3 Create three ¼" (6mm)-wide Link 073s using 16-gauge wire. Create one Link 053. Use two Link 073s to connect the Link 053 to the top connecting loop of the Link 043. Use one Link 073 to join the bottom connecting loop on the coil link with the wrapped straight-loop of the Link 265. The finished earring measures 2½" (64mm) from the wrapped straight-loop of the earring wire.

Brandywine

Casual Friday

Casual Friday (left) is created in the same manner as *Brandywine* (above right). This set of earrings uses a ¼" (6mm)-wide-by-8-full-turn-coil Link 043 and Link 266 simple end-loop 14mm glass bead dangles. The coil and dangle are connected with a chain created with six ⅛" (3mm)-wide Link 073s. The earring wires, Link 051, use a simple straight-loop to join the coils to the earring wires.

LIGHTNING AND THUNDER

Lightning and Thunder earrings are made by joining three coil-covered wrapped straight-loop bead links.

1 For each earring, cut a 24" (610mm) length of 18-gauge wire. Wrap the wire into a ³⁄₁₆"-wide-by-8"-long (5mm by 203mm) coil. Cut the coil into six sections—one ¾" (19mm) long, one 1⅛" (29mm) long, and one 1⅜" (35mm) long for each earring.

2 Cut three 9" (229mm) lengths of 26-gauge wire. Working one bead link at a time, slide one 8mm round silver foil bead onto the wire and move it to the center point of the wire. With your fingers, bend the wire into a tight U-bend with the bead in the center of the bend. Grip both wires above the bead in your fingers and create a small bend in both to bring the two wires together. Slide one section of coil over both wires. Grip both wires above the coil in your bent-nose pliers. Working both wires as if they were one, bend a right angle. Transfer the right-angle bend to your round-nose pliers. Roll the wires into a simple straight-loop. Wrap both wires at the base of the simple side-loop to create a wrapped straight-loop ending. Clip the excess wires from the wrap with your flush wire cutters. Repeat these steps for the two remaining coil lengths and beads.

3 Cut a 6" (152mm) length of 18-gauge wire. Create one Link 047. For this sample, the loops were worked around the barrel of an ink pen. To create this loop, place the wire against the ink pen about 1½" (38mm) from the end. Roll the wire into a turn-back loop. Make a second turn-back loop below the first with the ink pen barrel touching the base of the first. While this link is in the turn-back loop stage, slide the wrapped straight-loop of all three bead links onto one of the loops of the Link 047. Complete the link by gripping all of the loop wires at the intersection of the turn-back loops and wrap the center intersection two to three times with the excess working wire left from the bottom turn-back loop.

4 Create one Link 053. While the Link 053 is in the simple straight-loop stage, join the simple straight-loop to the top loop of the Link 047. The finished earrings measure 3" (76mm) from the top of the Link 053 to the bottom of the dangles.

TRIPLE PLAY EARRINGS

Triple Play uses three long simple straight-loop links, one of them bead covered, to create a long dangle.

1 For each earring, create two Link 023s by cutting two 5" (127mm) lengths of 18-gauge wire. Grip the wire 1½" (38mm) from the end in your bent-nose pliers and create a right-angle bend. Transfer the bend to your round-nose pliers and roll the wire into a simple straight-loop. Clip the excess wire from the simple straight-loop using flush wire cutters. Grip the working wire 1½" (38mm) from the simple straight-loop in your round-nose pliers. Roll the wire into a turn-back loop. Add one space to the turn-back loop. Clip the excess wire from the turn-back loop where it intersects the center wire of this link. You can use your bent-nose pliers to create a small bend in the wire at the beginning of the turn-back loop to center this loop under the link's simple straight-loop. Repeat these steps for the second cut wire.

2 For each earring, create one Link 023 by cutting one 5" (127mm) length of 18-gauge wire. Create a simple straight-loop as above using your round-nose pliers. Slide seven assorted color spacer beads onto the working wire. Measure 1½" (38mm) from the base of the simple straight-loop. Using your bent-nose pliers, create a right-angle bend. Transfer the bend to your round-nose pliers and roll the wire into a simple straight-loop. Clip the excess wire from the loop.

3 For each earring, create one ¼"(6mm)-wide-by-10-full-turns Link 043 from 18-gauge wire. Bend the first and last turns into connecting links. Open the connecting link at the bottom of the coil and join the three Link 023s to this loop.

4 For each earring, create one Link 051 using 20-gauge wire. Join the connecting loop at the top of the coil to the Link 051.

Lightning and Thunder

Triple Play

Hoops

SIX DIFFERENT EARRING SETS FROM THE SAME LINKS

Hoop earrings are a classic and essential part of every woman's jewelry collection. Whether you prefer small or large hoops, or either, depending on the occasion, they are easy to make, with a lot of options for dressing them up. If you can see it in your head, you can make it with your hands.

Links used in this project:

	Link 054	basic earring hoop link
	Link 064	simple side-loop earring wires
	Link 073	jump ring
	Link 075	open-eyelet spiral hoop link

Supplies needed for this project:
- 18-, 20- & 26-gauge wire
- 2 4mm beads
- 2 10mm x 6mm oval striped glass beads

SIMPLE LARGE-HOOP EARRINGS

Work both earrings at the same time through each of these steps to ensure all of the bends are the same size.

1 Create two Link 075s using 18-gauge wire. Place the loop against a large-sized form—a vitamin bottle lid or a baby food jar, for instance—and roll the wire into one full circle around the form, bringing the working wire back to the simple side-loop.

2 Remove the link from the form. Grip the working wire of the full circle just above the simple side-loop. Create a midwire-circle using your round-nose pliers. Clip the excess wire from the midwire-circle to make it a simple side-loop.

3 Cut an 8" (203mm) length of 26-gauge wire. Wire-wrap the link, working over both wires of the circle between the two simple side-loops. Clip the excess wrapping-wire and crimp it into place.

4 Create two Link 054 wrapped straight-loop earring wires. Interlock the wrapped loop of this link into the outside simple side-loop. The finished loops are 2" (51mm) long from the wrapped straight-loop of the earring wire.

Simple Small-Hoop Earrings follow the same instructions as the *Simple Large Hoop Earrings*. For this set, the two Link 075s were rolled around the barrel of a large marking pen to create a smaller circle.

BEADED HOOP EARRINGS

1 Create two Link 075s using two 8" (203mm)-long lengths of 18-gauge wire for each. Work the earrings together to ensure each bend and turn is the same size.

2 Grip the end of the working wire in your round-nose pliers and roll a simple side-loop. Hold the simple side-loop against a large form, such as a marker, and roll the working wire into a full circle around that form.

3 Remove the 1-turn loop from the form. Clip the unworked portion of the working wire to 1½" (38mm) long. Grip the end of this section of wire in your round-nose pliers and roll a simple side-loop.

4 Cut a length of 26-gauge wire 12" (305mm) long. Wrap the wire into fourteen tightly packed coils along one side of the full-circle wire. Add one 10mm by 6mm bead to the wrapping-wire. Pull the wrapping-wire to the opposite side of the circle, placing the bead inside of the circle. Wrap the wrapping-wire around this opposite side of the circle in fourteen tightly packed coiled wraps. Clip the excess wrapping-wire and crimp into place.

5 Create two Link 064s using 20-gauge wire. The finished earrings measure 1¼" (32mm) from the top of the Link 064 to the bottom of the loop.

Spiral Hoops also follow the instructions for *Simple Large-Hoop Earrings*. Here the large hoop has become a 1½-turn spiral. The ending simple side-loop has been replaced with a 4-turn spiral. These hoop earrings use a wire-wrapping of 20 tightly packed coils of 26-gauge wire. Because of the size of the end spiral, a Link 073 is used to connect the hoop to the earring wire link.

Simple, small changes in your links create entirely new designs, like *Spiral Large-Hoop Earrings*. This set of earring is worked in the same manner as the *Simple Large-Hoop Earrings* on page 166. The beginning simple side-loop has been replaced with a 3-turn spiral and the ending simple side-loop has become a 1½-turn spiral. The two spiral areas give extra visual weight to this earring set.

Large Coiled-Hoop Earrings are made in the same manner as the *Simple Large-Hoop* with the addition of a long wire-wrap at the top of the hoop Link 075. Begin by cutting a 20" (508mm) length of 26-gauge wire. Wire-wrap eight tightly packed coils along one side of the simple side-loops of the Link 075 hoop. Slide the wrapping to touch the simple side-loop area of the hoop. Work four tightly packed coils of wrapping-wire through both simple side-loops. Wrap 20 tightly packed coils along the other side of the hoop from the simple side-loops. Add a 4mm bead to the wrapping-wire. Hold the bead to the inside of the hoop link and continue wrapping eight more tightly packed coils. Cut and crimp the excess wrapping-wire.

Spiral Heart

FIVE SETS OF EARRINGS FROM ONE HEART-SHAPED LINK

VALENTINE HEARTS EARRINGS

1 Cut two lengths of 18-gauge wire 9" (229mm) long to create the spiral-heart links. Create two Link 156s by gripping one end of the working wire in your round-nose pliers and rolling a simple side-loop. Transfer the loop to your bent-nose pliers and continue rolling the working wire to create a 2½-turn spiral. Create this same spiral on the opposite end of the working wire.

2 Work each step on both earrings at the same time to ensure each wire bends and turns similarly, and both are the same size.

3 Measure the wire between the two spirals to find the center point. Grip the center point in your bent-nose pliers and bend the wire into a right-angle bend that allows the sides of the spirals to touch.

4 Working with 20-gauge wire, start with two lengths of wire 6" (152mm) long and create two Link 152s. Grip the center point of the wire in your round-nose pliers. Create a tight U-bend. Grip both working wires and ease the wires into a full-turn circle around the round-nose pliers. Release the outside working wire and continue rolling the inside working wire for one-half turn. This places the working wires on opposite sides of the link. Create a simple side-loop using your round-nose pliers on the ends of both working wires. Completed, this link measures ¾" (19mm) long.

5 Still working with 20-gauge wire, create six Link 036s, wrapped straight-loop bead dangles, using the oval and teardrop beads.

6 Create two ¼" (6mm)-wide Link 073s using 18-gauge wire. Open one Link 073 and thread it through the U-bend in the Link 156. Add two Link 036s to the jump ring. Add one Link 152 to the jump ring through one of its simple side-loops. Close the Link 073.

7 Open the remaining simple side-loop on the Link 152 and add the Link 036. Close the simple side-loop.

8 For each earring, cut a 12" (305mm) length of 26-gauge wire. Add a beaded wire-wrapping to the spiral-heart link through the two center holes in the spirals. Use one 6mm flat disc bead for the wrapping bead. Clip the excess wire and crimp into place.

9 Create two Link 054s using 20- or 26-gauge wire. Interlock the wrapped loop of the link through one of the center holes of one of the spirals in Link 156. The completed earring from the earring wire-wrapped loop measures 3½" (89mm) long.

Links used in these projects:

	Link 036	large bead wrapped straight-loop link
	Link 054	basic earring hoop link
	Link 073	jump ring
	Link 152	turn-back midwire-spiral link
	Link 156	spiral heart link

Supplies needed for this project:
- 18- & 20-gauge wire
- 4 6mm x 8mm oval bi-colored glass beads
- 2 12mm x 8mm teardrop-striped beads
- 2 6mm flat disc beads

Valentine Hearts

THREE VARIATIONS ON THE SPIRAL HEART

Gothic Black earrings

Gothic Black earrings were worked using 9" (229mm) lengths of 16-gauge wire for the Link 156s. The loops of the heart link are 2½-turn spirals. Three small beads—one spacer bead, one crow roller, and one spacer bead—were added to the working wire after the first spiral was worked. The second 2½-turn spiral was created then the link was bent into the open U-bend of the heart link at the center point between the spirals. Two Link 065s, open-curve earring wires, created using 20-gauge wire, complete the set.

Sweet Honey earrings

Sweet Honey earrings are created in the same manner as *Gothic Black*. Follow the *Gothic Black* instructions except in place of the spacer and crow roller beads, use one 10mm by 6mm oval striped frosted bead. The earring wire was worked using a wrapped straight-loop to join the Link 156 and Link 065.

Tip 10: Creating shapes.

Use common household items as a bending profile for creating shapes in your wire link. Pencils, ink pens, markers, and knitting needles will provide you with a variety of circle sizes. Often you can create oval shapes using the handle profiles of your jewelry tools.

Broken Heart earrings

Turning the 18-gauge Link 156 hearts upside down gives a Victorian scroll look to *Broken Heart* earrings. Two Link 018s, simple side-loop bead links, were created using 18-gauge wire and one 10mm flat disk lampwork bead for the top link, and one 16mm flat disk bead for the second link. A ¼"(6mm)-wide Link 073 jump ring connects the Link 156 to the bead links through the U-bend area of the heart. Link 065, worked in 20-gauge wire and added to the top of the bead links, completes the earring set.

LOOKING FOR LOVE EARRINGS

1 *Looking for Love* earrings are created in the same manner as *Sweet Honey* and *Gothic Black*—using 18-gauge wire for the heart Link 156s and one 10mm by 6mm oval-striped bead for each link.

2 Cut an extra-long length of 26-gauge wire. You will need about 24" (610mm) to work the wire-wrapping step. Create five tightly packed coils with the wrapping-wire on the side of the U-bend of the Link 156 that does not have the bead. Push this coil wrap against the base of the spiral. Add about 16 to 20 seed beads to the wrapping-wire. Loosely wrap the beaded wrapping-wire around the side of the U-bend. You will need to slide a few beads into place with each wrap. Wrap around the U-bend until you touch the bottom of the oval bead.

3 Cage-wrap the bead by taking the wrapping-wire over the bead and then coiling the wire one time around the spiral-heart wire at the top of the bead. Work the wrapping-wire back to the bottom of the bead and wrap one coil around the spiral-heart wire below the bead. Return the working wire to the top of the bead and wrap one coil around the spiral-heart wire.

4 Pick up your loose wire-wrapping with the seed beads above the oval bead. This should bring you to the base of the second spiral in the Link 156. Gently open the spiral using your bent-nose pliers. Wire-wrap along the top turn of the spiral using wire only, no seed beads. Work the wrapping-wire to where the two spirals of the spiral heart touch. Thread the wrapping-wire into one of the center holes of one spiral. Close the spiral that you opened to bring the wrapping-wire across the top of the link.

5 Wrap between the two center holes of the two spirals. Clip the excess wire and crimp the wrapping wire into position.

6 Create two Link 054s using 20- or 26-gauge wire. Interlock the wrapped straight-loop of the earring wire through one of the spiral-center holes in the spiral-heart link. The finished earrings measure 1½" (38mm) from the wrapped straight-loop of the earring wire.

Links used in this project:

	Link 156	spiral heart link
	Link 054	basic earring hoop link

Supplies needed for this project:
- 18- & 26-gauge wire
- 2 10mm x 6mm oval striped glass beads
- 40 bone seed beads

***Looking for Love* earrings**

Spiral-End

DIFFERENT SETS OF EARRINGS FROM SAME LINKS

Spiral-end bead dangles make quick-and-easy earrings while showcasing your favorite bright lampwork or semi-precious beads. You can change the size of the spiral ends by adding any number of turns to your spirals. Double-spirals are created by using both the end working wire at the base of the bead and the extra wire left from creating the wrapped straight-loop at the beginning of the bead dangle.

Springtime, *Marbled Spirals*, and *Agate Disc* earrings are all made using the same simple spiral-end bead link.

Links used in this project:

	Link 051	simple side-loop hook
	Link 052	wrapped straight-loop hook
	Link 310	simple straight-loop spiral bead link

Supplies used in this project:
- 18- & 20-gauge wire
- 2 6mm cracked-glass beads
- 6 3mm seed beads
- 2 12mm flat disc jade bead

SPRINGTIME, MARBLED & AGATE DISC SPIRALS

1 Begin by cutting an 8" (203mm) length of 18-gauge wire. Grip the working wire 1¼" (32mm) from the end and create a Link 004 wrapped straight-loop.

2 Add one or more beads to your working wire. *Springtime* uses two beads per earring—one 6mm round glass bead and one 8mm round glass bead. *Marbled Spirals* uses 10mm porcelain marbled tube beads and *Agate Disc* earrings use 18mm agate flat disc beads.

3 Clip the excess wire that comes from the base of the bead to 3" (76mm). Grip the end of the working wire in your round-nose pliers and roll the wire into a 2- to 3-turn spiral, rolling the spiral to touch the bottom of your beads. Transfer the simple side-loop to your bent-nose pliers and continue rolling the loop into a spiral. Roll the spiral until it touches the base of your bead.

4 Use 20-gauge wire to create your earring wire links. *Springtime* uses Link 051 and uses a ¼" (32mm)-wide Link 073 jump ring to join the bead links to the earring wires. *Marbled Spirals* and *Agate Disc* earrings use Link 052, working the wrapped straight-loop of the earring wire into the wrapped straight-loop of the bead links.

Springtime

Agate Disc

Marbled

Gypsy Moon

Just a Bit of Jade

Experiment with bead sizes. After you've learned how to make the earrings, let your own creativity rule and decide what size beads are right for you.

GYPSY MOON EARRINGS

Work *Gypsy Moon* with 6mm cracked-glass beads.

Include a midwire-circle between the bead and the spiral.

1 Cut a 10" (254mm) length of 20-gauge wire. Create a wrapped straight-loop at the top of the wire by bending a right-angle bend using your bent-nose pliers 1¼" (32mm) from the end. Grip the right-angle bend in your round-nose pliers and roll the wire into a simple straight-loop. Use the excess end wire from the loop to wrap the base of the loop three times. Clip the excess wire from the wrap using your flush cutters.

2 Add one 6mm cracked glass bead. Grip the working wire at the base of the bead in your round-nose pliers and create a Link 009 midwire-circle.

3 Clip the remaining wire, the wire below the midwire-circle, to a length of 4" (102mm). Add three 3mm seed beads to the working wire. Slide the beads into position near the midwire-circle. Grip the end of the working wire in your round-nose pliers and roll the wire into a Link 012 spiral. As you near the midwire-circle, allow the beads to drop to the bottom of the last spiral turn.

4 Use Link 052 earring wires, working the wrapped straight-loop on the earring wire into the wrapped straight-loop of the earring wire.

JUST A BIT OF JADE EARRINGS

Just a Bit of Jade spiral-end earrings use two spirals—one from the wrapped straight-loop wire and one from the base of the bead.

1 Cut a 10" (254mm) length of 20-gauge wire. Create a Link 004 wrapped straight-loop by gripping the wire 5" (127mm) from the end. You will have about 4" (102mm) of excess wire from this wrap. Do not cut the excess wire.

2 Slide one 12mm flat disc jade bead onto the working wire below the wrapped straight-loop. Clip the working wire below the bead to a length of 3" (76mm). Grip the end of the wire in your round-nose pliers and create a 3-turn spiral. Roll the spiral until it touches the base of the bead.

3 Grip the end of the wire left from the wrapped straight-loop at the top of the link in your round-nose pliers. Create a 3-turn spiral with about 1" (25mm) of unworked wire between the spiral and the wrap. Holding the bead link in one hand, guide the spiral end wrapping-wire over the front of the bead on the diagonal and tuck this spiral behind the end bead spiral.

4 Using 20–gauge wire, create a Link 052 wrapped straight-loop earring wire, working the loop of the earring wire into the wrapped straight-loop of the bead link.

U-Turn/Horseshoe

THREE SETS OF EARRINGS FROM THE SAME LINKS

MING DYNASTY

Link 044, a coil-covered simple straight-loop link, transforms into a Link 050 horseshoe by bending the link around the medium-sized form.

1 Create one Link 044 for each earring. Begin by making a ³⁄₁₆"-wide-by-3½" (5mm by 89mm)-long coil of 20-gauge wire. Next cut a 6" (152mm) length of 18-gauge wire and create a Link 004 1½" (38mm) from the end of the wire. Slide the 3½" (89mm) length of small coil over the working wire. Grip the working wire ½" (13mm) from the coil's end and create the link's second wrapped straight-loop. Clip the excess wire from the wrap. Stretch the coil covering to open the turns and fill the wire of the Link 044.

2 Place the center point of the coil-covered wrapped straight-loop against a medium-sized, 1" to 1½" (25mm to 38mm)-wide form. Bend the link into a horseshoe shape with the bend at the center of the link and the two wrapped loops at the top of the link touching.

3 Create a spiral bead dangle by cutting a 12" (305mm) length of 18-gauge wire. Measure to find the midpoint of the wire. Grip that point in your bent-nose pliers and create a wrapped straight-loop. Hold the wrapped straight-loop above the jade donut bead. Bend the wrapped loop slightly to center the loop to the bead. You will have two long wires extending from the bottom of the wrapped loop—one wire is left from the wrapping and one wire is the center wire that was wrapped.

4 Thread the wire you used to wrap the base of the wrapped straight-loop through the center hole of the donut bead. Bring the wire back to the wrapped area of the loop. Wrap this wire three times around the loop wrapping, working from the bottom toward that top. Clip the excess wire.

5 Clip the remaining long working wire to 3½" (89mm). Grip the end of the wire in your round-nose pliers and create a 2½-turn spiral. Stop the spiral turn about ¼" (6mm) from the bead.

6 Create five ¼" (6mm)-wide Link 073s. Open one Link 073 and thread it through both wrapped straight-loops of the coil-covered horseshoe link. Join one 073 to the same jump ring above the wrapped straight-loops. Add one 073 to this same jump ring below the wrapped straight-loops. You now have a three-jump-ring link chain with the horseshoe joined in the middle jump ring. Add one jump ring to the bottom ring of this chain. Add the last jump ring to the bottom of this chain, joining the Link 272 donut bead through its wrapped straight-loop.

7 Create two Link 053s using 20-gauge wire. For each earring open the top Link 073 and thread this ring through the joining ring of the Link 050 and the wrapped straight-loop of the earring wire. Close the jump ring.

ORIENT EXPRESS

1 Cut a 24" (610mm) length of 18-gauge wire for each earring. Roll the wire around a coil maker or knitting needle to create a ³⁄₁₆"-wide-by-3½" (5mm by 89mm)-long coil. Using your bent-nose pliers lift and bend the first turn on each end of the coil to create connecting loops. Hold the center point of the coil link against a small ½" (13mm)-wide form such as the barrel of an ink pen. Gently push the link into a horseshoe shape around the form with the connecting loops of the coil link touching.

2 Cut a 12" (305mm) length of 18-gauge wire and create a second coil that measures ³⁄₈"-wide-by-½"-long (10mm by 13mm). Slide this large coil onto the horseshoe-shaped shaped coil link. Move the large coil to the center bend of the horseshoe.

3 Cut a 6" (152mm) length of 20-gauge wire and create a wrapped-loop donut link using the oriental coin. Measure to a point 1½" (38mm) from the end of the wire. Roll this point of the working wire around a small, ½" (13mm)-wide form such as the barrel of an ink pen to create a turn-back loop. Slide the turn-back loop through the large coil that has been threaded onto the horseshoe coil ink. Wrap the base of the turn-back loop with the excess wire left from the loop's creation. Take the remaining center wire of the wrapped turn-back loop and thread it through the center hole of the oriental coin. Fold the threaded wire around the coin's inner edge and bring it back to the wrapped-loop area of the link. Wrap the threaded wire around the wrapped area of the turn-back loop two to three times. Clip the excess wire from the wrapping with your flush wire cutters.

4 For each earring, create two ¼" (6mm)-wide Link 073s using 18-gauge wire. Open the first Link 073 and thread it through both wrapped loops of the horseshoe-coil link. Open the remaining jump ring and thread it through the top of the first Link 073.

5 For each earring, create one Link 053 wrapped straight-loop earring wire using 20-gauge wire. Open the top Link 073 above the horseshoe-coil link and thread it through the wrapped straight-loop of the earring wires.

CROW ROLLERS EARRINGS

1 For each earring, cut a 12" (305mm) length of 20-gauge wire. Create a ¼" (6mm)-long coil worked over a ³⁄₁₆" (5mm)-wide knitting needle or coil maker. Remove the coil from the form and, using your bent-nose pliers, bend the working wire into two right-angle bends so that the working wire is above but parallel to the coil. Add three 3mm crow roller beads to the working wire. Bend two more right-angle bends at the end of the crow rollers to drop the working wire back into position to create a second set of coils. Hold the working wire against your form and roll a ¼" (6mm)-long coil. Clip the excess wire from the coil.

2 Cut a 5" (127mm) length of 20-gauge wire to create a Link 050 horseshoe. Begin this link with a simple side-loop. Slide two crow rollers onto the link wire. Now slide the beaded coil and then two more crow rollers onto the wire. Create a simple side-loop at the top of the last bead on the working wire. Clip the excess. Grip the working link wire at the midpoint in your round-nose pliers and create the U-bend of the horseshoe link.

3 With your fingers, gently press the sides of this link to bring the two simple side-loops together at the top of the link.

4 For each earring, create one Link 051 using 20-gauge wire.

5 For each earring, create one ¼" (6mm)-wide Link 073. Use the jump ring to connect the two simple side-loops of the Link 050 to the simple side-loop of the earring wire.

Links used in this project:

	Link 043	coil link
	Link 044	coil-covered simple straight-loop link
	Link 050	long horseshoe link
	Link 051	simple side-loop hook
	Link 053	wrapped straight-loop hook
	Link 073	jump ring
	Link 272	wrapped-donut straight-loop-dangle link
	Link 289	spiral bead dangle link

Supplies used in this project:
- 18- & 20-gauge wire
- 2 14mm green jade donut beads
- 2 20mm oriental coins
- 14 3mm crow rollers

Ming Dynasty

Orient Express

Oriental coins hang from a horseshoe-shaped coil link for this earring set.

Crow Rollers

Crow Rollers earrings uses a small beaded coil to add a little extra sparkle to the wires.

All Wrapped Up

The links for *All Wrapped Up* were created using heavy 16-gauge wire. Before they were joined into the chain, each link was placed on an old rough brick and lightly hammered. The hammering both flattened the wire and left each link textured. The bracelet is 7¼" (184mm) long.

1 Create a ⅜"-wide-by-2"-long (10mm by 51mm) coil using 16-gauge wire. Cut the coil into 3-loop Link 074 split rings.

2 Create one Link 051 from 16-gauge wire, using a 2-turn split ring bend in place of the simple side-loop. The finished hook measures ⅝" (16mm) long.

3 Create one 1" (25mm)-long Link 199 with two full turns in the center spiral with a simple side-loop at the end.

4 Create one Link 086 with four full turns in the spiral with a simple side-loop at the end. Wire-wrap nine tightly packed coils of 26-gauge wire through the center hole of the spiral, capturing the side leg of the raindrop. The link measures 1" (25mm) long.

5 Create two Link 241s using 16-gauge wire. The triangle raindrop is worked in a spiral fashion with each bend turning the working wire around the center point of the link. Grip your working wire ½" (13mm) from the end in your bent-nose pliers and bend a right-angle bend. Move your bent-nose pliers ¼" (6mm) from this right angle and create a second right-angle bend. With your round-nose pliers, grip the working wire ½" (13mm) from the second right-angle bend and create a U-bend. You have made

Links used in this project:		
	Link 051	simple side-loop hook
	Link 074	split ring
	Link 086	3-turn spiral link
	Link 199	2½-turn-spiral raindrop link
	Link 202	double-spiral raindrop link
	Link 241	triangle raindrop link
	Link 282	wrapped bead dangle link

Supplies used in this project:
- 16- & 26-gauge wire (for wrapping)
- 2 10mm yellow jade donuts
- 1 14mm lampwork bead

one complete spiral-type turn around the center of this link. Create a second spiral-type turn on the link in the same manner. End the link by creating a 1½-turn spiral at the topside or center of the triangle spiral. Cut an 8" (203mm) length of 26-gauge wire and wrap the two outside legs of the triangle raindrop with tightly packed coils. The completed link measures 1½" (38mm) long.

6 Create one Link 202 with three full turns to the center spiral and 2½ turns to the ending spiral. This link measures 1¾" (44mm) long.

7 Place the raindrop, triangle raindrop, and spiral links on a hard rough textured surface. Gently tap the wire of these links with a hammer to flatten the wire and to add texture. Both sides of the link can be tapped.

8 Join the bracelet chain by opening the split ring end of the Link 051 and threading it through the U-bend area of the Link 199. Using one ⅜" (10mm)-wide Link 074 for each, join the Link 086, Link 241, Link 202, and the remaining Link 241 to the chain.

9 Create three Link 282s using the yellow jade donuts and the lampwork bead as follows: Create a wrapped straight-loop in the beginning of the working wire. With your round-nose pliers, grip the working wire ½" (13mm) below the wrapped loop and make a wide U-bend. Slide one bead into the U-bend area. With your fingers, hold the bead and gently pull the open U-bend tight, bringing the working wire back toward the wrapped loop area of the link. Wrap the working wire over the original straight-loop wrapping two to three times. Clip the excess working wire using your flush wire cutters.

10 With a ⅜" (10mm)-wide Link 074 add the three bead dangles to the chain through the hole of the center spiral of the Link 202.

Apple Turnovers

Despite not having any icing or glaze, this *Apple Turnover* is sure to become one of your favorite pieces of jewelry. The easy-to-make bracelet is 7" (178mm) long.

1 Please review and practice Link 117 on page 92 before attempting this bracelet.

2 Create ten 1" (25mm)-long links 108s using 18-gauge wire.

3 Create one Link 052 using 18-gauge wire.

4 Create a hairpin chain using Link 052 as the first link of the chain. Begin by threading the U-bend turn area of one Link 108 through the wrapped straight-loop of the hook. Fold the simple side-loops of the Link 108 over the wrapped straight-loop to lock these two links. Press the fold area of Link 108 with your nylon pliers to compress the fold. Continue adding Link 108s to the chain, working each new link through the U-bend of the previous link until all ten Link 108s are added.

5 Cut an 8" (203mm) length of 20-gauge wire and bead-wrap the U-bend areas of the nine Link 108s, working from the hook. Add one 3mm agate bead to each wrapping. The last Link 108 is not wrapped.

6 Create two Link 266s using a 3mm agate for each dangle.

7 Create one ¼" (6mm)-wide Link 074. Add the two Link 266s, using the split ring, to the wrapped straight-loop of Link 052 hook.

Links used in this project:

	Link 052	wrapped straight-loop hook
	Link 074	split ring
	Link 108	long simple hairpin link
	Link 266	simple loop-end bead dangle link

Supplies needed for this project:

- 18- & 20-gauge wire
- 11 3mm agate beads, assorted colors

Carnival Ride

Bone beads accent this heavy-coiled 9½" (241mm) bracelet. Each of the links is worked using simple side-loops or simple straight-loops as the connecting loops. The bracelet ends with a six-jump-ring chain, making it easily adjustable to any wrist size.

1 Please review and practice Link 332 on page 136 before beginning this project to learn how to center the working wire to a coil so that hairpin turns, simple side-loops, or beads can be added to the link. All of the coils created in steps 2 through 4 in this bracelet were worked over a ⅜" (10mm)–diameter wooden kitchen spoon handle to create the extra-wide coils.

2 Create one 1⅜" (35mm)-long Link 061 by creating an eight-turn coil. Turn the first coil of the link into a connecting loop. Reposition the working wire on the opposite side of the coil and make a U-bend hook turn. Finish the hook with a small simple side-loop.

3 Make one seven-turn coil Link 043. Turn the first coil of the link into a connecting loop. Reposition the working wire on the opposite side of the coil to add one 10mm-by-8mm bone bead to the end of the link. Finish this link with a simple straight-loop at the top of the bead.

4 Make one 6-turn coil Link 043. Turn the first link of the coil into a connecting loop. Reposition the remaining working wire to add one 10mm-by-8mm bone bead on top of the coil. With the working wire at the top of the bead, create a 2-turn U-bend hairpin. Finish this link with a simple side-loop centered over the first hairpin turn. Compress the hairpin area of this link.

5 Make one Link 205, adding one 8mm copper disc bead to the link after the spiral.

6 Create two Link 018s using one 10mm-by-8mm bone bead for each.

7 Create one Link 018 using one 6mm copper cone bead.

8 Create one Link 135, repositioning the working wire to add one 10mm copper bead at the end of the 2-turn U-bend hairpin. Finish this link with a simple side-loop.

9 Create one ¼"-wide-by-2"-long (6mm by 51mm) Link 043. Cut this coil into Link 073 jump rings.

10 Create a six-link chain of Link 073 jump rings. Add the Link 018 to one end of this chain. To the other end of the chain, join the Link 043 made in step 4, one simple side-loop bone bead Link 018, the Link 135 made in step 8, one beaded Link 018, the Link 043 made in step 3, the Link 205 made in step 5, and finish with the coiled hook Link 061 made in step 2.

Links used in this project:

	Link 018	1-bead simple side-loop link
	Link 043	coil link
	Link 061	coiled hook
	Link 073	jump ring
	Link 135	double-hairpin link
	Link 205	2½-turn spiral hairpin raindrop link

Supplies needed for this project:
- 16-gauge wire
- 4 10mm x 8mm bone beads
- 1 10mm copper bead
- 1 8mm copper disc bead
- 1 6mm copper cone bead

Center of Attention

The *Center of Attention* is just what you'll be when you wear this spiral- and coil-adorned bracelet. The 8¾" (223mm) bracelet makes excellent use of various types of round glass beads to accentuate the spiral shapes that dominate the piece.

1 Make one 1½" (13mm)-long Link 223 ending with the simple side-loop facing into the link.

2 Make two Link 024s using the 12mm round lampwork glass beads.

3 Make one ⅜"-wide-by-1¾"-long (10mm by 41mm) Link 043.

4 Make one Link 024 using the 12mm flat disk glass bead.

5 Make one 1"-wide-by-1⅝"-long (25mm by 44mm) Link 152.

6 Make two Link 265s using a simple straight-loop in place of the wrapped straight-loop and the 8mm round frosted glass beads.

7 Make one Link 051 simple side-loop hook.

8 Make three ¼" (6mm)-wide Link 073s.

9 Make five ⅜"-wide Link 073s.

10 Link the bracelet as follows: Link 223, Link 073, Link 024 with round lampwork bead, Link 043, Link 024 with flat disk bead, Link 152, Link 024 with round lampwork bead link, Link 073, and end with Link 051.

11 Add the two Link 265s to the connecting loop of the Link 152.

12 Add three ⅜" (10mm) Link 073s to the Link 152, working them through the center hole of the spiral.

13 Add two ⅜" (10mm) Link 073s and one ¼" (6mm) Link 073 to the Link 223, working the jump rings through the center hole of the spiral.

Links used in this project:

	Link 024	1-bead simple straight-loop link
	Link 043	coil link
	Link 051	simple side-loop hook
	Link 073	jump ring
	Link 152	turn-back midwire-spiral link
	Link 223	4-turn spiral-raindrop link
	Link 265	crimped-end bead dangles

Supplies needed for this project:
- 16-gauge wire
- 2 12mm round lampwork glass beads
- 1 12mm flat disk glass bead
- 2 8mm round frosted glass beads

Choir Practice

Choir Practice uses simple side-loop links and jump rings to create an easy-to-make chain perfect for hanging a colorful mixture of India glass bead dangles. A long chain created from double jump rings at the end of this bracelet makes it adjustable in size.

1 Create a ¼"-wide-by-3"-long (6mm by 76mm) coil. Use the coil to cut Link 073s used in the bracelet chain and to hang the bead dangles from your bracelet.

2 Create nine ½" (13mm)-long Link 015s.

3 Create a chain using the nine Link 015s by connecting each link to the next using two ¼" (6mm)-wide Link 073s.

4 Create one ¾" (19mm)-long Link 056. Connect this hook to one end of the chain using two ¼" (6mm)-wide Link 073s.

5 Create a five-link chain using two ¼" (6mm)-wide Link 073s per link. Join this Link 073 chain using two ¼" (6mm)-wide Link 073s into the opposite end of the Link 015 chain.

6 Create 24 bead dangles using any combination of link bends and India glass beads. For *Choir Practice*, I used six Link 312s, three Link 299s, two Link 279s, six Link 266s, and seven Link 265s.

7 Cut twenty-four ¼" (6mm)-wide Link 073s from your original coil. Use the cut links to connect each bead dangle to one of the simple side-loops in the bracelet's Link 015s.

Links used in this project:

∞	Link 015	simple side-loop link
	Link 056	wrapped straight-loop hook link
○	Link 073	jump ring
	Link 265	crimped-end bead dangles
	Link 266	simple loop-end bead dangle link
	Link 279	wrapped bead-cap dangle link
	Link 299	rolled-wire-end bead dangle link
	Link 312	wrapped straight-loop spiral-end bead dangle link

Supplies used in this project:

- 18-gauge wire
- 24 6mm to 28mm assorted mixed India glass beads

Country Life

Country Life is a fun multi-link bracelet measuring 8½" (216mm) long. The links are created separately, then joined through their simple side-loops using ¼" (6mm)-wide jump rings.

1 Create a coil ¼"-wide-by-1"-long (6mm by 25mm). Cut the coil into six Link 073s.

2 Create one 1"-long (25mm) Link 053.

3 Create two Link 199s with 2½-turn spirals. The Link 199s measure 1¼" (32mm) long each.

4 Create two Link 141s by working a simple straight-loop and then adding one 12mm-by-10mm porcelain bead. Work two U-bend hairpin turns below the bead. Finish the link with a simple straight-loop.

5 Create one ¼" (6mm)-wide-by-six-turns Link 043. Bend the first turn of the coil into a connecting loop. Bend the working wire to cross the center of the opening in the coil. Bend the working wire into a right angle that brings the working wire out from the center of the link. Add one 12mm-by-8mm porcelain bead. Finish this link with a simple straight-loop.

6 Using ¼" (6mm)-wide Link 073s, join the links in the following order: Link 053, Link 199, Link 141, Link 199, Link 043, and Link 141. Add one ¼" (6mm)-wide Link 073 to the end of the chain as the eye for the hook.

Links used in this project:

	Link 043	coil link
	Link 053	wrapped straight-loop hook
	Link 073	jump ring
	Link 141	hairpin bead link
	Link 199	2½-turn-spiral raindrop link

Supplies needed for this project:
- 16-gauge wire
- 3 12 mm x 10mm glazed porcelain beads

Crystal Fairy

The sparkling chain bracelet *Crystal Fairy* is made by adding jump rings to the simple side-loop hairpin link. One large focal-point bead, a 20mm glass lampwork, finishes off this simple project.

1 Create one ¼"-wide-by-3"-long (6mm by 76mm) Link 043 and use it to cut 54 Link 073s and one 3-turn Link 074.

2 Create one ⅜"-wide-by-1½"-long (10mm by 38mm) Link 043 and use it to cut 12 Link 073s.

3 Create one ¾" (19mm)-long Link 053.

4 Create six Link 107s.

5 Create one Link 265 using one 10mm copper bead cap, one 20mm x 12mm lampwork bead, and one 10mm copper bead cap, in that order.

6 Following the photo of *Crystal Fairy*, lay out the ⅜" (10mm)-wide Link 073s and the Link 107s of your bracelet, alternating one ⅜" (10mm)-wide jump ring with one simple hairpin link. Begin the layout with a Link 073 and end it with a Link 107. Turn the simple side-loops of the first Link 107 to face the second ⅜" (10mm)-wide jump ring. Turn the simple side-loops of the second Link 107 to face this same jump ring. Continue turning the Link 107s in this manner.

7 Add one ⅜" (10mm) Link 073 over the ⅜" Link 073 you started with. When joining the chain, treat these two links as if they were one link. To the opposite side of the layout that ends with a Link 107, add Link 053 hook to the end of the bracelet.

8 Join the links you have laid out using ¼" (6mm)-wide Link 073 jump rings. Use two Link 073s to join one ⅜" (10mm)-wide Link 073 to the U-bend turn of each Link 107. Use three Link 073s for each simple side-loop of the Links 107s to join them to the adjacent ⅜" wide Link 073. Join the Link 053 hook to the chain using two ¼" (6mm) Link 073s worked through the last Link 107.

9 Join the Link 265 to the center two ⅜" (10mm)-wide Link 073s using one ¼" (6mm)-wide Link 074.

Links used in this project:

	Link 053	wrapped straight-loop hook
	Link 073	jump ring
	Link 074	split ring
	Link 107	simple hairpin link
	Link 265	crimped-end bead dangles

Supplies needed for this project:
- 16-gauge wire
- 1 20mm x 12mm yellow lampwork bead
- 2 10mm copper bead caps

Deep Sea Adventure

Green beads combined with hairpin turns echo the ocean's waves in *Deep Sea Adventure.* The finished necklace is 7½" (191mm) long.

1 Create three 1" (25mm)-long Link 036s using the 12mm flat foil-lined glass beads.

2 Bend two 1" (25mm)-wide Link 137s, using five U-bends for each hairpin link.

3 Create one ¾" (18mm)-wide Link 107.

4 Create two ¼" (6mm)-wide links 073s.

5 Create one Link 058 using the 20mm-by-18mm fish bead. As you work the wrapped straight-loop of the Link 058, interlock the loop with a loop on one of the Link 036s.

6 Using the simple side-loops of the Link 137 as your connecting loops, add one Link 137, one Link 036, one Link 137, and the last Link 036 with the attached Link 058 to the chain.

7 Connect the Link 107 to the wrapped straight-loop of the last Link 036 using one Link 073 for each simple side-loop of the hairpin.

Links used in this project:

	Link 036	large bead wrapped straight-loop link
	Link 058	beaded hook link
	Link 073	jump ring
	Link 107	simple hairpin link
	Link 137	5-turn hairpin link

Supplies needed for this project:

- 16-gauge wire
- 3 12mm square flat foil-lined glass beads
- 1 20mm x 18mm glass fish bead

Double Spiral

Double Spiral is a fun bracelet created with double-spiral hairpin links joined by jump rings. Practice making Link 112 on page 90 before beginning. Determine how much wire you need to create the link as outlined in the accompanying sidebar about estimating the amount of wire needed to create mirror image links.

1 Create ten Link 112s by cutting ten lengths of wire as determined by your practice links. For *Double Spiral*, I used 8" (203mm) of wire for each link. Create the links by making a 3-turn spiral on each end of the wire.

2 Create one Link 112 using a wire 2" (51mm) longer than you used for your first Link 112s. Create this link by working a 3-turn spiral on both ends of the wire. Grip the center point of the wire in the tip of your round-nose pliers and roll the link into a tight, small U-bend. Grip the U-bend in your bent-nose pliers and crimp the bend to tighten the turn as much as possible. This brings the two sides of the U-bend area of this link together as double wires. Grip the wires 1" (25mm) from the tight U-bend and roll the wire into a U-bend hook.

3 Create a ¼"-wide-by 2"-long (6mm by 51mm) coil. Cut the coil into Link 073s. You will need twenty Link 073s to join the Link 112s into a chain. Connect the links to this bracelet by threading one Link 073 through each of the holes in the center of the spirals. Join both of these Link 073s to the U-bend area of the next Link 112. The last Link 112 on the chain will be the one upon which you created the 1" (25mm) hook on the U-bend end.

4 Create three Link 073s. Thread one each through the hole in the spirals in the first Link 112. Join the two Link 073s together by threading them through one more Link 073. This last Link 073 will act as your hook eye for closing your bracelet.

Links used in this project:

◯	Link 073	jump ring
🌀	Link 112	3-turn double-spiral hairpin link

Supplies needed for this project:

- 18-gauge wire

How much wire is needed for a mirror image link?

There is an easy method to determine the amount of wire needed to create any mirror image link. Knowing the exact amount needed for a mirror link is especially important when you have a project using multiples of the same link and you want them all to be the same size.

Make one Link 112 as follows.

1. Begin by cutting a 12" (305mm) length of wire. Grip one end of the wire in your round-nose pliers and roll a simple side-loop. Transfer the loop to your bent-nose pliers and continue rolling the loop to create a 3-turn spiral. Grip the working wire ½" (13mm) from the base or end of the spiral and create a shallow, or partial, U-bend.

2. You have created one-half of the finished double-spiral link. Measure the length of working wire remaining from the center of the partial U-bend turn. Subtract that measurement from your original 12" (305mm) of wire. The remainder is the amount of wire you have used in creating the one-half of the link.

3. Double the remaining amount to determine how much wire you will need to work both sides of one Link 112.

4. The method works for any mirrored image link.

Moons of Jupiter

The quick-and-easy *Moons of Jupiter* bracelet uses the simple side-loop link to form a long chain at the end of the project, making it adjustable.

1 Working from the hook end of the bracelet, create one ¾" (19mm)-long Link 053.

2 Create two 1" (25mm)-long Link 036s using 10mm-by-6mm oval agate beads. Interlock one of these links to the Link 053 hook. Set the second link aside.

3 Create two 1¼"-long-by-⅝"-wide (32mm by 16mm) Link 186s. These links use five turns to the midwire-spiral. Wrap the link through the spiral hole using 26-gauge wire with six random wraps. Connect one Link 136 to the chain. Set the second link aside.

4 Create one 1" (25mm)-long Link 036 using the 18mm flat disc agate bead. Add this link to the chain.

5 Add the remaining Link 186 to the chain. Add the remaining oval agate Link 036 to the chain.

6 Create six Link 015s that measure ½" long each. Join these links to the chain at the Link 036 oval bead through their simple side-loops.

Links used in this project

	Link 015	simple side-loop link
	Link 036	large bead wrapped straight-loop link
	Link 053	wrapped straight-loop hook
	Link 186	midwire-spiral link

Supplies needed for this project:

- 18- & 26-gauge wire
- 1 18mm flat disc agate stone bead
- 2 10mm x 6mm oval agate stone beads

Raspberry Patch

Wire-wrapped beads are added to three of the links of the simple bent-wire links for *Raspberry Patch*, a 7½" (184mm) bracelet.

1 Working from the hook eye end of the bracelet, create one ⅜" (10mm)-wide Link 073.

2 Create two Link 091s with 2½ turns in each spiral. Cut a 10" (254mm) length of 26-gauge wire. Wire-wrap the link through the two holes in the spiral. Add a 6mm-by-4mm purple spacer bead to the wire-wrap. The finished link is 1" (25mm) long. Join one Link 091 to the Link 073; set the second Link 091 aside.

3 Create two 1" (25mm)-long Link 018s using one 10mm lampwork bead for each. Join one Link 018 to the chain; set the second one aside.

4 Make one ⅜" (10mm)-wide-by-eight-full-turns coil Link 043. Bend both end loops into connecting loops. Add this link to the chain.

5 Add the remaining Link 018 to the chain.

6 Create one 1"-long-by-1"-wide (25mm by 25mm) Link 138 using five U-bend turns. Using 26-gauge wire, coil-wrap one section of the hairpin link with five tightly packed coils. Add a 6mm-by-4mm bead to the wrapping-wire. Bring the wrapping-wire across one U-bend hairpin, placing the bead inside this U-bend area, and wrap the next wire leg of the hairpin with five tightly packed coils. See the photo for the exact placement. Join this link to the chain.

7 Create two ¾" (19mm)-long Link 015s. Add one of the Link 015s to the chain; set the second link aside.

8 Join the remaining Link 091 to the chain. Add the remaining Link 015 to the chain.

9 Create one Link 051; add it to the chain.

Links used in this project:

	Link 015	simple side-loop link
	Link 018	1-bead simple side-loop link
	Link 043	coil link
	Link 051	simple side-loop hook
	Link 073	jump ring
	Link 091	double 3½-turn spiral link
	Link 138	tapered hairpin link

Supplies needed for this project:

- 16- & 26-gauge wire
- 2 10mm clear floral lampwork beads
- 3 6mm x 4mm spacer beads

Links used in this project:

	Link 036	large bead wrapped straight-loop link
	Link 038	3-bead wrapped straight-loop link
	Link 043	coil link
	Link 051	simple side-loop hook
	Link 073	jump ring
	Link 338	hairpin bead link

Supplies needed for this project:

- 18- & 20-gauge wire
- 2 18mm glass swirl round beads
- 2 10mm copper cone beads
- 1 12mm flat disc copper bead
- 1 14mm barrel copper bead

Sable Swirls

Small sections of coil can be added to the working wire of your links as if they were beads. In *Sable Swirls*, three wrapped straight-loop links use a combination of beads and coils to accent this 8¼" (210mm) bracelet.

1 Create three ⅛"-wide-by-½"-long (3mm by 13 mm) 20-gauge wire coils. Create one ⅛"-wide-by-¾"-long (3mm by 19mm) coil.

2 Create one ¼"-wide-by-2"-long (6mm by 51mm) coil using 18-gauge wire. Cut this coil into Link 073 jump rings.

3 Working from the hook end of the bracelet and using 18-gauge wire for the links, make one Link 051 straight-loop hook.

4 Create one 1¼" (32mm)-long Link 038 using one ½" (13mm) coil, one 10mm copper bead, and one ½" (13mm) coil. Add this link to the simple straight-loop of Link 051.

5 Create one 2½" (57mm)-long Link 038 using one 18mm glass swirl bead, one ½" (13mm) coil, and one 14mm copper barrel bead. Add this link to the chain with one Link 073.

6 Create one 1¼" (32mm)-long Link 036 using one 18mm glass swirl bead. Add this link to the chain with one Link 073.

7 Create one Link 338 using one 12mm flat disc copper bead, one 10mm copper cone bead, and a ¾" (19mm) coil. Start this link with a wrapped straight-loop. Add the two beads. Using your round nose pliers, create a U-bend turn at the base of the second bead. Add the ¾" (19mm) coil. Position the coil near the U-bend and gripping the coil-covered working wire in your round-nose pliers, create a second U-bend turn. Add a third U-bend turn at the end of the coil. Finish the link with a wrapped straight-loop. Connect this link to the chain using a Link 073.

8 Add four Link 073s to the end of the chain.

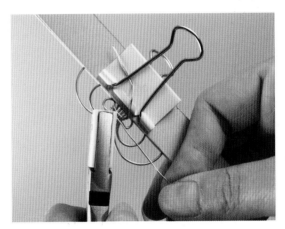

Tip 11: Homemade clamps.

Occasionally you will need a third hand to hold the wire link while you work the next step. A simple clamp can be made from two ¾" (19mm) wide strips of heavy cardboard and a large spring clip.

Saint Patty's Day

Saint Patty's Day, a cheery 7½" (191mm)-long bracelet, uses coils, hairpins, and spirals to accent one large black floral lampwork bead.

Working from the hook end and using 18-gauge wire, work the bracelet as follows:

1 Create one ¾" (19mm)-long Link 052.

2 Create one Link 141 using a wrapped straight-loop and adding one 8mm cat's eye bead. Add four U-bend turns after the bead. End with a wrapped straight-loop. Join this link to the hook using Link 074.

3 Create two ¼"-wide-by-¾" long (6mm by 19mm) Link 043s. Add one link to the chain; set the second link aside.

4 Create one Link 036 using the black lampwork bead, interlocking the wrapped straight-loop of the link to the chain.

5 Create one 1" (25mm)-long Link 036 using one 8mm cat's-eye bead, interlocking the wrapped straight-loop to the chain. Wire-wrap the bead using 18-gauge wire.

6 Add the second Link 043 to the chain.

7 Bend one ¼"-wide-by-¾"-high (6mm by 19mm) Link 123. Connect the link to the chain through the midwire-circle to the last connecting loop of the Link 043.

8 Create three ¼" (6mm)-wide Link 074s. Connect one Link 074 through each hole in the spirals of the midwire-circle hairpin link. Use the remaining Link 074 to join the first two Link 074s.

9 Make one 1" (25mm)-long Link 036 using one 6mm green spacer bead. Join the Link 036 to the Link 074.

Links used in this project:

	Link 036	large bead wrapped straight-loop link
	Link 043	coil link
	Link 052	wrapped straight-loop hook
	Link 074	split ring
	Link 084	6-turn wire-wrapped spiral link
	Link 123	2½-turn spiral midwire-circle hairpin link
	Link 141	hairpin bead link

Supplies used in this project:

- 18- & 26-gauge wire
- 2 8mm green cat's eye glass beads
- 1 6mm green spacer bead
- 1 20mm x 10mm black lampwork bead

Simply Pink

Sometimes, in jewelry designing, a very simple design or link can have a powerful effect. Interlock the links by sliding the first loop of the new link, during the simple straight-loop stage, into the last link loop on the chain. The finished bracelet measures 8" (203mm) long.

Each of the links in *Simply Pink* begins and ends in a wrapped straight-loop. Interlock the links by sliding the first loop of the next link into the end wrapped straight-loop of the previous link, and then wrapping the loop on the second bead link.

1 Make a chain of seven Link 036s, interlocking the loops as you work each progressive link. Alternate the beads, using first a cat's eye bead and then a flat square frosted bead. End the chain with a cat's eye bead link.

2 Create a Link 052 and interlock it with one end of the chain.

3 Create three Link 272s using the lampwork beads and one cat's eye bead. Interlock the loops of these links into the same bead link loop where you placed your bent-wire hook.

Links used in this project:

	Link 036	large bead wrapped straight-loop link
	Link 052	wrapped straight-loop hook
	Link 272	wrapped-donut straight-loop-dangle link

Supplies needed for this project:

- 20-gauge wire
- 5 10mm pink cat's eye glass beads
- 3 16mm flat square frosted glass beads
- 2 12mm to 14mm lampwork beads

Extra dangles

Extra dangles can be added to any bracelet. In *Saint Patty's Day*, three Link 084s using a 4-turn spiral center and wire-wrapped with 26-gauge wire were added to the loops of Link 036. For *Simply Pink*, I chose three Link 272s using small lampwork beads as my additional dangles.

Links used in this project:

	Link 073	jump ring
	Link 130	offset 2½-turn double-spiral hairpin link
	Link 139	3-turn open-hairpin link
	Link 211	2½-turn spiral-center double-raindrop link
	Link 332	coiled-spiral bead link

Supplies needed for this project:
- 16- & 26-gauge wire
- 4 3mm crow rollers
- 1 4mm x 6mm oval agate bead
- 1 16mm flat disc agate bead

Stone Road

Stone Road is full of a real country road's twists and turns. The 7¾" (197mm)-long bracelet takes a simple 3-turn hairpin link and changes it into a beaded hook. Extra flash and sparkle are added with the use of multiple jump rings and wire-wrapping.

1 Throughout this project, use 16-gauge wire to create links and 26-gauge wire for wrapping. This bracelet is worked from the hook end.

2 Create one Link 139 starting with a simple side-loop then adding two ½" (13mm) U-bend turns. Bend a right-angle ¼" (6mm) from the last U-bend turn. Add one 3mm crow roller, one 16mm flat agate bead, and one 3mm crow roller to the wire. Place the working wire against a medium-sized form and create a U-bend for the hook. Clip the hook bend to ½" (13mm).

3 Using about 8" (203mm) of 16-gauge wire for each, create two Link 130s. Begin with a 3-turn spiral. Create a U-bend ½" (13mm) from the spiral. Working the opposite end of the wire create a spiral that faces the same side of the link as the first. Roll this spiral until it touches the top of the first spiral.

4 For one Link 130, cut 12" (305mm) of 26-gauge wire. Wire-wrap the link below the top spiral with 12 tightly packed coils. When the wrapping-wire touches the centered spiral, wrap the link through the spiral hole, catching the outer arm of the link with six tightly packed coils.

5 For the second Link 130, cut 12" (305mm) of 26-gauge wire. Wire-wrap the link through the centered spiral hole, catching the outer arm for six tightly packed coils. Wrap three through the spiral hole, catching the U-bend arm. Wrap three tightly packed coils at the top of the spiral.

6 Create one Link 332, starting with 10" (254mm) of wire. Make a seven full-turn ¼" (6mm)-wide coil. Turn the first full turn into a connecting loop. Create two right-angle bends in the remaining working wire at the end of the coil to center the working wire. Add one 3mm crow roller, one 16mm flat agate disc, and one 3mm crow roller to the wire. Clip the remaining wire to a length of 3" (76mm). Roll the end of the wire into a spiral.

7 Create one Link 211. Using 8" (203mm) length of wire, create a 2½-turn spiral center surrounded by a double-raindrop turn. Finish this double-raindrop link with a simple side-loop. Cut a 12" (305mm) length of 26-gauge wire and wire-wrap this link through the spiral hole, catching both raindrop arms with six random coils.

8 Roll a ¼"-wide-by-2"-long (6mm by 51mm) coil. Using your flush cutters, create Link 073s from the coil.

9 Using three ¼" (6mm) Link 073s per connection, join the links as follows: one Link 139, one Link 130, one Link 332, one Link 130, and end with one Link 211.

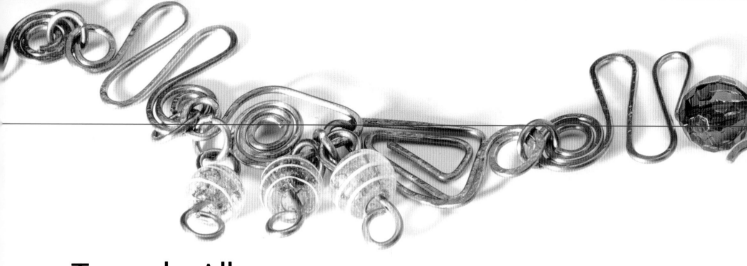

Tornado Alley

With more twists and turns than a good mystery novel, the 7" (178mm)-long *Tornado Alley* leads you down one winding curve and into a spiral. It's an eclectic collection of links representing the power and fury of nature.

1 Using 16-gauge wire, *Tornado Alley* is a quick project using five links in the chain, including the hook-and-eye.

2 Make one Link 090 with a 3-turn spiral on one side, and an open 1¼" (32mm)-long 2-turn spiral on the second end.

3 Create one 1¼"-wide-by-1"-high (32mm by 25mm) Link 151 using 1½ turns in the spiral on one end, three hairpin turns, and a 2-turn spiral on the second end.

4 Make one 1¼" (32mm) long Link 199 with three turns to the center spiral and one turn for the connecting loop.

5 Bend one 1½" (38mm)-long Link 241 using 2½ turns in the triangle and 1½ turns in the connecting loop.

6 Make one 2" (51mm)-wide Link 151 double-spiral hairpin using two turns in the spiral and three hairpin turns. Make a right-angle bend in the working wire at the midpoint of the last hairpin. Add one 14mm faceted glass bead. Make a right-angle bend in the working wire at the top of the bead. Bend the working wire into a large hook curve by working it over a wooden spoon handle. Bend a small open U-bend at the end of the hook. Cut the excess wire.

7 Make three 1" (25mm)-long Link 018s using the 12mm lampwork beads.

8 Make seven Link 073s.

9 Connect the links using the Link 073 following the photo for placement.

10 Add two of the Link 018s to the U-bend area of the Link 199. Add the remaining Link 018 to the connecting loop of this same link.

11 Test the bracelet for size and fit, gently bending the larger links into a gentle curve using your fingers.

Links used in this project:

	Link 018	1-bead simple side-loop link
	Link 073	jump ring
	Link 090	double 2½-turn-spiral link
	Link 151	double-spiral 5-bend hairpin link
	Link 199	2½-turn-spiral raindrop link
	Link 241	triangle raindrop link

Supplies used in this project:
- 16-gauge wire
- 3 12mm large hole lampwork glass beads
- 1 14mm faceted glass bead

Optional To add texture to this bracelet, place the links on a rough metal or stone surface. I used the iron head on an old sledgehammer.

White Chocolate

The multiple hairpin links make *White Chocolate* a wide ruffled bracelet. Bold 14mm lampwork beads add color to the design of this 7¾" (197mm) piece.

1 Create three 4-turn Link 137s with coiled ends. Begin by cutting an 8" (203mm) length of wire. Grip the end of the wire in the widest point of your round-nose pliers. Roll the wire into a simple side-loop.

2 Continue rolling the wire in the round-nose pliers two more times to create a 3-turn coil. Grip the working wire ½" (13mm) from the coil in your round-nose pliers and create a U-bend hairpin turn. The second hairpin turn is made 1" (25mm) from the first. The third and fourth hairpin U-bend turns are also made 1" (25mm) from the last. Using your round-nose pliers, grip the working wire ½" (13mm) from the last U-bend. Roll the wire into a 3-turn coil.

3 Clip the excess wire from the coil. Grip the coil ends of each link in your fingers and compress the hairpin turns so they overlap each other.

4 Create two links 141s using 8" (203mm) of wire. Following the same instructions, make a 3-turn coil end. Create a right-angle bend at the end of the third hairpin. Add one 14mm lampwork bead. Bend the wire at the end of the bead into a right angle. Using your round-nose pliers, create a 3-turn coil. Clip the excess wire from the coil.

5 Create one Link 036 using one 14mm lampwork bead. Interlock the wrapped straight-loops of the link into one Link 137 on the bead side of each link as you work the Link 036.

6 Create five ¼" (6mm)-wide links 073s. Using the jump rings to connect each link, add two Link 137s on each side of the bead chain.

7 Create one Link 051 with a 3-turn coil in place of the simple side-loop. Join this hook link to the side of the chain with the two 4-turn hairpin links.

Links used in this project:

	Link 036	large bead wrapped straight-loop link
	Link 051	simple side-loop hook
	Link 073	jump ring
	Link 137	5-turn hairpin link
	Link 141	hairpin bead link

Supplies needed for this project:

- 16-gauge wire
- 3 14mm round lampwork glass beads

Appalachian Trail

NECKLACE AND EARRING SET

The long wrapped-loop link made from 12-gauge wire makes *Appalachian Trail* a fast project. The finished necklace is 18½" (420mm) long.

1 Using 12-gauge wire, create ten 1½" (38mm)-long Link 047s. Start with at least 8" (203mm) of wire for each. Because 12-gauge wire can be hard to bend into tight turns, allow plenty of extra working wire as you create these links. (See "Ganging Up on Link 047" on page 83.)

2 Using your bent-nose pliers, grip the working wire 2½" (64mm) from the end. Create a simple straight-loop in the wire. Grip the working wire 1¼" (32mm) from the simple straight-loop in your round-nose pliers and roll the wire into a tight U-bend. This brings the working wire back to the simple straight-loop area of the link. Grip both arms of the U-bend under the simple straight-loop and use the excess wire from the simple straight-loop to create a 2-turn wrap. Clip the excess wire from the wrapping process.

3 Create one Link 152 with 15" (381mm) of 12-gauge wire, using two full turns in the midwire-spiral. Clip the top working wire to 1¼" (32mm) from the spiral and roll a simple side-loop. Bring the bottom working wire to the opposite side of the midwire-spiral. Roll the end into a simple side-loop.

Links used in this project:

	Link 047	wrapped long loop link
	Link 051	simple side-loop hook
	Link 073	jump ring
	Link 152	turn-back midwire-spiral link
	Link 156	spiral heart link
	Link 267	coil-end bead dangle link

Supplies needed for this project:

- 12-, 18- & 26-gauge wire
- 8 3mm black seed beads
- 2 6mm black crow roller beads
- 7 4mm black spacer beads
- 2 4mm spacer beads

4 Wire-wrap this link with 26-gauge wire working five loose random coils through the center hole. Add three 3mm seed beads to the wrapping-wire. Continue wire-wrapping for five more random coils. Clip and crimp the wrapping-wire.

5 Create one Link 156 open-eyelet heart link using 12-gauge wire. Cut an 8" length of wire. Grip the end of the working wire in your round-nose pliers and roll a 2-turn spiral. Slide one 4mm copper spacer bead, three 4mm black spacer beads, and one 4mm copper spacer bead onto the working wire. Repeat the spiral step for the opposite side of the working wire. Slide the beads toward one of the spiral ends. Grip the working wire between the two spirals at the center point in your round-nose pliers. Create a U-bend in the working wire that allows the sides of the spirals to touch.

6 Using 12-gauge wire, create one 1" (25mm)-long Link 051 hook.

7 Create eleven ¼" (6mm)-wide Link 073s using 12-gauge wire.

8 Join the links of the chain using one ¼" (6mm)-wide 12-gauge wire Link 073 to connect each link. Join five Link 047s. Join the Link 152. Add five Link 047s to the chain. End the chain by adding the one Link 051.

9 Cut two 12" (305mm) lengths of 26-gauge wire. Wire-wrap the two Link 047s that connect on either side of the Link 152. Work six tightly packed coils on one arm of the long U-bend. Add one 3mm seed bead to the wire and place it between the U-bend arms. Wrap six tightly packed coils on the opposite arm of the link. Clip and crimp the wire.

10 Create five ¼" (6mm)-wide links 073s using 18-gauge wire. Thread one jump ring through each spiral hole of Link 156. Join these two rings with the third jump ring. Use the last jump ring to join the Link 156 to the Link 152. Set the fifth jump ring aside.

11 Create three Link 267 using 26-gauge wire and one 3mm seed bead for each link. Use the remaining ¼" (6mm)-wide 18-gauge wire jump ring to join these three bead links to the same simple side-loop of the Link 152 to which you previously joined the Link 156.

EARRINGS

1 Create two Link 156s using 12-gauge wire as instructed for the necklace. For each earring, slide one 4mm black spacer bead, one 6mm black crow roller, and one 4mm black spacer bead onto the working wire after the first spiral is created.

2 Create two Link 051s using 18- or 20-gauge wire. Join the earring wires to the Link 156s with the simple side-loops of the earring wires.

Blue Denim Dreams

NECKLACE, BRACELET, AND EARRINGS SET

This eclectic *Blue Denim Dreams* necklace, bracelet, and earring set gives you a chance to sample many varieties of link styles. The repetition of blue glass beads holds these individual projects together as a set.

Supplies needed for necklace:

- 12-gauge wire
- 18-gauge wire
- 2 10mm turquoise glass round beads
- 2 10mm oval clear glass lampwork beads
- 1 10mm oval dark blue lampwork bead
- 1 24mm x 14mm tube lampwork bead
- 4 4mm medium blue round beads
- 1 8mm light blue round bead
- 1 8mm light blue lampwork bead
- 1 14mm square dark blue bead
- 2 12mm oval light blue glass beads

NECKLACE FOCAL POINT CHAIN

1 Create two Link 235s using 4" (102mm) of 12-gauge wire each. Begin the link with a right-angle bend ½" (13mm) from the end of the working wire with your bent-nose pliers. The right-angle bends in this link fall closer to a 60° angle to create the triangle shape. Create a second right-angle bend ½" (13mm) from the first. Create a right-angle bend ¾" (19mm) from the second. The fourth right-angle bend is worked ¾" (19mm) from the third. Grip the working wire ⅜" (10mm) from the last right-angle bend in your round-nose pliers and create a U-bend hairpin turn. Clip the working wire to 1½" (38mm) from the U-bend turn and roll the end of the working wire into a simple side-loop.

2 Create one Link 141 using 12-gauge wire and one 24mm-by-14mm tube lampwork bead. The link starts with an 8" (203mm) length of wire. Slide the bead onto the wire, moving it to the center point of the wire. Grip the working wire at one side of the bead in your round-nose pliers and roll the wire into a U-bend hairpin turn. Grip the working wire ½" (13mm) from the first U-bend hairpin turn and create a second U-bend hairpin. Clip the working wire to 2" (53mm) long. Grip the end of the working wire in your round-nose pliers and roll the wire into a spiral. Stop the spiral ½" (13mm) from the last U-bend hairpin turn. Repeat these steps for the second side of the working wire. Compress the hairpin links so they sit tightly on top of the tube lampwork bead.

Links used in this necklace:

	Link 018	1-bead simple side-loop link
	Link 023	long simple straight-loop link
	Link 036	large bead wrapped straight-loop link
	Link 043	coil link
	Link 050	long horseshoe link
	Link 051	simple side-loop hook
	Link 063	long-backed simple side-loop earring wire
	Link 073	jump ring
	Link 141	hairpin bead link
	Link 185	turn-back loop spiral link
	Link 212	2½-turn-spiral double-raindrop hairpin turn link
	Link 235	triangle raindrop hairpin link
	Link 322	compressed hairpin spiral bead link

3 Create two ¼" (6mm)-wide Link 073s using 12-gauge wire. Use one Link 073 to join the Link 235s through the bottom right-angle bend to the spiral holes of the Link 141.

4 Create one Link 023 using 4" (102mm) of 12-gauge wire and three 10mm oval glass beads. Create a simple straight-loop in one end of the wire. Slide the three oval beads onto the wire. Create a simple straight-loop at the opposite end of the working wire. Gently hold the end simple side-loops of this link and curve the center wire section into a half-circle.

5 Create two ¼" (6mm)-wide Link 073s using 12-gauge wire. Join the Link 023 to the Link 235s through their inside triangles.

6 Using 18-gauge wire, create one Link 043 that is ⅛"-wide-by-3"-long (3mm by 76mm). Hold the ends of the coil and stretch it to measure 5" (127mm) long.

7 Starting with 8" (203mm) of 12-gauge wire, create one Link 023. Create a simple straight-loop in one end of the working wire. Slide the stretched Link 043 onto the working wire. Create a simple straight-loop at the end of the coil in the working wire. Clip the excess wire from the simple straight-loop. Curve the link

8 Create two ¼" (6mm)-wide Link 073s using 12-gauge wire. Use the Link 073s to join the Link 023 to the Link 235s through the tight U-bends next to the simple side-loops of the triangle links.

9 Create two Link 036s using 12-gauge wire and one 10mm turquoise glass bead for each.

10 Create two ¼" (6mm)-wide Link 073s using 12-gauge wire and join the Link 036s to the Link 235s through the simple side-loop at the end of the triangle links.

11 Create a chain of fourteen 1¼" (32mm) Link 023s using 12-gauge wire joined with one ¼" (6mm)-wide Link 073 made from 12-gauge wire between each link.

12 Create two ¼" (6mm)-wide Link 073s using 12-gauge wire. Join the Link 023 chain ends to the focal point chain through the end-wrapped straight-loop of the last Link 036. The finished necklace measures 26" (660mm) long.

BRACELET

1 Create one Link 051 using 12-gauge wire.

2 Using 8" (203mm) of wire, create one Link 185 using 12-gauge wire. Create a 3-turn spiral in the end of the wire. Roll the working wire into a turn-back loop. Hold the spiral in your hand and bend the working wire from the turn-back loop under the spiral to the opposite side of the link. Create a simple side-loop. Clip the excess wire.

3 Create one Link 212 using 10" (254mm) of 12-gauge wire. Add three 4mm round glass beads to the outer raindrop wire as you make this link. Create one Link 212 using one 4mm round glass bead to the outer raindrop.

4 Create one Link 018 using 12-gauge wire and one 14mm square bead.

5 Create one Link 018 using 12-gauge wire and one 8mm round bead.

6 Create one Link 141 using 8" (203mm) 12-gauge wire and one 8mm lampwork bead.

7 Create seven ¼" (6mm)-wide Link 073s using 12-gauge wire. Join the links to the bracelet using one Link 073 between each link in the following order: one Link 051, one Link 185, one Link 212, one Link 018, one Link 141, one Link 018 and end with one Link 212. Add the last Link 073 to the U-bend of the last Link 212. The finished bracelet measures 8" (203mm) long.

EARRINGS

1 Create two Link 023s using 12-gauge wire and one 12mm oval bead each. The link measures 1½" (38mm) long.

2 Starting with 4" (102mm) of 12-gauge wire, create two Link 050s. Create a simple straight-loop on both ends of the wire. Roll the center point of the wire around a large 1" (25mm)-wide form to create a half-circle bend in the link. Compress the simple straight-loop area of these links so the loops are within ¼" (6mm) of each other.

3 Create two ¼" (6mm)-wide Link 073s using 12-gauge wire.

4 Place one simple straight-loop of one Link 023 between the simple straight-loops of one Link 050. Thread one ¼" (6mm)-wide Link 073 through all three simple straight-loops.

5 Starting with 4" (102mm) of 18- or 20-gauge wire, create one Link 063. Create a small tight U-bend in one end of the wire. The U-bend will latch to the back wire of the earring wire loop. Create a right-angle bend ⅛" (3mm) from the tight U-bend. Create a second U-bend ¼" (6mm) from the first. This second U-bend will hold the jump ring of the earring bead dangle. Place the working wire against a medium-sized ½" (13mm)-wide form and roll the wire into a half-circle. Clip the end of the working wire 1" (25mm) from the half-circle bend. Create a gentle curve in this back earring wire. Join the bead dangle to the earring wire by threading the jump ring through the second U-bend of the earring wires. Each earring measures 1¾" (44mm) long from the earring wire bend.

sets

EASY & ELEGANT **beaded copper** JEWELRY

Gentle Touch & Gentle Touch S-Link

Links used in this project:

	Link 033	wrapped straight-loop link
	Link 036	large bead wrapped straight-loop link
	Link 038	3-bead wrapped straight-loop link
	Link 053	wrapped straight-loop hook
	Link 073	jump ring
	Link 306	S-shaped wrapped-bead link

Supplies used in this project:
- 18- & 26-gauge wire

Beads for *Gentle Touch* Necklace:
- 33 3mm lavender marbled beads
- 11 3mm oval gray-lavender beads

Beads for *Gentle Touch S-Link* Necklace:
- 36 3mm lavender marbled beads
- 10 3mm oval gray-lavender beads

Beads for *Gentle Touch* Earrings:
- 6 3mm lavender marbled beads

NECKLACE WITH ALTERNATE AND MATCHING EARRINGS

How you plan the bead layout for a simple wrapped straight-loop link necklace can dramatically change the finished look of the project. *Gentle Touch* and *Gentle Touch S-Link* use the same link and the same beads; the only change between these two necklace chains is the bead placement on the links. Both necklaces are simple beginner designs.

REGULAR NECKLACE

1 Working with 26-gauge wire, create eleven Link 038s using three 3mm lavender marbled beads for each. Create eleven Link 036s using one 3mm gray-lavender oval bead for each link. Using 26-gauge wire, create a ³⁄₁₆"-wide-by-3"-long (10mm by 76mm) coil. (A number 4 to 6 knitting needle works well for this size coil.) Cut the coil into Link 073s. Join the links of the chain using one Link 073 between each Link 038, alternating one Link 038 and one Link 036. Join the last link of the chain to the first using a Link 073. The finished necklace measures 25" (635mm).

S-LINK NECKLACE

Working with 18-gauge wire:

1 Create a series of Link 036-038s using 3mm lavender marbled beads and 26-gauge wire as follows: two five-bead links, two four-bead links, two three-bead links, two two-bead links, and two one-bead links. Make ten one-bead links with the gray beads.

2 Create one Link 033 and one Link 053, both using 18-gauge wire.

3 Create a ³⁄₁₆"–wide-by-3"-long (10mm by 76mm) coil Link 043 using 18-gauge wire. Cut this coil into Link 073s.

4 On your work table, lay out the two side chains by placing the links with one five-bead, one four-bead, one three-bead, one-two-bead, and one one-bead links. Add one gray 1-bead link at the beginning of each layout. Add one gray 1-bead link between each multiple bead link. End each lavender chain with one 1-bead link. There are a total of ten links per chain. Add Link 033 to one chain end and Link 053 to the second chain end. Join the links of each chain using one Link 073.

5 To create a Link 306, cut 7" (178mm) of 18-gauge wire. Grip the end of the working wire in your round-nose pliers and roll the end into a simple side-loop. Place the simple side-loop against a medium-sized 1" (25mm)-wide form as the barrel of a marking pen. Roll the wire into one-half of a circle. Remove the wire from the form, turn the working wire over, and again using the form, roll the working wire into a second half circle that bends in the opposite direction as the first. This gives the link the S-shape. Grip the working wire in your round-nose pliers at the end of the second half circle and roll the wire into a simple side-loop. Clip the excess wire.

6 Cut an 18" (457mm) length of 26-gauge wire for wire-wrapping. Create seven tightly packed coils in the center of one of the half-circle areas of the S-shaped link. Add one 3mm marbled bead to the wrapping-wire. Wrap the wire into three tightly packed coils around the link wire. Continue adding one marbled bead to the wrapping-wire

and securing it to the link wire with three tightly packed coils five more times. Add one more marbled bead for a total of six wrapped beads on this S-shaped link. End the wrapping-wire with seven tightly packed coils. Clip the excess wrapping-wire and crimp it tightly.

7 Join the two side neck chains, on the five marbled bead link ends, to the simple side-loops of the Link 306 using one jump ring for each side. This finished necklace measures 26" (660mm) long.

EARRINGS

1 For each earring, create one Link 306 following the instructions in *Gentle Touch S-Link* necklace using a ½" (38mm) wide form to create the S-bends and creating those bends 1½" (38mm) from the end of the working wires. Add a simple side-loop to each end of the S-bend curve.

2 Cut a 20" (508mm) length of 26-gauge wire for wrapping. Wrap the wire five times around the S-shaped link ¼" (6mm) from the first simple side-loop. Add one 3mm bead. Wrap the wire one time around the link. Add the remaining two beads in the same manner. Finish the wrapping with fifteen loosely spaced wraps. Clip and crimp the wire.

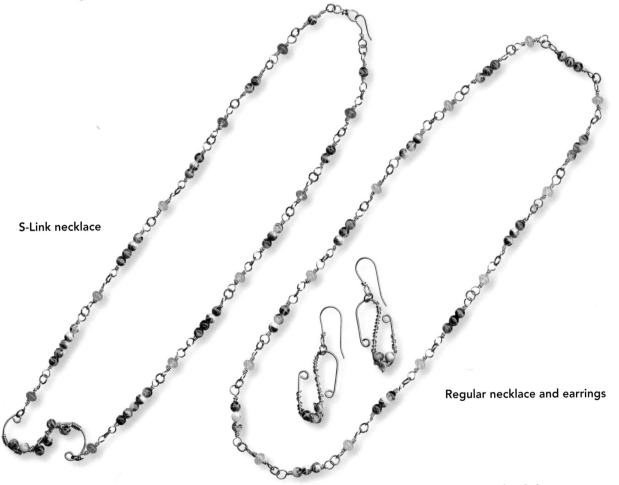

S-Link necklace

Regular necklace and earrings

EASY & ELEGANT **beaded copper** JEWELRY

Links used in this project:

	Link 023	long simple straight-loop link
	Link 024	1-bead simple straight-loop link
	Link 026	3-bead simple straight-loop link
	Link 033	wrapped straight-loop link
	Link 043	coil link
	Link 049	horseshoe bead link
	Link 051	simple side-loop hook
	Link 052	wrapped straight-loop hook
	Link 073	jump ring
	Link 185	turn-back loop spiral link
	Link 265	crimped-end bead dangles

Love's Reflection

NECKLACE, BRACELET, AND EARRING SET HIGHLIGHTS SPIRAL LINKS

A large abalone shell heart is suspended by a coil-end horseshoe link from a simple side-loop link in *Love's Reflection.* Blue green porcelain beads add the color accents to this necklace, bracelet, and earring set. The necklace is 18" (457mm) long, the bracelet 7¼"(184mm) long, and the earrings 3" (76) long.

Supplies used in this project:
- 16-, 20- & 26-gauge wire
- 8 12mm porcelain round beads
- 8 6mm porcelain round beads
- 1 50mm abalone heart

FOCAL-POINT CHAIN

1 Create one ¼" (6mm)-wide Link 073 using 16-gauge wire and thread it through the hole in the top of the abalone shell heart bead.

2 Cut a 4" (102mm) length of 16-gauge wire. Grip the center of the wire in your round-nose pliers and bend the wire into an open U-bend. Place the working wire sides against a small ¼" (6mm)-wide form with the U-bend area ¼" (6mm) below the form. Roll the two end wires around the form for five full turns. Clip the excess wire from both sides at the ends of the coils. This creates a coil-ended Link 049.

3 Join the Link 073 attached to the abalone shell heart bead to the center U-bend of the Link 049.

4 Cut a 2½" (64mm)-long length of 16-gauge wire. Slide the wire through the center of the two coils of the Link 049. Grip the ends of this wire in your round-nose pliers and create a simple side-loop on each end of the wire, both facing in the same direction.

5 Create two Link 185s using a 10" (254mm) length of 16-gauge wire and a 4½-turn center spiral. Cut a 10" (254mm) length of 26-gauge wire. Wrap the spiral hole of this link with ten tightly packed coil wraps. Clip and crimp the wrapping-wire.

6 Create two Link 026s using 16-gauge wire, adding one 6mm porcelain bead, one 12mm porcelain bead, and one 6mm porcelain bead, in that order, to each.

7 Create two long Link 023s using 6" (152mm) of 16-gauge wire each.

8 Using 16-gauge wire, create one Link 033 that will act as your hook eye.

9 Create one Link 051 using 16-gauge wire.

10 Create a ¼"-wide-by-2"-long (6mm by 51mm) Link 043 using 16-gauge wire. Cut the coil into Link 073s.

11 Join the necklace links using one Link 073 for each connection in the following order: one Link 033, one 6" (152mm) long Link 023, one Link 026, one Link 185, the Link 049 with the abalone heart bead, one Link 185, one Link 026, one 6" (152mm) long Link 023, and one Link 051.

BRACELET

1 Create four Link 026s using 16-gauge wire and one 12mm porcelain bead for each.

2 Create one 2" (51mm)-long Link 023 using 16-gauge wire.

3 Create one Link 051 using 16-gauge wire.

4 Join the links to the bracelet using one Link 073 for each connection, joining first the four Link 026s, adding the one 2"-long (51mm) Link 023, and ending with the Link 051.

EARRINGS

1 Work one earring at a time. Create one Link 052 using 20-gauge wire.

2 Using 16-gauge wire, create three Link 024s that are 1" (25mm) long, 1¼" (32mm) long, and 1½" (38mm) long.

3 Using 16-gauge wire, create three Link 265s. Use one 6mm porcelain bead and one 12mm porcelain bead for each.

4 Using one ¼" (6mm)-wide Link 073 created from 16-gauge wire, connect one Link 265 6mm bead link to the 1½" (38mm)-long Link 024, one Link 265 6mm bead link to the 1¼" (32mm)-long Link 024, and the Link 265 12mm bead link to the 1" (25mm)-long Link 024.

5 Join all three Link 024s using one ¼"-wide Link 073. Join the Link 024 to the Link 052.

6 Repeat steps for the second earring.

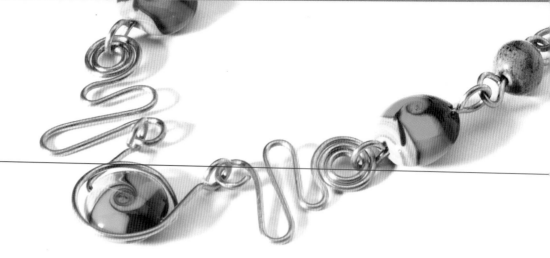

Trip Around the World

Trip Around the World is a 16" (406mm) modern-style necklace using two tapered-hairpin and one beaded horseshoe links to drop the center bead of the necklace below the line of the necklace chain. The move makes the necklace an attractive piece suitable for all types of occasions.

This necklace is worked from the center focal point link towards the hook-and-eye ends.

CENTER FOCAL POINT LINK

1 Create one Link 049 horseshoe bead link with a 10" (254mm) length of 16-gauge wire. Slide one 16mm lampwork disc bead onto the wire, moving it to the center point of the wire. Hold the bead in one hand. With the other hand, gently bend the wire into a right-angle bend at the base of the bead. Bend the working wire on the second side of the bead into a right-angle bend so that both wires point in the same direction. Still holding the bead, grip one working wire and roll the wire around the outside edge of the bead for one full turn. This brings the working wire back to its starting point. Grip this working wire ½" (13mm) from the bead in your bent-nose pliers and create a right-angle bend. Transfer the bend to your round-nose pliers and roll the wire into a simple-straight-loop. Grip the remaining working wire ½" (13mm) from the bead in your bent-nose pliers and bend it into a right-angle bend. Transfer this bend to your round-nose pliers and roll the wire into a simple-straight-loop. Clip the excess wire from both simple straight-loops. The finished link is 1¼" long by 1" wide (32mm by 25mm).

Links used in this project:

	Link 017	long simple-side-loop link
	Link 018	1-bead simple side-loop link
	Link 049	horseshoe bead link
	Link 051	simple side-loop hook
	Link 053	wrapped straight-loop hook
	Link 073	jump ring
	Link 148	2½-turn spiral 4-turn hairpin link

Supplies needed for this project:

- 16- & 18-gauge wire
- 5 16mm lampwork disc beads
- 2 8mm porcelain beads
- 2 6mm porcelain beads

SIDE NECKLACE CHAINS

1 Using 16-gauge wire, create two Link 148s. This hairpin uses three U-bend hairpin turns with a 2½-turn spiral. Join these links to the simple straight-loops of the Link 049 through their simple side-loops. One Link 148 link is added to each side of the center focal-point link.

2 Create two Link 018s using one 16mm lampwork disc bead for each. Add the links to the end of the center chain by threading the simple side-loop through the spiral hole in the Link 148.

3 Create two Link 018s using one 8mm porcelain bead for each link. Add one of the links to the end of the center chain.

4 Create two Link 018s using one 6mm porcelain bead for each. Add one of these links to each end of the center chain. The center chain measures 8½" (216mm) long.

LONG SIMPLE SIDE-LOOP LINKS

1 Cut two 4¼" (108mm) lengths of 16-gauge wire to create two Link 017s. With your round-nose pliers, create a simple side-loop in each end of the wire so the loops fall on the same side of the wire. Hold the long link in one hand and, with the thumb on the second hand, gently press your thumb pad along the inside (loop side) of the link wire to give it a gentle curve. Create two ¼" (6mm)-wide Link 073s. Use one Link 073 to connect the Link 017 to the ends of the center chain, one on each side.

2 Working on one end of the chain, create three ¼" (6mm)-wide Link 073s. Add the Link 073s to the end of the chain. Create one large ½" (13mm) wide Link 073 and add it to the end of the chain. This large Link 073 becomes the hook eye for this necklace.

3 Working on the opposite end of the chain, create three ¼" (6mm)-wide Link 073s. Add the Link 073s to the end of the chain. Create one large, 1¼" (32mm)-long Link 051 and add it to the end of the chain.

EARRINGS

1 Working with 16-gauge wire, create a Link 148. Make the link by creating a simple straight-loop at the end of the wire. Slide one 16mm lampwork disc bead onto the working wire. Using your fingers, bend the working wire at the base of the lampwork bead into a right-angle bend. With your round-nose pliers, create the first hairpin U-bend ½" (13mm) from the base of the bead. The second hairpin is worked 1" (25mm) from the first, and the third 1" (25mm) from the second. Clip the working wire to a measurement of 3" (76mm). Grip the end of the working wire in your round-nose pliers and roll the end into a simple side-loop. Transfer the loop to your bent-nose pliers and continue rolling the loop into a spiral until the spiral is centered under the link.

2 Repeat this link for the second earring.

3 Using either 18- or 20-gauge wire, create two Link 053s. Add one of these to each Link 148 through the simple-straight-loop at the top of the link.

Winter Waves

NECKLACE AND EARRINGS

Hairpin turn links and spiral end hairpin links create the wave effect of this quick design. Before the evening movie is over, you will be wearing your version of *Winter Waves*, a 20½" (521mm)-long necklace with matching earrings.

1 Create four Link 147s. Begin with 9" (229mm) of wire and create a 2-turn spiral in the end of the wire. Add three hairpin U-bend turns in a tapered manner, each U-bend made slightly closer to the last with the first U-bend 1" (26mm) from the spiral. End this link with a simple side-loop.

2 Beginning with 12" (305mm) of wire, create one Link 151. This link begins with a 2-turn spiral. Add three U-bend hairpin turns ½", 1", and ½" (13mm, 25mm, and 13mm) apart. Clip the working wire 2½" (64mm) from the last U-bend turn to end the link with a 2-turn spiral.

3 Create four Link 024s using one 8mm foil glass bead for each.

4 Create one ¼"-wide-by-2" long (6mm by 51mm) Link 043. Cut the coil into Link 073s.

5 Join the links into the focal-point chain using one Link 073 for each connection in the following order: one Link 147, one Link 024, one Link 147, one Link 024, one Link 151, one Link 024, one Link 147, one Link 024, and end with one Link 147.

6 Cut two 10" (254mm) lengths of 2mm black rattail cord. Work one side at a time. Thread one end of the rattail cord through the center hole of the spiral in the Link 147 at the end of the chain. Bring the two ends of the cord together to make two even lengths. Create one ¼" (6mm)-wide Link 043 that has ten full turns. Slide both ends of the rattail cord through the center of the coil. Slide the coil to within 1" (25mm) of the spiral end of the chain. Crimp both end loops of the coil to secure the rattail cords. Repeat these steps for the second rattail cord side.

7 Create one ¼" (6mm)-wide-by-ten-full-turns-long Link 043. Slide one coil over the two ends of the rattail cord on one side of the necklace. Crimp the bottom inside loop of the coil to secure the rattail cord. Bend the top loop of the coil into a connecting loop using your bent-nose pliers. Repeat these steps for the second rattail cord side.

8 Create one Link 033. Create one ¼"-wide (6mm) Link 073. Use the Link 073 to connect the Link 033 to the connecting loop on one of the end Link 043s. This link becomes the hook eye of the necklace.

9 Create one Link 052. Create one ¼" (6mm)-wide Link 073. Use the Link 073 to connect the Link 052 to the connecting loop on one of the end Link 043s.

Links used in this project:

	Link 024	1-bead simple straight-loop link
	Link 033	wrapped straight-loop link
	Link 043	coil link
	Link 051	simple side-loop hook
	Link 052	wrapped straight-loop hook
	Link 073	jump ring
	Link 147	3½-turn spiral 3-turn hairpin link
	Link 151	double-spiral 5-bend hairpin link

Supplies needed for this project:
- 18-gauge wire
- 6 8mm foil glass beads
- 20" (508mm) 2mm black rattail cord

EARRINGS

1 Create two Link 147s following the instructions in step one for the *Winter Wave* necklace.

2 Create two Link 024s using one 8mm foil glass bead each. Interlock the wrapped straight-loop of this link through the center hole of the Link 147's spiral.

3 Create two Link 051s. Join these links to the simple side-loops of the Link 147s.

Professional Woman's Necklace Set

Both easy to make and classic to wear, the *Professional Woman's Necklace Set* is designed to easily mix and match four basic necklace chains with twelve different link styles as focal point dangles. Each of the large links has an added extra-large split ring at the top of the link that can be threaded onto any of the chains.

Before you begin this project, read through the step-by-step instructions for each of the individual links. Take time to create a few practice links to make yourself comfortable with the bending pattern, to familiarize yourself with the method used to attach the link to the chain, and to check the finished size of the link in relationship to the gauge of your wire.

Links used in this project:

	Link 015	simple side-loop link
	Link 018	1-bead simple side-loop link
	Link 036	large bead wrapped straight-loop link
	Link 038	3-bead wrapped straight-loop link
	Link 039	double wire-wrapped straight-loop link
	Link 047	wrapped long loop link
	Link 051	simple side-loop hook
	Link 052	wrapped straight-loop hook
	Link 057	double-wire hook link
	Link 074	split ring
	Link 075	open-eyelet spiral hoop link
	Link 076	medium wire-beaded hoop link
	Link 077	medium wire-beaded hoop link
	Link 152	turn-back midwire-spiral link
	Link 155	open-heart link
	Link 159	open-heart wire bead-wrapped link
	Link 165	open hairpin-bend center open-eyelet link
	Link 170	wire-wrapped double-circle eyelet link
	Link 199	2½-turn-spiral raindrop link
	Link 235	triangle raindrop hairpin link
	Link 265	crimped-end bead dangles
	Link 272	wrapped-donut straight-loop-dangle link
	Link 286	centered spiral-end bead link

As you work on the focal-point dangles for this mix-and-match set, check the practice links you have created in learning how to make bent-wire links. Many of the links can have small bead dangles added, wire-wrapped accents worked, or wire-wrapped beads attached to the link to add to your *Professional Woman's* set.

Simple Side-Loop Necklace

Long Loop Necklace

Wrapped-Loop Bead Links Chain

Hand-Wrapped Necklace

NECKLACE 1: SIMPLE SIDE-LOOP NECKLACE

Measures 14¾" (375mm). Worked in 18-gauge wire.

1 This simple side-loop necklace is worked from the center of the chain out toward the ends. You can easily increase the size of this necklace by adding either simple side-loop links or simple side-loop bead links to both sides of the necklace.

2 This necklace begins with a center chain of five ½" (13mm)-wide Link 015s. Create two Link 018s using 8mm red round glass beads. Add one each to the ends of the necklace chain. Create two chains of thirteen ½" (13mm)-wide Link 015s. Add one chain each to the ends of the necklace chain. Create one Link 051 and add it to one end of the chain.

NECKLACE 2: LONG LOOP NECKLACE

Measures 14¾" (375mm). Worked in 18-gauge wire.

1 This simple chain is worked using 1⅝" (41mm)-long wrapped-loop link. As you create the chain, remember to thread the simple loop on one end of the link into the loop of the last link on the chain before you wrap the loops on the working link.

2 Create a chain of twenty-four Link 047s. Create one Link 052 and interlock the wrapped loop of the hook into the end of the chain.

NECKLACE 3: WRAPPED-LOOP BEAD LINKS CHAIN

Measures 15" (381mm) long. Worked in 18-gauge wire.

1 This beaded chain uses fourteen 10mm-by-6mm frosted oval glass beads and one 10mm-by-6mm frosted bead for the Link 057 hook. Chose a bead color that will be complementary to your beaded dangles.

2 Create a chain of fourteen 1" (25mm)-long Link 036s using one frosted bead for each link. Remember to interlock the new link to the chain while it is in the simple straight-loop stage.

3 Create one Link 057 by cutting an 8" (203mm) length of wire. With your bent-nose pliers, create a right-angle bend to the working wire 1½" (39mm) from the end. Using your round-nose pliers, roll the working wire into a simple side-loop. Interlock the simple side-loop to the end of the chain and wrap the working wire around the base of the simple side-loop two to three times.

4 Add one frosted bead to the working wire. With your round-nose pliers, grip the working wire 1¼" above the bead—work as closely to the tips of the pliers as possible. Bend the wire into a tight U-bend. With your bent-nose pliers, crimp the U-bend tightly to create the double-wire portion of the hook.

5 Grip the double wire in your bent-nose pliers at the top of the bead. Holding the double wires in your pliers, use your fingers to roll the working wire around the bead to wire-wrap it. Roll the working wire to the base of the bead and wrap the wire around the wrapped loop. Clip the excess wire using your flush wire cutters. Grip the double wire area of this link in your round-nose pliers and roll the double wire into the hook shape.

NECKLACE 4: HAND-WRAPPED NECKLACE

Measures 15½" (394mm). Worked in 18-gauge wire.

1 This hand-wrapped link necklace is worked from the center out toward the ends. Remember to interlock both styles of links while the working link is still in the simple side-loop stage.

2 Create a center chain of five 1" (25mm)-long Link 039s. Work one ½" (13mm)-long Link 047 and one Link 039 to each end of the chain twice. Add five Link 047s to each end of the chain. Finish the chain by creating one Link 052 worked into one end of the chain.

FOCAL-POINT DANGLES:

Any of your practice links can become focal-point dangles for this *Professional Woman's* set of necklaces.

For each dangle, create a large Link 074 worked over a ½" (13mm)-wide marking pen. Thread the Link 074 onto the decorative link, either through the simple side-loop or wrapped-loop at the top of the link, or through an outside spiral arm of the link. A 26-gauge wire-wrapping can be added to the Link 074 to cover the cut ends of the coil.

DANGLE 1

1 Our first focal-point dangle was created following the step-by-step instructions for Link 170. This sample was worked using 18-gauge wire for the open-eyelet link and 26-gauge wire for the wire-wrapping at the center of the open-eyelet. The finished dangle measures 2" (51mm) long and 1" (25mm) wide.

DANGLE 2

1 This medium hoop link has a wire-wrapped 6mm green glass bead. It was worked following the step-by-step instructions for links 075, 076, and 077. The basic hoop link was worked in 18-gauge wire with a 26-gauge wire-wrapping. The finished dangle measures 1½" (38mm) long.

DANGLE 3

1 This heart-beaded triangle link is a variation of Link 235.

2 Cut a 12" (305mm) length of 18-gauge wire. Roll a simple side-loop in the end of the wire using your round-nose pliers. With your bent-nose pliers, create a right-angle bend ¼" (6mm) from the simple side-loop. Make a second right-angle bend ¾" (19mm) from the first. The third right-angle bend falls 1" (25mm) from the second and the fourth. The last right-angle bend of the triangle is worked 1" (25mm) from the third. Measure 1⅛" (29mm) from the last right-angle bend and create a small bend in the wire. The bend will hold the bead above the triangle area.

3 Add a 12mm-by-16mm lampwork heart bead to the working wire. Create a wrapped straight-loop above the bead.

4 Cut a 15" (381mm) length of 26-gauge wire. Wire-wrap ten tightly packed coils to the outer non-beaded leg of the triangle raindrop. Add one 4mm-to-6mm glass bead to the wrapping-wire. Bring the wrapping-wire across to the opposite side on the triangle link. Wrap three to four tightly coiled wraps, catching both the beaded wire and triangle wire. Clip and crimp the wrapping-wire. The finished dangle measures 2" (51mm) long.

DANGLE 4

1 This large open-eyelet heart was worked following the instructions for Link 155. It was created with 18-gauge wire for the link and 26-gauge wire for the center eyelet wire-wrap. A wire-wrapped bead could easily be added to either one side of open-eyelets or to the V-shape area below the eyelet spirals. The finished dangle measures 1¾" (44mm) wide by 1" (25mm) high.

DANGLE 5

1 Link 159 is worked using 18-gauge wire for the link and 26-gauge wire for the wire-wrapping steps. A 12mm-by-6mm tube bead was added to the wire-wrap. The finished dangle measures 1½" (38mm) wide by 1" (25mm) high.

DANGLE 6

1 Dangle 6 is made following the step-by-step instructions for Link 165. Using 18-gauge wire, create an open-eyelet link with one full-turn spiral for one side of the link and a simple side-loop for the second side. A 26-gauge wire-wrapping is added between the two simple side-loops of this link.

2 Create one Link 038 using one 6mm round glass bead, one 14mm bead, and one 6mm bead, working the wrapped straight-loop of the link into the U-bend of the open-eyelet link.

DANGLE 7

1 This large foil-lined bead dangle was worked as a variation of the step-by-step instructions for Link 286. The large flat disc foil bead measures 35mm in diameter.

2 Cut a 15" (381mm) length of 18-gauge wire. Create a wrapped straight-loop at the center point of the wire. Add the foil disc bead to the wire. Clip the excess wrapping-wire from the wrapped straight-loop to a length of 4" (102mm) and create an open-spiral. Stop the spiral 1" (25mm) from the wrapped loop.

3 Cut the wire at the bottom of the bead to 4" (102mm) long. Create an open-spiral that ends 1" (25mm) from the base of the bead.

4 Bend the top spiral wire toward the center of the foil bead. Bend the bottom spiral toward the center of the bead. Slide the outer ring of one spiral across the extra working wire of the other bead to interlock them. Use your fingers to tighten the spirals, using the excess working wire on both spirals until both spirals lie flat against the bead. You can add a drop of cyanoacrylate glue behind the spiral wires to secure them.

DANGLE 8

1 This simple donut with Link 272, adds a large zebra-striped bead to your dangle selection. The donut zebra bead measures 45mm in diameter. To create Dangle 8, cut an 8" (203mm) length of 18-gauge wire. Make a right-angle bend in the working wire 1½" (38mm) from the end. Transfer the bend to your round-nose pliers and create a simple side-loop. Use the excess wire from the side-loop to wrap the base of the loop two to three times. Clip the excess wire.

2 Hold the wrapped straight-loop above the donut bead. Bend the straight-loop slightly to center it over the bead. Thread the working wire through the donut hole and bend it around the bead hole to bring the working wire back to the wrapped straight-loop area of the link. Hold the wrapped straight-loop in one hand and wrap the donut hole wire around the base of the wrapped straight-loop two to three times. Wrap the wire from the bottom of the wrapped area toward the loop area. This step double-wraps the loop. Clip the excess wire from the wrapping with your flush wire cutters.

DANGLES 9 & 10

1 These two dangles were worked by following the step-by-step instructions for Link 075, 076, and 077. Please also refer to Link 170 for creating multiple graduated spirals.

2 By using different-sized forms for the open-eyelets, you can create a hoop of gradually widening spirals. Working with 18-gauge wire, cut a 15" (381mm) length. Grip the end of the wire in your round-nose pliers and roll a simple side-loop. Place the loop against the side of a small form, such as an ink pen barrel, and roll a full-circle spiral. Flatten the simple side-loop into the small spiral. Place the spiral against a medium-sized form, such as a marking pen, and roll the wire into the second full spiral. Flatten the spiral using your nylon-grip pliers. The third spiral is made around an extra-large form, such as a bottle cap or medicine jar lid. Flatten the spirals. With your round-nose pliers, roll a simple side-loop at the top of the spiral. Clip the excess wire using your flush wire cutters. For a fourth roll, select a slightly bigger object.

3 Add a wire-wrapping to this link using 26-gauge wire. Cut the wrapping-wire 8" (203mm) long. Wrap the wire at the top of the link near the outside simple side-loop, catching all inside spiral wires. A bead can easily be added to the wire-wrapping. The finished four-spiral hoop link measures 1½" (38mm) long.

DANGLE 11

1 This spiral raindrop link has four donut wrapped-bead dangles added to give the finished project a little touch of color. The beads are 8mm cat's eye beads.

2 Work this raindrop following the step-by-step instructions for Link 199 using 18-gauge wire. The finished link measures 2" (51mm) long.

3 Create four Link 272s using one glass bead per link following the step-by-step instructions for a donut-wrapped link in Dangle 8. One bead link is worked into the spiral hole and the remaining three bead links are worked in the U-bend area of Link 199.

DANGLE 12

1 This turn-back spiral dangle follows the step-by-step instructions for Link 152. This example is worked in 18-gauge wire and measures 1⅜" (35mm) when complete.

2 Create a Link 265 following the instructions for Link 265. Use 18-gauge wire and a 14mm-by-6mm rectangle glass bead.

3 Create two ⅜" (10mm)-wide Link 073s using 18-gauge wire. Thread one Link 073 through the top simple side-loop to the top center hole in the midwire-spiral. Thread the second Link 073 through the bottom simple side-loop and the lower-center hole in the midwire-spiral. Create one ¼" (6mm)-wide Link 073 using 18-gauge wire. Thread the Link 073 through the lower simple side-loop and the wrapped loop of the bead dangle. With the bead dangle, this focal-point pendant measures 2½" (64mm) long.

DANGLE 13

1 The last focal-point dangle for this set is a large open hoop created in 16-gauge wire following the step-by-step instructions for links 075 to 077. For this hoop, a 10" (254mm) length of wire was wrapped once around a large 2" (51mm)-diameter medicine bottle lid. Simple side-loops begin and end the hoop.

2 Wire-wrap one arm of the hoop at the simple side-loop with ten tightly packed coils using 26-gauge wire. Work three tightly packed coils going through the center of both simple side-loops. Work ten tightly packed coils on the opposite side of the simple side-loops on the hoop arm.

3 Cut a 10" (254mm) length of 26-gauge wire for wrapping. Work ten tightly packed coils along one side of the top simple side-loop, working toward that loop. Work three tightly packed coils through the loop and catch the full circle wire. Work ten tightly packed coils on the opposite side of the loop. Clip and crimp the excess wire from the wrapping-wire.

4 Create three Link 265s using the 12mm-to-14mm beads and 18-gauge wire. Create one ¼" (6mm) Link 073 using 18-gauge wire. Join the three bead dangles to the inside simple side-loop of the hoop link using the Link 073. The finished hoop link measures 2¼" (57mm) long.

Tip 12: Split Rings

Split rings are commonly used to connect bent-wire links to create a chain. They can also become part of your focal point as in the dangles used in the *Professional Woman's Necklace Set*. These split rings were worked over a ½" (13mm)-wide form then threaded onto the individual dangle link. A 26-gauge wire-wrapping adds a little sparkle to the oversized split ring. Working the rings over a large form allows plenty of space to slide your dangle onto the necklace chain.

Links used in this project:

	Link 056	wrapped straight-loop hook link
	Link 073	jump ring
	Link 074	split ring
	Link 266	simple loop-end bead dangle link
	Link 289	spiral bead dangle link
	Link 310	simple straight-loop spiral bead link

Supplies needed for this project:
- 20-gauge wire
- 6 6mm dark green jade beads (optional)
- 2 16mm flat disc fire agate beads (optional)
- 1 26mm flat disc fire agate bead (optional)

Aztec Maiden

Create this jump ring chain by joining multiple jump rings for each link. The 16½" (419mm) necklace is worked in three sections, joined by larger split rings to add variation to the chain. Use the chain alone for a strong, masculine design or add your favorite bead dangles to the center chain section.

1 Make a ¼"-wide-by-15"-long (6mm x 381mm)-long coil. (You may need more coil depending on how many jump rings you use for each link.) Cut the coil into Link 073 jump rings.

2 Create three separate chains using three jump rings per link. The two side chains use 18 links and measure 3½" (89mm) long. The center jump ring chain uses 38 links and measures 7" (178mm) long.

3 When creating multiple Link 073 chains, first create the chain using one Link 073 for each link until the chain is the desired length. Then return to the beginning of the chain and add one Link 073 to each link. Continue the process, adding one Link 073 at a time across the entire length, until you have the desired number of Link 073s per link. You can easily add up to five Link 073s per link.

4 Create two ⅜" (10mm)-wide Link 074s. Use these split rings to join the 3" (76mm)-long Link 073 chains to the ends of the 7" (178mm)-long Link 073 chain.

5 Create two ¼" (6mm)-wide Link 074s. Add these to the ends of the necklace. Create one ⅜" (10mm)-wide Link 074. Add the Link 074 to one end of the chain as the hook eye. Create one Link 056 to use at the other end of the chain as a hook.

6 If you are adding beads, create six Link 266s using one 6mm dark green jade bead for each. Create two Link 310s using one 16mm flat disc fire agate bead each. Create one Link 289 using the 26mm flat disc fire agate bead.

7 Create eight ¼" (6mm)-wide Link 073s. Use one Link 073 to connect each bead link to the center focal point chain. Complete this step by finding the center link on the chain and adding the 26mm agate bead link to it. Count three links to both sides of this bead link and add one 6mm jade bead link and one 16mm fire agate bead link. Count two links to both sides of these bead links and add two 6mm dark green bead links to these links.

Links used in this project:

	Link 036	large bead wrapped straight-loop link
	Link 039	double wire-wrapped straight-loop link
	Link 052	wrapped straight-loop hook

Supplies used in this project:

- 18- & 26-gauge wire
- 16" (406mm) 1/8" (3mm)-wide suede leather cord
- 2 14mm gold-foil-lined glass beads
- 2 16mm hexagon stone beads
- 1 12mm round stone bead
- 2 8mm hexagon stone beads
- 1 6mm stone bead

Ancient Temple

Ancient Temple's design uses seven wrapped straight-loops to create a chain, yet each link has a different look and texture because of the use of different bead styles and wire-wrapping. This simple project will be done before you know it, so plan to make several during your jewelry session.

1 Create one Link 039 using 9" (229mm) of 18-gauge wire and one 12mm round stone bead. Start this link with a wrapped straight-loop made 4" (102mm) from one end of the wire. Do not cut the excess wrapping-wire. Add one 12mm round bead to the wire. Grip the working wire 1¼" (32mm) from the first wrapped straight-loop and create a second wrapped straight-loop. Do not cut the excess wrapping-wire. Wrap the excess wire on both sides of the link around the working wire until the wraps meet the bead in the center of the link. Clip the excess wires.

2 Create two Link 036s using 18-gauge wire and one 14mm gold foil glass bead for each link, interlocking the wrapped straight-loops of these links to Link 039.

3 Create two Link 036s using 18-gauge wire and one 16mm hexagon stone bead for each link, interlocking the wrapped straight-loops of these links to the gold foil bead links. Cut two 12" (305mm) lengths of 26-gauge wire. Wire-wrap these bead links following the step-by-step instructions on page 142.

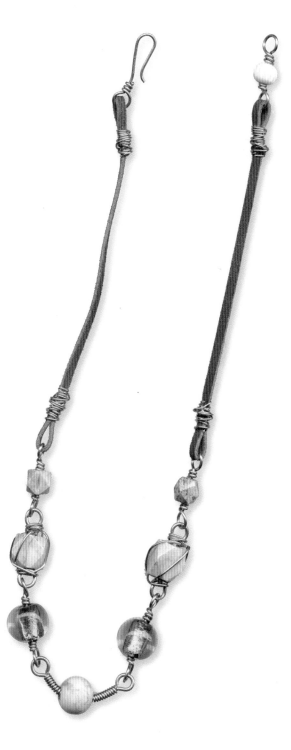

4 Create two Link 036s using 18-gauge wire and 8mm hexagon beads, interlocking these to the chain during the wrapped straight-loop construction.

5 Cut two 8" (203mm) lengths of ⅛" (3mm) suede leather cord. Work one side cord at a time. Thread one end of the leather cord through the end-wrapped straight-loop of one end of the 8mm hexagon bead Link 036. Fold the leather cording back on itself 1" (25mm). Cut a 12" (305mm) length of 26-gauge wire. Tightly wire-wrap the fold area of the leather cording with fifteen random coils. Clip and crimp the ends of the wrapping-wire to secure the cord.

6 Fold the remaining end of the leather cord back on itself 1" (25mm). Cut a 12" (305mm) length of 26-gauge wire and wire-wrap this area of the cord with fifteen random coils. Clip and crimp the ends of the wrapping-wire to secure the cord.

7 Create one Link 036 using 18-gauge wire and one 6mm stone bead, interlocking this link through one leather end loop.

9 Repeat the leather cord side steps for the second side of the necklace substituting one Link 052 for the Link 036.

Autumn Affair

Autumn Affair features two coil-covered coiled links that support a large fire agate heart bead. The finished necklace is 23" (584mm) long.

1 Using 15" (381mm) of 18-gauge wire and the 35mm heart bead, create one Link 290. Start this link with a wrapped straight-loop 6" (152mm) from the end of the wire. Bend the wire at the base of the loop into a right angle. Add the heart bead to the wire at the right-angle bend threading the working wire from the back of the bead, to the front. Clip this working wire to a 3" (76mm) length and roll the end into a 3-turn spiral, stopping the spiral ½" (13mm) from the hole. Curve the spiral slightly to bring it to one side of the heart bead.

2 Grip the long, unworked wire and wrap it one time around the heart, taking it to the back of the heart bead and then up to the wrapped straight-loop. Wrap the wire for a full second turn around the bead. Wrap this wire one time around the base of the wrapped straight-loop to lock the wire into place. Clip the wire to a 4" (102mm) length and roll the end into a 3-turn spiral, stopping the spiral 1" (25mm) from the wrapped straight-loop of the link. Thread this spiral under one of the wire-wraps, bringing it to the bottom side of the bead.

3 Create one ⅛"-wide-by-6"-long (3mm by 152mm) Link 043 using 26-gauge wire. Pull the coil apart slightly to allow some space between the loops. Cut a 9" (229mm) length of 18-gauge wire. Create a wrapped straight-loop in one end of the wire. Slide the coil onto the wire. Create a wrapped straight-loop using 18-gauge wire at the base of the coil. Place one wrapped straight-loop against a ¼" (6mm) form, such as a knitting needle, and roll the coil-covered link into a loose coil. Do not remove this link from the form.

4 Cut a 9" (229mm) length of 18-gauge wire. Secure the wire to the coil-covered Link 043 by wrapping the end of the wire at the base of one wrapped straight-loop for two to three tight turns. Coil the wire around the form, working the wire between the coil-covered wraps. Secure the remaining end of the wire to the opposite wrapped straight-loop with two to three tight turns. Clip the excess wire from the wrapping. Remove the link from the form.

5 Repeat the steps to create a second coil-covered wire-wrapped Link 043.

6 Create two Link 074s using 18-gauge wire to join the coil-covered Link 043s to the wrapped straight-loop of Link 290.

7 Cut two 16" (406mm) lengths of 2mm black rattail cord. Work one side of rattail cord at a time. Thread one end of the rattail cord through the end-wrapped straight-loop of the coil-covered wire-wrapped Link 043. Bring the ends of the rattail cord together to create two even lengths.

8 Create three ¼" (6mm)-wide Link 073s using 18-gauge wire. Slide the jump rings over both ends of the rattail cord and move them to the wrapped-straight-loop of the coil-covered Link 043 coil.

9 Create two ⅛"-wide-by-½"-long (2mm by 13mm) Link 043s using 18-gauge wire. Slide one coil over one end of the rattail cord and crimp the inside (bottom) loop of the coil to secure it to the cord. Repeat the

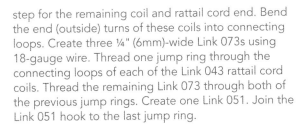

step for the remaining coil and rattail cord end. Bend the end (outside) turns of these coils into connecting loops. Create three ¼" (6mm)-wide Link 073s using 18-gauge wire. Thread one jump ring through the connecting loops of each of the Link 043 rattail cord coils. Thread the remaining Link 073 through both of the previous jump rings. Create one Link 051. Join the Link 051 hook to the last jump ring.

10 Repeat these steps for the second rattail cord side—substituting one Link 086 made with 18-gauge wire for the Link 051 hook.

Tip 13: Wrapping beads.

Add beads to a finished wire link by wire-wrapping them with fine, 24-gauge wire, through the loops of the bends or by wrapping along an open bend of the link.

Links used in this project:

	Link 035	long wrapped straight-loop link
	Link 043	coil link
	Link 051	simple side-loop hook
	Link 073	jump ring
	Link 074	split ring
	Link 086	3-turn spiral link
	Link 290	double-spiral bead dangle link

Supplies needed for this project:

- 18- & 26-gauge wire
- 32" (813mm) 2mm black rattail cord
- 1 35mm fire agate heart

Bold Statement

With its large coils and multiple spirals, *Bold Statement* is just that, providing an attractive adjustable-length necklace for casual wear. The necklace is adjustable in size, with a maximum of 24" (610mm).

Links used in this project:

	Link 043	coil link
	Link 073	jump ring
	Link 089	double 2-turn spiral link
	Link 135	double-hairpin link
	Link 304	open-cage link

Supplies needed for this project:

- 12-gauge wire
- 20" (508mm) 2mm black rattail cord

CREATING THE WIRE LINKS

1 Using a household wooden spoon with a ½" (13mm)-diameter handle, create a coil roll approximately 4" (102mm) long. From the coil, cut two sections nine turns long. Bend the end turns to create connection loops. Using your bent-nose pliers, pull the coils apart until the link measures 1½" (38mm) from connecting loop to connecting loop. You now have two Link 043s.

2 Bend two 1" (25mm)-long Link 089s.

3 Create two ½" (25mm)-high Link 304s that measure 1" (25mm) long.

4 Make one Link 135 hairpin that uses two spiral turns on one side and 2½ turns to the spiral on the second side that measures 1½" (38mm).

5 Create four ⅜" (10mm)-wide Link 073s.

6 Join the links by joining one Link 043, one Link 089, one Link 073, one Link 304, one Link 073, one Link 135, one Link 073, one Link 304, one Link 073, one Link 089, and ending with one Link 043. The wire link chain measures 8½" (216mm) long.

7 Cut a 20" (508mm) length of black 2mm rattail cord. Feed one end through the connecting loop on the end of the Link 043. Tie a simple-slide knot. Repeat this step with the second side of the rattail cord on the opposite end of the wire-link chain.

8 Make four Link 073s. Open the Link 073s and slide them over the turn-back area of the rattail cord. Close the links.

Caged Ruby

Caged Ruby features seven iridescent red beads inside of the ball-and-cage link. The necklace measures 17" (432mm) in length.

Links used in this project:

	Link 036	large bead wrapped straight-loop link
	Link 037	2-bead wrapped straight-loop link
	Link 052	wrapped straight-loop hook
	Link 091	double 3½-turn spiral link
	Link 303	ball-and-cage bead link

Supplies needed for this project:
- 18-gauge wire
- 25 8mm iridescent red round beads

BALL-AND-CAGE LINKS

1 Using 18-gauge wire and one 8mm red bead per link, create seven Link 303s following the step-by-step instructions on page 130.

CREATING THE CHAIN

1 This necklace uses wrapped straight-loop bead links throughout to create the chain. Join each new link to the chain during the simple straight-loop stage of the link.

2 Using 18-gauge wire and two 8mm beads for each, create and join two Link 037s. Join one Link 303 to the second Link 037.

3 Join one Link 036 that uses one 8mm bead to the end loop of the Link 303. Join one Link 303 to the last wrapped straight-loop of the Link 036.

4 Work a Link 037 with two 8mm beads into the end loop of the last Link 303. Join the chain's third Link 303 to the end-wrapped straight-loop of the Link 037.

5 Repeat this last step three times, working and joining one Link 037 to one Link 303. You will have six Link 303s on your chain when this step is completed.

6 Work one Link 036 with one 8mm bead into the end loop of the last Link 303 on the chain. Add the remaining Link 303 to the end-wrapped straight-loop of this Link 036.

7 Work two Link 037s onto the chain.

8 Create one Link 052 at one end of the chain.

Crescent Moon

Wire-wrapping and small hematite stars decorate the multi-turn spiral hoop of *Crescent Moon*. This strong modern design is perfect for that little black dress evening. The finished necklace is 26" (660mm) long.

Links used in this project:

	Link 033	wrapped straight-loop link
	Link 043	coil link
	Link 053	wrapped straight-loop hook
	Link 074	split ring
	Link 081	large wire-bead-wrapped hoop link
	Link 283	wrapped straight-loop bead link

Supplies needed for this project:
- 16-, 18- & 26-gauge wire
- 2 16mm lampwork beads
- 3 6mm hematite star beads
- 36" (914mm) 2mm rattail cord

1 Cut 15" (381mm) of 16-gauge wire and create one Link 081, following the step-by-step instructions for Links 080-081, using a simple side-loop, a ½" (13mm) full-turn loop, a 1" (25mm) full-turn loop and a 1¼" (32mm) full-turn loop. End the hoop link with a simple side-loop.

2 Cut 6" (152mm) of 26-gauge wire and wire-wrap all of the spiral arms by working through both simple side-loops for eight to ten coils.

3 Cut 24" (610mm) of 26-gauge wire. Begin this wire-wrapping by working over the ½" and 1" (13mm and 25mm) inner loops with ten loose random coils. Wrap the wire one time around the 1" (25mm) hoop, then one time around both hoops. Repeat this twice. Move the wrapping-wire to the outer largest hoop and wrap it one time. Wrap the wire, catching the outer large hoop and the 1" (25mm) hoop. Repeat this twice. Add one hematite star bead to the wire. Continue in the 'over one, over both' pattern five times. Add the second hematite bead. Repeat the wrapping pattern seven times. Add the last hematite bead. Wrap in the pattern seven times. Move the wrapping-wire to the outer largest hoop only and create tightly packed coils until you touch the simple side-loop area of the link. Clip and crimp the wrapping-wire.

CENTER CHAIN

1 Create two Link 283s using 18-gauge wire and one 16mm lampwork bead for each. Cut a 12" (305mm)-long wire. Make a wrapped straight-loop 1½" from one end of the wire. Clip the excess wire from the wrapping. Add the lampwork bead to the working wire. Create a wrapped straight-loop at the base of the bead. Using the excess wire from the wrapped-loop to wrap the working wire around the bead for two full turns. Secure the wire by wrapping it around the wrapped straight-loop twice. Clip the excess wire.

2 Create four Link 074s form 18-gauge wire. Create a chain of one Link 074, one Link 283, one Link 074, one Link 283, and one Link 074. Join Link 081 to with a Link 074 to the center 074 of the chain. Cut a 6" (152mm) length of 26-gauge wire and wire-wrap the front side of this last Link 074 for five tightly packed coils. Clip and crimp the wrapping-wire.

RATTAIL CORD SIDES

1 Using 18-gauge wire, create a 4"-long-by-¼"-wide (102mm by 6mm) Link 043. Cut the coil into four 1" (25mm)-long sections. Cut two 18" (457mm) lengths of 2mm black rattail cord.

2 Work one side of the necklace at a time, thread one end of the rattail cord through the ending split ring on the center chain. Bring the ends of the rattail cord together to create a double-corded side necklace. Slide one section of Link 043 over both rattail cords. Slide the coil to within ¼" (6mm) for the ending split ring. Using your bent-nose pliers, crimp both end loops of the coil against the cording to secure the coil.

3 Slide one section of coil over the two ends of the cord. Crimp the end loops of the coil to secure it to the cording. With your bent-nose pliers, create a connecting loop at the top of the coil. Repeat the steps for the second side of your necklace.

4 Create one Link 033 using 18-gauge wire. Add this link to one side of the necklace through the connecting loop on the end coil. Create one Link 053 using 18-gauge wire. Add the link to the remaining side of the necklace.

HOOK AND EYE

1 Create one Link 033 using 18-gauge wire. Add this link to one side of the necklace through the connecting loop on the end coil. Create one Link 053 using 18-gauge wire. Add the link to the remaining side of the necklace.

Links used in this project:

	Link 039	double wire-wrapped straight-loop link
	Link 043	coil link
	Link 052	wrapped straight-loop hook
	Link 073	jump ring
	Link 272	wrapped-donut straight-loop-dangle link

Supplies needed for this project:
- 18- & 26-gauge wire
- 5 14mm black jade donut beads

Dragon Flight

Small coil lengths create wonderful chains, as *Dragon Flight* shows. Black jade donuts accent the focal-point center in bead dangles and are used as part of the side chain area of the necklace, which measures 15" (381mm) in length.

STARTING OUT

1 Using 18-gauge wire, create a ¼"-wide-by-4"-long (6mm by 102mm) Link 043. You will need up to four long coils to complete this necklace chain. Cut the 4" (102mm) coil into smaller sections of eight full turns each. Bend the end coils on both sides of each smaller section into connecting loops using your bent-nose pliers. You need a total of eighteen Link 043s.

TOP SIDE CHAIN

1 Create two chains of six Link 043s by opening the connecting end loops and threading the new coil link onto that connecting loop.

BOTTOM SIDE CHAIN

1 Create eight ¼" (6mm)-wide Link 073s using 18-gauge wire. Create two chains of three Link 043s using one Link 073 between each coil link. Add one Link 073 to both ends of these chains.

2 Working one side chain area at a time, create one Link 039 using 18-gauge wire. During the simple straight-loop stage of Link 039, join the first loop to the chain of five Link 043s. Join the second loop of the Link 039 to one 14mm jade donut during the simple straight-loop stage. Create a second Link 039 using 18-gauge wire. Join this link to the jade donut and to the end Link 073 of one of the three Link 043 chains during the simple straight-loop stage. Repeat these steps for the second side chain.

JOINING THE SIDE CHAINS

1 Create one Link 039 using 18-gauge wire. Open the end Link 073 on both side chains and add them to one wrapped loop of the Link 039.

2 Using 26-gauge wire, create three Link 272s using one 14mm jade donut for each dangle.

3 Create one ¼" (6mm)-wide Link 073 using 18-gauge wire. Join the three Link 272s to the unused wrapped loop of the center Link 039 using the Link 073 you just created. Attach a Link 052 to the end of one chain.

Links used in this project:

●	Link 036	large bead wrapped straight-loop link
⬤▬▬▬▬⬤	Link 043	coil link
◯	Link 073	jump ring
◯	Link 074	split ring
∞◎∞	Link 186	midwire-spiral link

Supplies needed for this project:
- 18- & 26-gauge wire
- 1 25mm gold foil-lined disc bead
- 2 14mm x 10mm bumpy lampwork tube beads
- 36" (914mm) 1/8" (3mm) suede leather cord

Frosted Suede

You will be ready for the next post-grunge concert by Theory of a Deadman in this rugged leather cord necklace, *Frosted Suede.* One extra-large foil-lined bead creates the center focal point of this adjustable-length necklace.

1 Create one Link 036 using 18-gauge wire and the 25mm gold foil bead. Cut a 15" (381mm) length of 26-gauge wire and wire-wrap this link following the step-by-step instructions on page 142.

2 Create two Link 186s using 18-gauge wire and one 14mm-by-10mm bumpy lampwork bead each. Begin this link by creating a wrapped straight-loop in one end of the wire. Add the bead. Grip the working wire ¼" from the end of the bead and create a 3-turn midwire-spiral. Create a simple side-loop at the end of the spiral. Clip the excess wire. Cut a 10" (254mm) length of 26-gauge wire and wire-wrap the center spiral hole with eight tightly packed coils.

3 Create one ¼"-wide-by-3"-long (6mm by 76mm) Link 043 using 18-gauge wire. From the coil, cut 12 Link 074s and six Link 073s.

4 For each side of Link 036 create a chain of three Link 073s and join them to Link 036s wrapped straight-loop. Open the last 073 jump ring and add the wrapped straight-loop of Link 186 to the chain. Create a chain of three Link 074s. Thread the last Link 074 through the wrapped straight-loop of Link 186.

5 Cut a 36" (914mm) length of ⅛" (3mm)-wide suede leather cord. Thread the leather cord through the Link 074s joined to the Link 186. Center the two split rings to the length of the leather. Move the split rings so they are 2" (51mm) apart. Tie a simple knot in the leather cord over each split ring that catches the split ring in the knot.

6 Create two chains of three Link 074s. Add one chain to the simple side-loop of both Link 186s.

7 Thread the ends of the leather cord through the Link 074s at the end of the necklace chain. Move these Link 074s to 1½" (38mm) from the first Link 074s. Tie a simple knot to the leather cord catching the Link 074 in the knot.

8 This necklace is worn by holding the chain in the front. The leather cords are brought around the neck and crossed in the back. The cords are then returned to the front and tied in a loose knot or bow at the base of the throat. The extra length of the leather cords dangles to accent the metal area of the necklace.

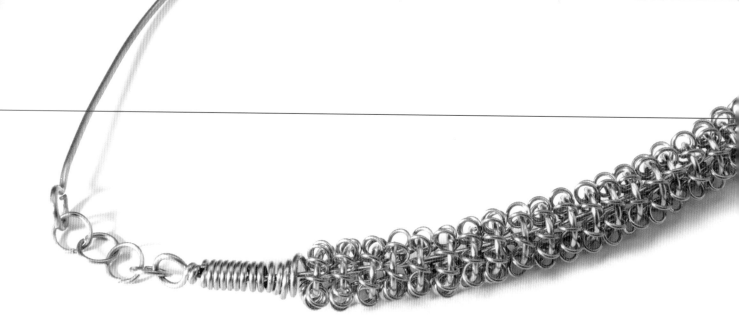

Links used in this project:

⊙——⊙	Link 023	long simple straight-loop link
🔗	Link 043	coil link
🔗	Link 055	wrapped side-loop hook link
⊙	Link 073	jump ring

Supplies needed for this project:
• 18-, 20- & 26-gauge wire

Galaxy

Galaxy is created using a fine 26-gauge wire coil that is wrapped repeatedly around a central wrapped straight-loop link. This focal link is fun and simple to create but gives this 16" (406mm) necklace an intriguing look.

FOCAL-POINT LINK

1 Create a ⅛"-wide-by-12"-long (3mm by 305mm) Link 043 using 26-gauge wire. Stretch the 26-gauge coil to measure 22" to 24" (559mm to 610mm) long—twice its original size.

2 Cut a 30" (762mm) length of 20-gauge wire. Wrap the wire around a ⅛" (3mm)-wide form for twelve full turns. Remove the wire from the coil form and slide the Link 043 coil over the wire to touch the last full turn. Return the link to the coil form and work the coil-covered wire over the form until all of the coil area has been wrapped. Finish this link by wrapping just the 20-gauge wire at the end of the coil cover for twelve full turns.

3 Cut a 9" (229mm) length of 18-gauge wire. Create a wrapped straight-loop in one end. Slide the coiled coil-covered link onto the working wire. Create a wrapped straight-loop at the end of the coil-covered link.

BACK NECK LINK

1 Create two 6½" (165mm) long Link 023s using 18-gauge wire. Gently curve the links.

2 Create seven ¼" (6mm)-wide Link 073s using 20-gauge wire.

3 Create one Link 055 using 20-gauge wire.

4 Join the necklace in this order: one Link 055, one Link 073, one Link 023, three Link 073s, the coiled coil-covered link, three Link 073s, and one Link 023.

Links used in this project:

∞	Link 015	simple side-loop link
	Link 033	wrapped straight-loop link
	Link 043	coil link
	Link 056	wrapped straight-loop hook link
○	Link 073	jump ring

Supplies needed for this project:
• 16-, 18- & 20-gauge wire

Gothic Coils

Coil-wrapped coils are the focal point of *Gothic Coils*.
The necklace measures 17" (432mm).

CENTER COIL LINK

1 Create one Link 043 that is ⅜"-wide-by-2½"–long (10mm by 64mm) using 16-gauge wire. Begin the coiling of this link 4" (102mm) from the end of the wire. End the link with 4" (102mm) of working wire remaining.

2 Create one Link 043 using 20-gauge wire that measures ³⁄₁₆"-wide-by-4"long (4mm by 104mm). Cut a 7" (178mm) length of 20-gauge wire. Create a wrapped straight-loop in the wire. Slide the small coil over the working wire. Slide this wrapped straight-loop over one 4" (102mm) end of the large coil link. Wrap the small coil link around the large coil link one full turn. Create a wrapped straight-loop at the end of the small coil link interlocking it over the end 4" (102mm) wire on the large coil.

3 Cut the two end wires of the large coil to 2½" (64mm) long. Roll both wires into 2½-turn spirals.

SIDE COIL LINKS

1 Create two 16-gauge wire Link 043s that measure ⅜"-wide-by-2" (10mm by 51mm)-long.

2 Create two Link 043s using 16-gauge wire that measure ¼"-wide-by-2" (6mm by 51mm)-long.

3 Following the photo example, join the five Link 043s to create the center chain.

4 Using 18-gauge wire, create eighteen Link 015s. Make two chains of nine Link 015s each. Join one chain to each side of the coil chain.

5 Create four ¼" (6mm)-wide Link 073s using 18-gauge wire. Join two Link 073s to each end of the necklace.

6 Make one Link 056 using 18-gauge wire and add this to one end of the necklace.

7 Create one Link 033 using 18-gauge wire and add it to the remaining end of the necklace.

Links used in this project:

	Link 015	simple side-loop link
	Link 033	wrapped straight-loop link
	Link 038	3-bead wrapped straight-loop link
	Link 043	coil link
	Link 056	wrapped straight-loop hook link
	Link 073	jump ring
	Link 156	spiral heart link

Supplies needed for this project:

- 18-gauge wire
- 2 8mm crow rollers
- 4 6mm crow rollers
- 4 4mm spacer beads

Heart Breaker

1 Create one Link 156 using 8" (203mm) of 18-gauge wire and 2½-turn spirals as shown in the step-by-step instructions for this link (page 106).

2 Create two ⅜" (10mm)-wide-by-14-turns Link 043s, bending the end turns into connecting loops.

3 Create two Link 038s using the following beads: 6mm crow roller, 4mm spacer bead, 8mm crow roller, 4mm spacer bead, and 6mm crow roller.

4 Create one Link 033. This link will become the hook eye of your necklace.

5 Create one Link 056.

6 Create eight Link 015s.

7 Create sixteen ⅜" (10mm)-wide Link 073s.

8 To join the links, work from the center Link 156 toward one end of the necklace, working one side of the necklace at a time. The links are joined in the following pattern with Link 073s between each: one Link 156, one Link 043, one Link 038, and four Link 015s, joined to the chain using one Link 073 for each connection. Add one extra Link 073 to the connection between the Link 156 and the adjacent Link 043. Repeat this pattern of joining for the second side of the necklace.

9 Join the Link 033 to one end of the chain using one Link 073. Join the Link 056 to the opposite end of the chain using one Link 073.

Tip 14: Hole size.

Beads come with a variety of hole sizes, so check what gauge wire will fit the beads you will be using in a project. You can use different gauges of wire in one project if you are consistent throughout the project with where each is used. At left, I used 18-gauge wire on all of the large spiral bent-wire links and 20-gauge wire on all of the bead links.

Links used in this project:

	Link 033	wrapped straight-loop link
	Link 036	large bead wrapped straight-loop link
	Link 051	simple side-loop hook
	Link 073	jump ring
	Link 186	midwire-spiral bead link
	Link 286	centered spiral-end bead link

Supplies needed for this project:

• 16" (406mm) necklace
• 16 gauge wire
• 4 20mm x 16mm flat oval foil glass beads

In the Mood

In the Mood (shown on cover) is a simple yet elegant design using various wrapped straight-loop links, including two that feature wrapped beads.

1 Create eighteen ¼" (6mm) Link 073s.

2 Create eight Link 033s that measure ¾" (19mm) long.

3 Create two Link 036s, using one flat oval foil bead each, that measure 1⅜" (35mm) long.

4 Create one Link 051 that measures ¾" (19mm) long.

5 Create one Link 186 using four turns for the midwire-spiral, and wrapped straight-loop ends.

6 Create two Link 286s using one flat oval foil bead each. Work this link with 10" (254mm) of wire. Create a wrapped straight-loop in one end of the wire. Add the foil bead. Create a wrapped straight-loop at the base of the bead. With the excess wrapping-wire, create a midwire-spiral using four turns, working the spiral ⅜" (10mm) from the second wrapped straight-loop. Lay the midwire-spiral at the center of the bead. Wrap the working wire from the midwire-spiral once around the first wrapped straight-loop of this link. Clip the excess wire.

7 Link the necklace using the jump rings to connect the links with the following pattern: four Link 033s, one Link 036, one Link 286, one Link 186, one Link 286, one Link 036, and four Link 033s.

8 Add three Link 073s to one end of the necklace. To the remaining end, add three Link 073s and oneLink 051.

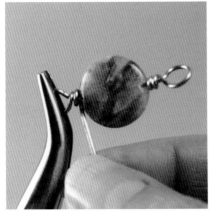

Tip 15: Extra room.

Allow a small amount of extra room or play in the wire-wrap when you are securing a bead. Wrapping the bead too tight can easily break glass and semi-precious stone beads.

Links used in this project:

○—○	Link 023	long simple straight-loop link
	Link 041	3-bead random-wrap straight-loop link
○	Link 073	jump ring

Supplies needed for this project:
- 20- & 26-gauge wire
- 16 antique brass 16mm bells
- 32 fringe seed beads
- 12 4mm tube spacer beads

Jingle Bells

Jingle Bells is constructed out of just simple straight-loop links. Wire-wrapping adds beads, bells, and sparkle to this fun project. Read through the step-by-step instructions for beaded wire-wrap on page 142 before starting this project.

1 Create one Link 043 coil ³⁄₁₆"-wide-by-3"-long (5mm by 76mm) using 20-gauge wire. Cut the coil into Link 073 jump rings.

BEADED WIRE-WRAP BELL LINKS

1 Make sixteen Link 041s as follows. For each link, create one Link 023 ¾" (19mm) long, using 20-gauge wire. Beaded-wire-wrap this link using 26-gauge wire with three tightly packed coils on the link, adding one seed bead, two tightly packed coils, one brass bell bead, two tightly packed coils, one seed bead and ending with three tightly packed coils.

2 Join twelve of these links into a chain using one Link 073 between each link. Join four of these links into a chain using one Link 073 between each link.

BEAD-WRAPPED SPACER LINKS

1 Make four Link 041s as follows. For each link, create one 1" (25mm)-long Link 023 using 20-gauge wire. Add a beaded wire-wrap to the link using 26-gauge wire. Random wire-wrap the links, adding three 4mm tube spacer beads to the wrap. Join the four links into a chain using Link 073s between each link.

NECKLACE CHAIN

1 Create and join twenty-eight 1" (25mm)-long Link 023s using one Link 073 between each link.

2 Join the ends of this Link 023 chain to the twelve-link brass bell chain using one Link 073 on each side of the chain.

MIDDLE FOCAL-POINT CHAIN

1 Join the four-link spacer bead chain to the necklace with one Link 073 on each side of the chain, looped through the lower simple straight-loop of the second brass bell links.

TOP FOCAL-POINT CHAIN

1 Join the four-link brass bell chain to the necklace using one Link 073 on each side of the chain and looped into the same brass bell link of the necklace as the middle focal point chain.

EASY & ELEGANT **beaded copper** JEWELRY

Links used in this project:

	Link 024	1-bead simple straight-loop link
	Link 043	coil link
	Link 047	wrapped long loop link
	Link 073	jump ring
	Link 135	double-hairpin link
	Link 158	wire-wrapped heart eyelet link

Supplies needed for this 19" project:
- 12- & 26-gauge wire
- 4 8mm-by-4mm white marble oval beads
- 3 3mm white marble round beads

Maiden's Blush

Three large open-eyelet hearts make *Maiden's Blush* a perfect necklace for Valentine's Day. White marble oval and round beads provide soft wrapped bead accents for the 19" (483mm) completed piece.

1 Create three Link 158s using 8" (203mm) of 12-gauge wire, working the open-eyelet over a 1" (25mm) form. Each heart link measures 1¾" (44mm) long.

2 For each Link 158, cut a 12" (305mm) length of 26-gauge wire and wire-wrap the open-eyelet arms where they touch with fifteen tightly packed coils.

3 For each Link 158, cut a 12" (305mm) length of 26-gauge wire and wire-wrap one simple side-loop of the link with five packed coils. Add one 3mm marble bead to the wire. Wire-wrap the second simple side-loop with five packed coils.

4 Create two Link 024s using 12-gauge wire one 8mm oval bead. Use these links to join the three Link 158s.

5 Create two Link 047s using 12-gauge wire that measure 1⅜" (35mm) long. Cut a 12" (305mm) length of 26-gauge wire for each link. Working in the large loop of the link, wire-wrap six packed coils to one arm of the link. Add one 8mm oval bead to the wire. Wire-wrap the opposite arm of the link with six packed coils.

6 Create four ¼" (6mm)-wide Link 073s using 12-gauge wire. Use two Link 073s to join each Link 047 to the ends of the chain.

7 Cut six 12" (305mm) lengths of 26-gauge wire. Wire-wrap each link connection of the chain by working five to six tightly packed coils on one outside arm of a Link 158 below the connecting loop of the next link. Loosely bring the wrapping-wire over the connecting loop of the next link and create five to six tightly packed coils above the connection of the arm of the Link 158.

8 Create a ¼"-wide-by-4"-long (6mm by 102mm) Link 043 coil using 12-gauge wire. Cut the coil into Link 073s. Create two chains of 24 Link 073s. Join the end link of each chain to the smaller loop of the Link 047s at the ends of the focal-point chain.

9 Create one Link 135. Join this link to one end of the chain using one Link 073 through one of the U-bend turns.

Links used in this project:

	Link 018	1-bead simple side-loop link
	Link 038	3-bead wrapped straight-loop link
	Link 042	small coil link
	Link 057	double-wire hook link
	Link 073	jump ring
	Link 276	2-wire-wrapped-donut link

Night Owl

1 Create one ⅜"-wide-by-4"-long (10mm by 102mm) Link 043. Cut ten coils with six full turns each from the Link 043. Use your bent-nose pliers to bend the end coils of these smaller sections into connecting loops.

2 Create six Link 018s using one spacer bead for each link.

3 Create four Link 038s. To each link, add one spacer bead, one 8mm crow roller, and one spacer bead.

4 Create one ⅛"-wide-by-2"-long (3mm by 51mm) Link 043. Cut this coil into jump rings.

5 Create two side neck chains using one ⅛" (3mm) Link 073 as the connector between each link in the following order: one Link 038, one Link 042, one Link 038, one Link 042, one Link 018, one Link 042, one Link 018, one Link 042, one Link 018, and one Link 042.

6 Create one ⅜" (10mm)-wide Link 073. Join this Link 073 to the coil end of one of the side neck chains to become the hook eye.

Supplies needed for this 18" project:

- 18-gauge wire
- 1 1" (25mm)-wide wooden ring
- 4 8mm iridescent crow rollers
- 14 6mm copper spacer beads
- Liver of Sulfur

7 Create one Link 057. Join the link to the second side neck chain end using two ⅜" (10mm)-wide Link 073s.

8 Create one Link 276 using the 1" (25mm)-wide wooden ring. Cut two 6" (152mm) lengths of wire. In one wire, create a wrapped straight-loop in the end. Thread the wire through one of the holes in the side of the wooden ring so that the wrapped straight-loop is against the outside edge of the wooden ring. Grip the working wire on the inside of the wooden ring and wrap the wire around the ring for four tight turns. Clip the excess wire. Repeat these steps for the second working wire and the remaining hole in the wooden ring. Wrap this second wire onto the opposite side of the hole from the first wrapping.

9 Create two ⅛" (3mm)-wide Link 073s. Use one Link 073 on each side of the Link 276 to link it to the inside of each side neck chain.

10 The sample necklace was dipped in Liver of Sulfur to create the deep brown patina tone. Please read the instructions for use on your container of Liver of Sulfur. Please especially follow all safety and safe use rules.

Links used in this project:

	Link 036	large bead wrapped straight-loop link
	Link 043	coil link
	Link 051	simple side-loop hook
	Link 073	jump ring
	Link 137	5-turn hairpin link
	Link 154	wire-wrapped turn-back midwire-spiral link

Supplies used in this project:

- 16-, 18- & 20-gauge wire
- 2 14mm burgundy lampwork beads
- 32" (813mm) ⅛" (3mm) suede leather cord

Rush Hour

Five quick links make the focal-point chain for *Rush Hour*, with two bold lampwork beads added for a touch of color. The side neck area of the necklace is worked in suede leather for very comfortable wear all day long.

1 Using 18-gauge wire, create one Link 154 following the step-by-step instructions on pages 108 and 109, beginning with a one full-turn variation to the turn-back loop spiral. End one working wire with a 1½-turn spiral. End the opposite side with a 2½-turn spiral.

Cut two 10" (254mm) lengths of 20-gauge wire. Create eight tightly packed coil wire-wrappings on each side of the turn-back spiral.

2 Create two Link 137s with five U-bends, each 1" (25mm) long. Compress these links.

3 Create two Link 036s using 18-gauge wire and one 14mm lampwork bead for each link. Interlock the wrapped straight-loop of one Link 036 to one spiral end of Link 154. Interlock the second Link 036 to the remaining spiral end of Link 154.

4 Join the compressed Link 137s to the end of the chain.

5 Cut two 16" (406mm) lengths of ⅛" (3mm)-wide suede leather cord. Work one side neck cord at a time. Thread one end of the suede through the overlapped U-bends of one of the Link 137 hairpin links. Bring the ends of the leather together to even the cord. Create two Link 043 18-gauge wires that measure eight full turns each. Slide one coil over both ends of the leather suede cord. Slide the coil down the leather to touch the focal-point chain. Do not crimp this coil; allow it to float freely. Slide the remaining coil over both ends of the leather suede, keeping the coil at the neck end of the leather. Crimp the inside (bottom) loop of the coil to secure the leather cords. Bend the outside loop of the coil into a connecting loop. Create one ¼" (6mm)-wide Link 073 jump ring using 18-gauge wire. Join this to the side neck leather cord through the connecting loop of the coil.

6 Using 18-gauge wire, repeat the above steps for the second leather cord side neck area of the design substituting one Link 051 for the Link 073 used in the first side.

Salsa

Five separate bead link chains come together to create the 26" (660mm)-long *Salsa*. The beads for this project came from an India glass mixture that provided a variety of bead shapes all in one complementary range of color tones.

TOP FOCAL POINT CHAIN

1 Create ten Link 018s using one 12mm-by-1mm twisted rectangle bead for each link.

2 Create eleven Link 018s using one 8mm-by-4mm disc bead for each link.

3 Join the chain by using the simple side-loops of the links: alternate one Link 018 rectangular bead and one Link 018 disc bead. End the chain with one Link 018 disc bead. The finished chain measures 16" (406mm) long.

MIDDLE FOCAL POINT CHAIN

1 Create two Link 018s using one 8mm-by-4mm disc bead for each.

2 Create four Link 018s using one 8mm lantern-shaped bead for each.

3 Create four Link 310s. To each link, add one lantern-shaped bead, one disc bead, and one lantern-shaped bead. The spirals for the Link 310s use two full turns.

4 Create one Link 101 using one 16mm-by-12mm large oval bead.

5 Join this chain using the simple side-loops of the links. Place as follows: one Link 310, one Link 018 lantern bead, one Link 310, one Link 018 lantern bead, one Link 018 disc bead, and the one Link 101. The spiral ends of the Link 310s face toward the center of the chain. Repeat this link order in reverse for the second side of the chain. The finished chain measures 11½" (292mm).

Links used in this project:

	Link 018	1-bead simple side-loop link
	Link 033	wrapped straight-loop link
	Link 052	wrapped straight-loop hook
	Link 073	jump ring
	Link 101	3-turn parallel spiral bead link
	Link 141	hairpin bead link
	Link 310	simple straight-loop spiral bead link

Supplies used in this project:

- 18-gauge wire
- 2 16mm x 12mm large oval beads
- 14 16mm x 10mm ribbed oval beads
- 12 12mm x 10mm twisted rectangular beads
- 19 8mm x 4mm disc beads
- 16 8mm lantern shaped beads

BOTTOM FOCAL POINT CHAIN

1 Create eight Link 141s using one 16mm-by-10mm ribbed bead for each. Begin the link with 9" (229mm) of wire. Create a simple side-loop in one end of the wire using your round-nose pliers. Create a U-bend ¼" (6mm) from the simple side-loop using your round-nose pliers. Create a series of four hairpin U-bends each ¾" (19mm) from the last. Bend the wire into a right-angle bend ¼" (6mm) from the last U-bend turn. Slide one bead onto the working wire. End the link with a simple straight-loop at the top of the bead.

2 Create one Link 141 using one 16mm-by-12mm large oval bead. Begin with 9" (229mm) of wire. Create a simple side-loop in one end of the wire. Grip the working wire ½" (13mm) from the simple side-loop in your round-nose pliers and create a U-bend hairpin turn. Grip the working wire ¾" (19mm) from the first U-bend and create a second U-bend hairpin turn. Using your bent-nose pliers, create a right-angle bend ⅜" (10mm) from the second hairpin turn. Slide the bead onto the working wire. Create a right-angle bend at the base of the bead. Create one hairpin turn ⅜" (10mm) from the right-angle bend and a second hairpin turn ¾" (19mm) from the first. Finish the link with a simple side-loop ½" (13mm) from the second hairpin turn. Clip any excess wire from the simple side-loop.

3 Create two ¼" (6mm)-wide Link 073s.

4 Join four Link 141s using their simple side-loops. Face the hairpin-turn area of these links toward the center of the chain. Join the one different Link 141 to the chain using one Link 073. Create a second chain of four Link 141 five-hairpin-turn bead links using their simple side-loops. Face the hairpin turn area of these links towards the center of the chain. Connect this chain to the open end of the center Link 141 with a Link 073. This finished chain measures 13½" (343mm) long.

SIDE NECK CHAINS

1 Create one Link 018 using one 12mm-by-10mm twisted rectangle bead.

2 Create three Link 018s using one 16mm-by-10mm ribbed oval bead for each.

3 Create one Link 018 simple side-loop bead link using one 8mm disc bead.

4 Create two Link 018s using one 8mm lantern-shaped bead for each.

5 Create five ¼" (6mm)-wide Link 073s.

6 Join the side neck chain in the following order using the simple side-loops of the links: one Link 018 with twisted rectangle bead, three Link 018 with ribbed oval beads, two Link 073s, one Link 018 with disc bead, three Link 073s, and ending with two Link 018s with lantern-shaped beads.

7 Repeat the steps to create your second side neck chain.

JOINING THE CHAINS

1 To the last Link 018 of one side chain, join the middle focal-point chain through the simple side-loop at the end Link 310.

2 Join the bottom focal point chain through the simple side-loop at the end Link 310 of the middle focal-point chain.

3 Join the top focal-point chain to the side neck chain through the bottom simple side-loop of the side neck chain Link 018 with disc bead.

4 Repeat these joining steps for the opposite side of the necklace.

5 Create one Link 033 that will be the hook eye for the necklace. Join this link to one end of one of the side neck chains.

6 Create one Link 052. Join this link to the opposite end of the necklace.

Soccer Match

Soccer Match uses the double-spiral hairpin link to create a quick, fun, and brightly beaded necklace for casual wear. The 15" (381mm)-long necklace is easily extended by adding pairs of double-hairpin spirals to the chain.

1 Please read through the instructions "How much wire is needed for a mirror image link" on page 185 before beginning this project.

2 Create a ¼"-wide-by-3"-long (6mm by 76mm) Link 043. Cut the coil into Link 073s.

3 Create four Link 112s, using 2½-turn spirals on each end, that measure ¾" (19mm) long.

4 Create twelve Link 112s using 2½-turn spiral ends and adding two 4mm tube beads, one for each U-bend arm, to the working wire before the second spiral end. Each link measures ¾" (19mm) long.

5 Create one Link 033 using 18-gauge wire that measures ½" (13mm) long.

6 Create one Link 053 using 18-gauge wire that measures ⅝" (16mm) long.

7 Lay out the Link 112s in pairs on your worktable so that the spiral ends of one link touch the spiral ends of another. Begin the first pair with non-beaded Link 112. The next six pairs are beaded links; end with one pair of non-beaded links.

8. Join each pair of Link 112s using two Link 073s between each spiral hole.

9. Join the pairs of links to each other using two Link 073s through the U-bend areas of the Link 112s.

10 Create a chain of four Link 073s at both ends of the necklace, adding the first link to the U-bend of the last Link 112 and using two Link 073s per link.

11 Add the Link 033 to one end of the chain interlocking it with both Link 073s.

12 Add the Link 053 to the remaining end of the chain, interlocking it with both Link 073s.

Links used in this project:

	Link 033	wrapped straight-loop link
	Link 043	coil link
	Link 053	wrapped straight-loop hook
	Link 073	jump ring
	Link 112	3-turn double-spiral hairpin link

Supplies needed for this 15" (381mm) project:
- 18-gauge wire
- 24 4mm tube spacer beads of assorted colors

Sweet Whispers

Sweet Whispers is a simple 18" (457mm)-long necklace created with jump rings and simple side-loop bead links. It's a perfect design for those fun assorted color and shape bead mixtures offered at your local or online bead store.

1 Create twenty-six Link 018s using one 4mm oval glass bead for each.

2 Create a ⅛"-wide-by-3"-long (3mm by 76mm) Link 043. A #2 or #3 knitting needle will create the correct size coil. Cut the coil into Link 073s.

3 Join the Link 018s into a 17" (432mm)-long chain using one Link 073 between each link.

4 Create one Link 033. Add this to one end of the chain with a Link 073.

5 Create one Link 053 and add it to the opposite end of the chain.

6 Create one Link 035 using three 4mm oval beads. Start with 4" (102mm) of wire. Create a wrapped straight-loop at one end of the wire. Add three 4mm oval beads. Grip the working wire 1¾" (44mm) from the top of the wrapped straight-loop in your bent-nose pliers and create the second wrapped straight-loop of this link.

7 Create one 1½" (38mm)-long Link 035 with three 4mm oval beads.

8 Create one 2" (51mm)-long Link 035 with three 4mm oval beads.

9 Create one ¼" (6mm) -wide Link 073. Find the center Link 073 of the chain. Thread the ¼" (6mm) jump ring through the same simple side-loops on the chain as the center Link 073. Add the three Link 035s to the ¼" (6mm) Link 073.

Links used in this project:

	Link	Description
	Link 018	1-bead simple side-loop link
	Link 033	wrapped straight-loop link
	Link 035	long wrapped straight-loop link
	Link 043	coil link
	Link 053	wrapped straight-loop hook
	Link 073	jump ring

Supplies needed for this project:

- 20-gauge wire
- 35 4mm oval glass beads

Appendix: Additional Project Instructions

Many projects appear in reference photos throughout this book but not all projects are included in the detailed step-by-step projects section. A shortened format of the instructions for those necklaces follows. The name of the jewelry piece is listed along with the page(s) upon which it appears.

ALL THAT JAZZ BRACELET (PAGES 152 & 156)

Using 18-gauge wire, create one Link 332. Add one 8mm bead ending with a simple side-loop, two Link 141s with 8mm beads, one Link 018 with one 8mm bead, two Link 198s with 2-turn spirals, one Link 186 with one 8mm bead, one Link 051, and six ¼" (6mm)-wide Link 073s.

BENT-WIRE BRACELET (PAGE 158)

Using 18-gauge wire, create two Link 088s using a 4-turn spiral and a 2-turn spiral, two Link 086s using a 3-turn spiral and a wrapped straight-loop, two Link 136s using a wrapped straight-loop on one end and a 3-turn spiral on the other, and one ¼"-wide-by-4" (6mm by 100mm)-long Link 043. Cut the coil into Link 073s. Follow the photo on page 158 to see how the bracelet is joined by Link 073s.

BIG BLUE MARBLES NECKLACE (PAGE 60)

Using 18-gauge wire, create two ¼"-wide-by-4"-long (6mm by 100mm) Link 043 coils. Cut the coils into Link 073s. Create two ⅜"-wide-by-4" (10mm by 100mm) long Link 043 coils and cut them into Link 073s. Create one chain that measures 6" (152mm) long using one ¼" (6mm), one ⅜" (10mm), and then another ¼ (6mm) Link 073 per chain link. Add one link of three ⅜" (10mm) Link 073s to both ends of the chain. Create two Link 148s and add to the chain. Add two 20-gauge wire-wrapped 10" (254mm) long 2mm rattail cords with one Link 052 on one side and one Link 033 on the second side. Add twenty-one bead dangles to the Link 073 chain using 4mm-to-14mm beads and your choice of link designs. *Big Blue Marble* uses Link 279, Link 265, and Link 281.

BLUEBERRY MUFFIN BRACELET (PAGE 156)

Using 18-gauge wire, create one Link 060 using one 10mm-by-6mm bead, one Link 015, one Link 036 with one 18mm bead, one Link 306 with three 6mm beads on the spiral followed by a midwire-circle and one 16mm on the wrapped straight-loop end, two 2½-turn spiral Link 310s with one 18mm bead, and one Link 336 with one 16mm-by-12mm beaded wire-wrap on the simple side-loops. Create six Link 073s, using four to join the

bracelet. For the bead dangles, create one Link 310 using a 8mm bead, one Link 157 using three beads, and one Link 257 with one 16mm bead-wrapping on the straight-loop area with fifteen loose coils.

BLUEBERRY PIE BRACELET (PAGE 156)

Blueberry Pie uses 18-gauge wire and is created in the same manner as *Blueberry Muffin* (above) using a variety of beads including two 8mm beads, two 12mm beads, a 16mm jade donut, a 28mm by 12mm glass teardrop, seven assorted spacer beads, one 6mm crow roller, and three 6mm-by-4mm oval beads.

CHARM BRACELET (PAGE 159)

Using 18-gauge wire, create four ¼"-wide-by-4" (6mm by 100mm) long Link 043 coils. Cut the coils into Link 073s. Create a chain, using four Link 073s per link, that measures 7½" (191mm) long. Create one Link 057; interlock it to the last four-jump-ring link of the chain. Create one 4-turn Link 074 and join this to the opposite end of the chain. Create fifty-two Link 265 bead dangles using 3mm-to-10mm assorted beads. Join each dangle to the chain using one Link 073.

CHOCOLATE SUNDAE NECKLACE (PAGE 58)

Using 18-gauge wire, create one Link 292 using a 30mm foil-lined bead, two Link 141s with one U-bend and one 14mm lampwork bead each, two Link 147s with 4-turn U-bend hairpins and one 14mm lampwork bead each, and two Link 136s with 3-turn U-bends. Compress the hairpin links. Join the chain using six ¼" (6mm) Link 074s. Add two 26-gauge wire-wrapped 10" (254mm) long 2mm rattail cord ends. Add one Link 052 to one cord end and one Link 033 to the second cord end. Add one Link 036 using a 6mm spacer bead and five ¼" (6mm) Link 073s to the Link 033.

COPPER COILS BRACELET (PAGE 152)

Using 20-gauge wire, create one nine-coil Link 043, two five-coil Link 043s, two three-bead Link 038s with 6mm crow rollers, two one-bead Link 036s using 6mm copper spacers, seven ⅜"-wide (10mm) Link 073s, five ³⁄₁₆" (5mm) wide Link 073s and one Link 052. Use 26-gauge wire to wrap one ⅜" (10mm) Link 073.

DAY BREAK BRACELET (PAGES 22 & 152)

Using 16-gauge wire, create one Link 052, three one-bead Link 036s with 10mm copper round beads, one fifteen-coil Link 043, one Line 204 with a 26-gauge wrap, one ³⁄₁₆"(5mm)-wide coil-covered Link 135, and four ³⁄₈" (10mm)-wide Link 073s.

EASY GOING BRACELET (PAGE 22 & 157)

Using 18-gauge wire, create one Link 057, one Link 141 with one 6mm glass bead, two twelve-turn Link 043s, one Link 036 with one 10mm lampwork bead, one Link 036 with one wrapped 6mm bead, one Link 123 using 2½-turn spirals, one Link 036 using a spacer bead, four ¼"-wide (6mm) Link 074s, and three Link 084s using 5-turn spirals with an added wrap. Follow the photo to interlock the links and to use the Link 074 split rings for joining.

GOLDEN MOMENTS NECKLACE (PAGE 153)

Using 18-gauge wire, create four ¼" (6mm) Link 043 coils that measure 4" (102mm) long each. Stretch each coil to measure 6" (152mm). Create two Link 036s using 8mm flat disc beads. Create one Link 036 using seven beads from 8mm to 12mm. Create one Link 052 and one Link 033. Join this necklace using the connecting loops of the Link 043 coils.

HIGH TIDE BRACELET (PAGE 159)

Using 16-gauge wire, create one Link 051, two Link 185s using a 4-turn midwire-spiral, two Link 139s using five U-bend turns, five ¼"-wide (6mm) Link 073s, and one Link 036 using a 35mm frosted disc bead. Wire-wrap the Link 036 with 20-gauge wire for three turns. Use your bent-nose pliers to crimp the wrapping-wire into angles. Join the links using Link 073s.

HOT SUMMER NIGHT BRACELET (PAGE 159)

Worked in 16-gauge wire, *Hot Summer Night* uses one Link 015, two Link 090s, two Link 283s with one 10mm bead each, two Link 087s with a wire-wrap on one link and a 3mm beaded wire-wrap on the second, two ¼" (6mm)-wide Link 073s, one six-coil Link 043, and one Link 135 worked as a 6mm beaded hook. Interlock the links as they are created. Add three Link 265s with one 6mm-to-8mm bead each as dangles.

PARTY LIGHTS NECKLACE (PAGE 19)

Using 16-gauge wire, create four Link 107s, two Link 199s with 3-turn spirals, two Link 018s using one 14mm lampwork bead each, one seven-coil Link 043, one Link 230 with a beaded wire-wrapping using 20-gauge wire and one 14mm bead, one twelve-coil Link 043, eight ¼" (6mm)-wide Link 073s. Join the links following the photo using the simple side-loops of the links or Link 073s. Add two 26-gauge 3mm beaded wire-wrapped 8" (203mm) lengths of 2mm rattail cord—one ending with Link 051, and one ending with a ¼" (6mm)-wide Link 073. Add three wire-wrapped 3mm beaded Link 135s as dangles.

RAINBOW ROAD BRACELET (PAGES 27 & 157)

Rainbow Road uses six 8mm-by-14mm frosted glass beads, three spacer beads, and 16-gauge wire. Create one Link 051, one Link 037 using one frosted bead, one Link 156 with 2½-turn spirals, one Link 037 using two frosted beads, one Link 090 with 3-turn spirals, one Link 137, one Link 015, and six ³⁄₈" (10mm)-wide Link 073s. Join the links using the Link 073s. Create three Link 265s, using one frosted bead each, interlocking the beads to the chain. Create three Link 015s, adding one spacer bead to each and joining them to the chain.

RIBBON ROCK BRACELET (PAGE 153)

Using 18-gauge wire, create six Link 136s, adding one 8mm-by-6mm nugget bead to each link, five ¼" (6mm)-wide Link 074s, one Link 051 ending with a 3-turn split ring, and one Link 015 ending with a 3-turn split ring.

SOLITUDE BRACELET (PAGE 158)

Using 20-gauge wire, create two chains of eight Link 036s using one 6mm crow roller each and interlocking the links. Create one Link 057, interlocking both chains at one end of the chains. Create one Link 039, interlocking both chains. Create fifteen bead dangles of your choice using one 8mm frosted swirl bead each. The links used in *Solitude* bracelet are three Link 265s, one Link 279, two Link 312s, one Link 287, one Link 274, one Link 291, two Link 281s, two Link 286s, one Link 291, and one Link 280.

Complete Link Set Index

Index

INDEX

254

COVER & LAYOUT DESIGNER/IMAGE CONCEPT: Lindsay Hess
LAYOUT: Jason Deller
ACQUISITION EDITOR: Paul M. Hambke
COPY EDITOR: Kerri Landis
EDITOR: Paul M. Hambke

EDITORIAL ASSISTANT: Heather Stauffer
PHOTOGRAPHY: Scott Kriner/Lora S. Irish
PROOFREADER: Lynda Jo Runkle
INDEXER: Jay Kreider

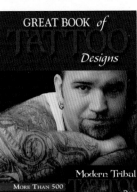

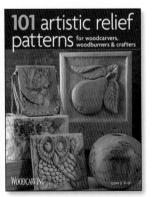
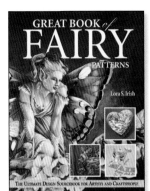
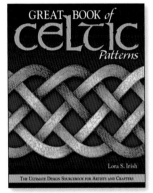

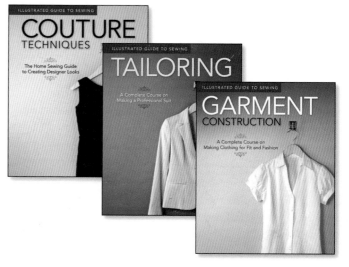